WEiRD MiChiGAN

Sterling Publishing Co., Inc.
New York

WEiRD MiChiGAN

Your Travel Guide to Michigan's Local Legends and Best Kept Secrets

by LINDA S. GODFREY

Mark Sceurman and Mark Moran, Executive Editors

WEiRD MiChiGAN

Published by Sterling Publishing Co., Inc.
387 Park Avenue South, New York, NY 10016
© 2006 Mark Sceurman and Mark Moran
Distributed in Canada by Sterling Publishing
c/o Canadian Manda Group, 165 Dufferin Street
Toronto, Ontario, Canada M6K 3H6
Distributed in Great Britain by Chrysalis Books Group PLC
The Chrysalis Building, Bramley Road, London W10 6SP, England
Distributed in Australia by Capricorn Link (Australia) Pty. Ltd.
P. O. Box 704, Windsor, NSW 2756, Australia

10 9 8 7 6 5 4 3 2 1

Manufactured in the United States of America.

Photography and illustration credits are found on page 254
and constitute an extension of this copyright page.

Sterling ISBN-13: 978-1-4027-3907-1
Sterling ISBN-10: 1-4027-3907-9

For information about custom editions, special sales, premium
and corporate purchases, please contact Sterling Special Sales
Department at 800-805-5489 or specialsales@sterlingpub.com.

Design: Richard J. Berenson
        Berenson Design & Books, LLC, New York, NY

DEDICATION

This book is dedicated to the marvelous people of Michigan, every Yooper, each Lower Peninsula inhabitant, young and old, alive on this earth or elsewhere, outwardly strange or sans noticeable eccentricities, without exception.

CONTENTS

Foreword: A Note from the Marks

Our weird journey began a long, long time ago in a far-off land called New Jersey. Once a year or so, we'd compile a homespun newsletter called *Weird N.J.*, then pass it on to our friends. The pamphlet was a collection of odd news clippings, bizarre facts, little-known historical anecdotes, and anomalous encounters from our home state. The newsletter also included the kinds of localized legends that were often whispered around a particular town but seldom heard outside the boundaries of the community where they originated.

We had started *Weird N.J.* on the simple theory that every town in the state had at least one good tale to tell. The publication soon became a full-fledged magazine, and we made the decision to actually do our own investigating to see if we could track down where all of these seemingly unbelievable stories were coming from. Was there, we wondered, any factual basis for the fantastic local legends people were telling us about? Armed with not much more than a camera and a notepad, we set off on a mystical journey of discovery. Much to our surprise and amazement, a lot of what we had initially presumed to be nothing more than urban legends turned out to be real—or at least to contain a grain of truth, which had sparked the lore to begin with.

After a dozen years of documenting the bizarre, we were asked to write a book about our adventures, and so *Weird N.J.: Your Travel Guide to New Jersey's Local Legends and Best Kept Secrets* was published in 2003. Soon people from all over the country began writing to us, telling us strange tales from their home state. As it turned out, what we had perceived to be something of very local interest was actually just a small part of a larger and more universal phenomenon.

When our publisher asked us what we wanted to do next, the answer was simple: "We'd like to do a book called *Weird U.S.*, in which we could document the local legends and strangest stories from all over the country." So for the next twelve months, we set out in search of weirdness wherever it might be found in the fifty states. And indeed, we found plenty of it!

After *Weird U.S.* was published, we came to the conclusion that this country had more great tales than could be contained in just one book. Everywhere we looked, we found unwritten folklore, creepy cemeteries, cursed locations, and outlandish roadside oddities. With this in mind, we told our publisher that we wanted

to document it ALL and to do it in a series of books, each focusing on the peculiarities of a particular state.

But where would we begin this state-by-state excursion into the weirdest territory ever explored, and whom would we invite to take this fantastic journey along with us? Our first inclination was to turn to some of the esteemed authors we had the pleasure of collaborating with on *Weird U.S.* One such writer was Linda Godfrey, a Wisconsin native who has been tracking down the strange and unexplained for years. With her books *The Beast of Bray Road* and *Hunting the American Werewolf,* Linda forces her readers to reexamine their own beliefs as to just what is myth and what might actually exist. Her comprehensive research on "dogmen" or "manwolves" in this country is too well documented to write off those creatures as mere fantasy. And her gift for vivid, spine-tingling storytelling would keep the most diehard skeptic looking over his shoulder while walking alone on a dark night. Linda also has a sly sense of humor that makes her investigations into her subjects such an inviting journey.

We recruited Linda to co-author *Weird Wisconsin,* one of the first state books outside our own home state of New Jersey to be published in the *Weird U.S.* series. In the year we spent collaborating on that tome, it became apparent that Linda definitely had what we like to call the "Weird Eye." The Weird Eye is what is

needed to search out the sort of stories we were looking for. It requires one to see the world in a different way, with a renewed sense of wonder. And once you have it, there is no going back—you'll never see things the same way again. All of a sudden you begin to reexamine your own environs, noticing your everyday surroundings as if for the first time. And you begin to ask yourself questions like, "What the heck is *that* thing all about, anyway?" and "Doesn't anybody else think *that's* kinda weird?"

In Linda, we knew we had found a true kindred spirit in the weird. So when she threw her author's cap into the ring in a bid to write *Weird Michigan,* we told her to hit the road in search of all the weirdness that the Wolverine State has to offer. Over the past year, Linda has chronicled a broad array of the odd and unique people, places, and stories that make Michigan the fascinating and just downright weird place that it is. So please read on and let Linda be your tour guide through one of the most intriguing and bewildering states of them all. It's a place we like to call *Weird Michigan.*

— *Mark Sceurman and Mark Moran*

Introduction

So *how did a Cheesehead chick* get to be author of a book about the weirdness of Michigan? Please don't blame the editors. Early on, before I had even started working on *Weird Wisconsin,* I called dibs on all the states shaped like mittens. Naturally, Mark and Mark, originators of the *Weird* series, are hip to all things mystical. They know about the sacred nature of dibs and the doom that can befall people who disregard them. What choice did they have?

Besides, during my years of hunting and cataloging weirdness in Wisconsin, Michigan oddities kept cropping up. It seemed only logical to start chucking Wolverine articles into a drawer right next to my Badger files. After all, it's just a quick swim across the big pond, and the two states share a lot of things: huge canines that walk on their hind feet, Cornish pasties, more snow than we know what to do with, Paul Bunyan, big auto plants, bizarre serial killers, and lots of amateur artists who like to make things from tractor parts and cement. Don't even get me started on the Paulding Light. Michigan felt like Wisconsin's parallel universe, albeit one with a lot more water frontage.

More than that, though, I had a secret weapon . . . the people of Michigan. As I racked up the miles on my *Weird*mobile seeking strangeness around the Upper and Lower Peninsulas, I never failed to be impressed with the goodwill and helpfulness of the folks I met along the way. On top of that, many other Wolverine Staters e-mailed me their personal experiences with Victorian-era specters or contributed articles on their areas of bizarre expertise. The authentic Michigander presence hangs heavy in this book, breathed onto its pages by the Vernors-laced exhalations of those who know the place best.

And, as with all the books in the *Weird* series, the term "travel guide" is meant to be taken loosely. We're all for road trips. By all means, toss *Weird Michigan* in your back seat, gas up the buggy, and go! There are shoe trees out there just begging for another pair of worn Reeboks. But you will find that some places featured in this book can't really be visited in the real world, where NO TRESPASSING signs are an uncontestable fact of life and wrecking balls often

pound the past into oblivion before we can arrive to pay our respects. And some interviewees kindly told their stories but stipulated they didn't want us to print a giant map to their door. Naturally, we respect their wishes. But we did take pictures: They last longer.

Bottom line: This book is meant to entertain, enlighten, and occasionally whisk you into a vortex to the twilight zone, whether you're lounging in your Kalamazoo living room or navigating "Michigan left turns" on the highway from Paradise to Hell. My standing invitation: take a walk on the weird side. It's a nice place to visit, and you just may find that you really do want to live there.

– *Linda S. Godfrey*

Local Legends

Teenage girls vanish. Small red-faced creatures with glittering eyes foretell doom. Someone usually dies, and sometimes there is treasure. Often some dissolute ghost disturbs the living, its twisted face pressed flat against a dark windowpane as mutely it screams for shelter or, perhaps, fresh blood.

Inside every legend, true or false, urban or rural, roils some primal fear common to mankind. Its telling is crammed with imagery stolen from the shadowed warehouse of our nightmares. And it is precisely because legends speak to our innermost fears that they survive over time and from generation to generation. Legends, unlike those unfortunates whose ghastly ends they chronicle, are never consumed by worm or microbe. People should be so lucky.

Michigan's long-lived cache of local legends spans three centuries, inching forth from the first eerie tales of the French émigrés in the 1700s. Go ahead and repeat these tales, the spirits won't mind. The spoken word—*your* spoken word—is the only sustenance they require to survive another eon or two.

The *Feu Follet*

In the mid-1700s, the old French legend goes, an aristocratic family built a mansion on the largest of a small group of islands in the Detroit straits, known as Grosse (French for fat) Ile. A young woman and her brother were stranded there during a thunderstorm while paying a visit to the owner, who unfortunately had been called to another settlement and was on his way back. The woman and her brother settled in to wait, and as the rain finally began to ebb, everyone in the house heard a loud, mocking shriek from somewhere out on the island.

The young woman instantly proclaimed it to be the *feu follet*, enigmatic spirit lights that leaped around the meadows in search of helpless travelers. Today they would be called will-o'-the-wisps, or spook lights. Her rational-minded brother scoffed, saying they were nothing more than gases seeping from the decaying vegetation in the marsh. But the young woman rushed around the house in terror, slamming all the windows, because tradition said that if permitted entrance to the house, the *feu follet* would curl themselves through the nostrils and into the windpipes of everyone present and choke them to death. She explained that when the lights were sighted out in the wetlands, they also had the power to lure the unwary deep into the wilds until the traveler became completely lost.

The owner of the mansion was still out in the stormy weather, and the pair was worried about his safety. They lit torches and set out to find him in the darkness, slogging their way through snake-infested swamps and dense thickets, until at last they located the frightened man in the middle of a watery quicksand. After the brother and sister managed to rescue him, he confessed that he had become lost in the storm when he followed a beautiful, bright light to what nearly became his boggy grave. The young woman no longer had a problem convincing anyone that the *feu follet*, trickster imp lights of the marshes, were *très très* real.

The Monguagon Ghost

In Trenton, near the corner of West Jefferson and Slocum, stands a historical marker that claims to be near the lost Indian village of Monguagon, where America's only Michigan victory in the War of 1812 was won. What the marker doesn't tell is that one of the young British soldiers who took a bullet to his temple managed to come back from the dead—for a few minutes, anyway.

On August 9, the night the young officer named Muir was killed, an apparition all sweaty and bloody from battle showed up in the boudoir of his sweetheart, Marie. Muir's ghost told Marie that his inert body lay in a thicket and begged her to bury it before it could be found and mutilated by one party or another. Before he left, he touched her hand with his cold, lifeless fingers.

When Marie awoke the next morning, she thought she had been dreaming—until she looked at her hand. There, pressed deep into her fair skin, was a strange dark mark where Muir's shade had touched her. She was stricken with guilt because she had flirtatiously pretended to spurn him the last time they were together. Deciding she must right her wrong, she hightailed it to the battle site with a servant and was somehow able to find her lover's body and make sure that it was properly buried. It was said that from then on, she always wore a black glove on her hand to cover the ghost mark.

The legend continued to grow because every year on the anniversary of Muir's death, Marie would put on a coarse, hooded beggar's robe and wander from house to house, asking for money to feed the poor. Some say she steals through the streets of Trenton to this day every August ninth, in her dark cloak, stretching forth her black-gloved hand and begging for alms to salve her eternally torn conscience.

Le Nain Rouge—That Cursed Red Dwarf

Detroit Lions fans might be forgiven if they think they've seen some of the worst disasters known to man. Superstitious ones might blame outside forces, the occult. Truth be told, the players have only themselves to blame. Or management.

Dark specters haunt the imaginations of Lions players and fans alike. Many have been jolted screaming from sleep by dreams of "a shambling, red-faced creature, with cold, glittering eyes and teeth protruding from a grinning mouth." Seasoned veterans will sit back and say, "Yes, we've seen that nightmare before. Green Bay Packers fans."

Close, but in this case they're wrong.

This particular nightmare has a more ancient pedigree, going back to the very founding of Detroit over three hundred years ago. The little beast in question stands a mere two and a half feet tall and weighs several hundred pounds less than your average bratwurst-stuffed Wisconsinite. And unlike its green-and-gold–clad demonic brethren, this one is red, devilishly red.

It's Detroit's very own Le Nain Rouge, the Red Dwarf.

Le Nain Rouge is frequently described as having "blazing red eyes with rotten teeth" or looking like a "baboon with a horned head . . . brilliant restless eyes and a devilish leer on its face." He appears just before disaster strikes.

Consider Antoine de la Mothe Cadillac, founder of Detroit. In 1701, he was warned by a gorgeous fortune-telling gypsy to "appease the Nain Rouge" lest he lose his riches and vast land holdings. Cadillac ignored the warning and continued to live the high life until six years later when, following a May Day celebration, he and his wife were strolling home and the red dwarf crossed their path.

"It is the Nain Rouge," whispered Cadillac's wife.

Not one for appeasement of any kind, the strutting Cadillac shouted, "Get out my way, you red imp!" and swung his cane, striking the aberrant creature. It vanished amid echoing, mocking laughter.

"Misfortune will soon be our portion," wailed Cadillac's wife. And, true to prophecy, cue disaster. Cadillac was arrested shortly afterward in Montreal for questionable trading activities. Later he was removed to Louisiana, where life continued its downward spiral. Eventually, he returned to France, where he died, mostly forgotten, his fortune gone.

As for the city of Detroit, it may have been all downhill from there. In 1805, the dancing beast was seen just before a massive fire broke out. The city's two hundred buildings were quickly engulfed in flame and consumed. Only a small stone structure survived the conflagration.

In 1884, a lonely woman was attacked by a leering red, baboon-headed dwarf. Several citizens reported an infernal imp brazenly strolling the streets during the infamous five days of rioting that left forty-three people dead in July 1967. Two Detroit Edison workers feared for the life of a small "child" they saw scampering up a utility pole on March 19, 1976. As they went to rescue it, the "child" took a twenty-foot leap to the ground and scurried away. The very next day Detroit was hit by a crippling snow-and-ice storm, one of the worst in the city's history. Lightning that day set off the bell in city hall, its ringing peal reminding some of the red dwarf's sardonic cackle.

As for the Detroit Lions, the less said the better. Flattery, the gypsy prophesied, is the only thing to appease Le Nain Rouge. Anything less offends it. Players and fans alike may well heed this advice should some shambling, red-faced creature, with cold, glittering eyes and teeth protruding from a grinning mouth cross their path. Should the Lions somehow reach the playoffs, instead of turning to soothsaying sports analysts for predictions, look out the window to the streets. Is there a rude red imp dancing in the snow?–*Richard D. Hendricks*

The Legend of the Melon Heads

For as long as anyone can seem to remember, tales have been told around Michigan of a strange race of subhuman creatures who live in the woods near the towns of Saugatuck and Bridgeman. These mutated beings are known as Melon Heads (or sometimes Melonheads) because of their small bodies and disproportionately bulbous craniums. Local children are warned not to venture into the forest, lest they be attacked by these vicious little monsters, which are said to kill and even eat anyone unlucky enough to wander onto their turf. The reason they are filled with such hatred toward us "normals" is because of the twisted way they were once treated at a mysterious institution known in local lore as the Junction Insane Asylum. It was here that experiments were conducted on unfortunate children that led to the horrid physical and mental conditions the Melon Heads now suffer.

The story goes that the facility was commissioned by the state government to treat children who were afflicted with a rare condition known as hydrocephalus, which causes large pockets of fluids within the brain. The Melon Heads suffered severe physical and mental retardation due not only to the disease, but also to their brains being experimented on by those whose care they were in. They continued to mutate until they were hardly human anymore. They became little more than wild animals.

Eventually, the decision was made to close the facility.

By this time, though, the Melon Heads had become feral to the point where the asylum deemed they could no longer be placed in more humane institutions. Supposedly, many of them escaped or, unable to be relocated, were simply released into the surrounding forest to fend for themselves.

Located near the Felt Mansion, behind the BMX track, is a small building that local lore dictates is all that remains of the Junction Insane Asylum, birthplace of the Melon Heads. Heavily vandalized over the years, this ramshackle building is a remnant of the Dunes Correctional Facility. It is the Trustee Building, which once housed about eighty inmates.

According to the Allegan County Historical Society, the Junction Insane Asylum is a myth and never existed; however, that does little to dissuade late-night seekers of the weird, who continue to flock to the site and report seeing curtains moving in the windows of the vacant old building and strange noises emanating from its dark recesses. Witnesses tell tales of the sounds of heavy breathing and tiny footsteps and of seeing shadowy silhouettes darting around inside and around the forlorn structure. And always, there is the feeling that they are being watched.

Is it possible that the Melon Heads have returned here, to this lonely and abandoned place, to live out their miserable existence in the only home they have ever known?–*Myke LaVey*

Encounter with a Melon Head

I used to go to the Felt Mansion in Saugatuck at night with friends when I was in high school. The building back then (only 5 years ago) was abandoned and falling apart. One night while my friends and I were exploring the grounds we heard something rustling in the woods. I tried to just brush it off as a deer or maybe a fat raccoon, but a man with what appeared to be an overly-sized head emerged from the woods about 50 yards away and, saying nothing, started to walk slowly towards us.

Not knowing who this man could be, my friend yelled, "Hello!" to try and be friendly, but all we got was a loud grunt and the man continued to walk towards us, but now at a faster pace. At this point the same idea hit all of us and we all started sprinting towards our car. We scrambled in and peeled out of the parking lot at full speed not slowing down until we were several miles from the mansion. When we all settled down we started to laugh at how we must have overreacted, nervously hoping that it was just a neighbor or possibly a night watchman.

Several days later I told the story to my dad and he suddenly got very serious. He told me that I was never to go back to the Felt Mansion at night. When I asked him why, he told me the story of the Melon Heads.

Years ago the Felt family sold the mansion to a seminary and a small insane asylum was built on the grounds. It was then sold to the state of Michigan and the state turned it into a low-security prison. My father told me that the asylum specialized in patients with extra fluid in the brain, causing their heads to swell. After funding for the asylum was cut, most of the patients were "set free." Many of the Melon Heads had already developed an intense hatred for normal-looking people and chose to stay on the grounds away from society, and they built homes out of the tunnels that run under the mansion. Supposedly they continued to live there and interbreed for decades and still live there to this day. I don't know if the man we saw was a Melon Head, but after I heard that story I never went back there at night again.

P.S. The Felt Mansion has recently been restored and now offers tours to the public. The mansion is located within the Saugatuck State Park and is well worth seeing. Also, Agnes Felt, for whom the house was built, died there three days after it was finished and is said to haunt the place to this day.

—Kellie Topp-Bedrosian

her money. So he concocted a plan: kill his wife, keep her fortune, and marry his sweetheart.

He lured his wife to a swampy area of Grosse Ile and murdered her, sinking her body beneath the muck. She lost her fur muff during the struggle, and not wanting to leave behind a clue, the faithless husband backtracked to hunt it up. An eighteenth century muff had little in common with the modern diminutive hand-warmer. As a wealthy bourgeois, our lady would have worn a large muff of ermine, fox, or sable. Many of the larger muffs covered about a third of their owners and incorporated a ribbon suspended from the neck to help support the muff and free up the wearer's arms.

Returning to our crime scene, the murderer finally spotted the muff and reached to pick it up. Just before he could reach it, however, the muff rolled away from him. Startled but not deterred, he bent down and reached for it again. Once more, it rolled away. The man continued to chase the muff for a while but it always rolled beyond his grasp. Then in a shocking turnaround, the muff began to chase the husband! It chased him right off Grosse Ile. The ordeal so terrified the killer that he fled back to Detroit and confessed his crime.

The muff continued rolling around Grosse Ile, each turn spewing forth the stench of rotting death. Several victims of rolling muff sightings returned bearing the

smuggled Canadian liquor into Detroit. Two men landed on Grosse Ile with a shipment of the goods, only to be turned back by the olfactory persuasion of the rolling muff. By all accounts, Grosse Ile remains today a peaceful and sweet-smelling community, untroubled by the rolling muff. But we say, may it ever roll on!

—Daniel J. Wood

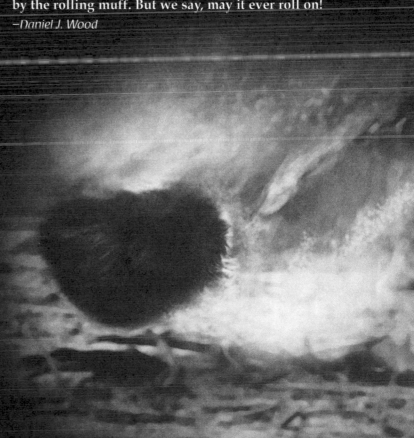

The Lost Painting and the Ghost of Little Grace

In the fall of 1885, in her bedroom in the village of Ontonagon, a thin young woman sat working on a small watercolor painting. On the parchment paper attached to her easel, a cherubic face beneath yellow curls smiled up at her. Grace Johnson Adams had worked on that face for days, trying to capture a feeling and expression that she held within her own being. The subject on the easel, a child's figure cloaked in a cowled garment, clutched a small empty bowl in her tiny fingers.

Grace, in frail health since a childhood bout with scarlet fever, had always been something of a prodigy. Now, at eighteen, she was a maturing artist. The picture upon which she was placing her attention today was intended as a Christmas gift for Grace Hill Mercer, the wife of James Mercer, the legislative representative whose stately home was located at the southeast corner of the village. Mrs. Mercer, herself an artisan, had shown a great deal of interest in young Grace's talents. The Mercers were very well connected, with many visitors to their home, and to have one of her pictures exhibited there would be a great honor for Grace.

In mid-November, though, the girl became ill and took to her bed. She was able to sit at her easel for only a few minutes a day. Nevertheless, by early December, she had finished what would turn out to be her last painting. By then, the picture had taken on a certain gloom. An eerie light source seemed to illuminate the scene from the upper left, as though coming from on high. The child's little hands still clutched an empty bowl, but the very emptiness of the bowl was now the central point. It was almost as if the artist had given the last contents of herself to this work and that the empty bowl was symbolic of events to come.

Grace's mother delivered the beautiful watercolor to the Mercer home just before Christmas, 1885. Only a few

days later young Grace Adams quietly passed away. Her mother was devastated. Shortly after her daughter's funeral, the distraught woman removed all of Grace's paintings, drawings, and other artwork from the family's home, unable to bear the reminders of her lost child.

Mrs. Mercer, fearing the mother would ask for the return of Grace's beautiful watercolor, hid the picture under a built-in set of drawers in a stairwell at her home. Sure enough, a few days later, Elizabeth Adams called at the Mercer home and asked for the painting. The older woman told a little fib. The picture, she said, had been sent off to be more suitably framed, and it had been lost by the express company. The last creation of Grace Adams was never again to be displayed while the Mercers lived in the house.

In 1945, the old Mercer house was purchased by Charles and Ellen Willman, who moved in with their two sons, Royce and John. Royce, the older boy, was helping do a general cleanup when he pulled out the drawers in the stairwell and found the lovely picture. The Willmans were captivated, and hung the watercolor in their new home.

Years went by, and it was by chance that the identity of the artist was revealed. Mrs. Betty Burke of Ellsinore, California, was doing genealogical research on her family. As it turned out, the young artist, Grace Johnson Adams, would have been Betty Burke's great-aunt. In 1997, Betty paid a visit to the Ontonagon County Historical Society Museum, knowing that it contained many pictures of her family members.

By that time, the elder Willmans had passed away and Royce had inherited the house. When he learned that Mrs. Burke was in Ontonagon researching family ancestry, Royce acted on a hunch and brought the mystery painting down to the museum for her to examine. Mrs. Burke confirmed that the painting was one of the last surviving works of her ancestor Grace Johnson Adams. Happy to have at last discovered something about the artist who had painted his "girl on the wall," Royce cleaned the picture up a bit and replaced it in an ornate gold frame. Almost miraculously, the picture seemed to assume a new presence.

In August 2001, he and a few friends were discussing the painting, which had been dubbed *Little Grace*, and decided to try reproducing it for sale. It took two attempts, but the results were very successful.

The rest of the story moves in a very different direction. Maureen Guzek, a friend who had helped Royce Willman reproduce the watercolor, was asleep in her bedroom shortly after the reproduction was done. Inexplicably she awoke from a sound sleep at four thirty-seven a.m. A few minutes later a very cold draft suddenly entered the room. And with the cold came what Maureen described as "fingers of light," which streamed into the room through her window almost as a mist. The fingers stretched across the room, gathered, swirled, and formed a ball from which a face began to emerge.

"No! No! Get away!" Maureen cried out as she struggled to control herself. The face in the ball of light began to take on detail, and Maureen asked, "Who are you?" to which there was no response. Again she asked, "What do you want? Who sent you?"

A clear feminine voice answered, "Royce sent me."

Suddenly it all fell into place. "Grace Johnson!" she exclaimed. In Maureen's own words: "She came out in full form. She sat on the love seat beside my bed. She was smaller than me, maybe five three or five four and very thin. She had medium-dark brown hair, with a little natural curl, that lay just below her collarbones. She wore a long printed dress that fell gracefully over her legs. . . ."

Maureen, sensing the apparition's mission, said, "You're here about the painting? It's absolutely beautiful! We aren't going to hurt it. We're reproducing it because we feel everyone should be able to have one in their home."

Maureen said that at this point, words were no longer necessary; that her thoughts were as one with that of the young girl before her and that ideas passed more quickly than words. Grace Johnson Adams, for the apparition had revealed to Maureen her identity, expressed her unfulfilled need for recognition for her work. Maureen replied that she understood, and she assured Grace that there was no intention to injure this last creation of hers, but to use it to bring her the recognition she deserved.

Maureen states that after exchanging these thoughts, she and the apparition both stood up and exchanged hugs. "I can still feel the warmth of her arms around my shoulders, and I can feel the skeletal structure of her back on the palms of my hands," Maureen relates. As they stepped apart, Grace began to drift off. "Don't go. . . . I have so many questions," Maureen implored.

Grace whispered audibly, "I can't stay . . ." and with that, quietly faded away.

Maureen turned to go back to bed and was startled to see herself lying there, eyes closed, exactly as she had lain down hours before. She realized that she was out of her body, actually viewing herself lying in bed! She knew that the struggling she had felt earlier had actually been her spirit taking temporary leave of her body.

On her way to work that morning, Maureen dropped by to see Royce Willman to tell him what had happened. Royce did not seem surprised in the least. He told her that he had himself talked to Grace Adams the night before and told her that Maureen was only copying her work! He assured Maureen that he had not sent anyone to see her.

When the first dozen copies of *Little Grace* were prepared and offered for sale, the first one was sold in hours. The search goes on for more works by Grace Johnson Adams, whose spirit has reached out of the past, calling for recognition.—*Bruce Johanson*

The following, eerily similar, haunted painting story came to us via e-mail:

Great Grandma Likes Being Framed

This took place in Dearborn in the early '80s to my dad's brother and his family.

A little history is needed first. There is a very quaint Victorian house on a main street in Dearborn that once belonged to my great great grandparents. My uncle lived at the time not too far from the house. One day as he passed the house he noticed that the current owners were selling it. He was curious as to what the inside looked like so he came back later with my aunt.

While touring the open house he struck up a conversation with the owners and said that the house used to belong to our family. The owner then said they had just found an old picture of a severe looking woman with intense eyes behind the chimney in the attic. The owner brought out the picture and there was my uncle's great grandmother staring back at everyone in a 3/4 profile.

The owner let my uncle have the picture, but insisted on keeping the ornate old frame that the picture was in. My uncle agreed, as he was more interested in the picture than the frame. My aunt took the picture home and placed it in the front room on the mantle piece over the fireplace until they could get it reframed.

Weird stuff started happening. Coupons that had been rubber-banded together on the table were found scattered all over the floor with the rubber band on the table. A bird landed on the ledge outside the kitchen window while my aunt was doing dishes and started pecking at the window. While my cousins were home one day the answering machine displayed a message even though no one heard the phone ring and there was no message on the tape. The dog would no longer go in the front room.

After two weeks my aunt went back to the house to beg for the frame. They were getting the feeling that great grandma wanted her frame back. The owner was eager to give it back as weird stuff had been happening there also since the frame and picture were parted. Once the picture was back in the frame all the strange stuff stopped.—*Ememsquared*

The Witch of Seven Gables Lane

Adventurers who tread the back road called Seven Gables near Dansville in Ingham County still sniff the air to see if they can smell the acrid, burnt flesh of the witch who supposedly lived there in years past. As the legend goes, local marauders locked the woman into her house, which was then set on fire. She perished in the flames, but the stories say she remains to wreak vengeance on those who still dare to venture near her property. The place became such a teen mecca that a fence was erected to keep snoopers out of the area. The effort proved fruitless as thrill seekers still found their way back to the deceased woman's old place. But they didn't get away scot-free. It was said that the ghost witch would scream at trespassers and that the scream meant instant doom to its hearers if the premises weren't cleared immediately.

Cheating Witch in Seidman Park

Seidman Park (in Ada Township south of Grand Rapids) is said to be haunted by a woman who was caught cheating there by her husband. It is said that a fight broke out and all three ended up dead. She has been seen by many people, and you can see the fight on a full moon. Some people call her the Ada Witch.–*Melissa Troast, Grand Rapids*

Mecosta Death Car

The little town of Mecosta, about an hour northeast of Grand Rapids, spawned a national legend that continues to spread horror through used car lots everywhere and may even have been the inspiration for an episode of the TV series *Seinfeld.*

It started back in 1929, when a Mecostan named Demings bought a spanking new Model A Ford to impress a lady friend. Little did Demings know he'd soon be riding in a hearse, courtesy of his shiny new wheels.

It turned out Demings's intended sweetheart did not return his feelings. Despondent over the rejection, Demings did himself in by using his Model A to inflict carbon monoxide poisoning. Since he carried out his plan on a deserted country road, no one found him for two months. By that time, his corpse had really stunk up the vehicle. Nonetheless, the death car was hauled to a nearby town, where an auto dealer was alleged to have sold it to one Clifford Cross.

Cross hadn't owned the car long before he realized why the Ford had been such a bargain. It smelled like rotting flesh. Nothing would remove the smell, no matter how hard Cross scrubbed or what cleaning potion he applied. Of course no one else could be induced to buy it, and Cross finally had to consign the odoriferous vehicle to the junkyard.

The death car tale has been repeated in endless variations and has doubtless contributed to the proliferation of the pine-scented, cardboard Scooby-Doos and Hawaiian girls that swing from thousands of rearview mirrors today.

Ancient Mysteries

In *Michigan,* the ancient past is not some dimly perceived, fuzzy dreamscape with no relationship to our techno-world of today. The past and its many mysteries intrude upon the modern consciousness everywhere. Remnants of primitive statues lurk in small-town museums, ancient rocks carved with silly grins lie half hidden in forests, and tantalizing earth berm designs dot the landscape like tattoos on a strongman's back.

Many of the ancient wonders are related to what has been called the Old Copper Culture, the unknown people who figured out how to cold-hammer the "red metal" of Lake Superior and dug something like five thousand mines eons ago. Other evidence keeps turning up to convince us that people from the Old World—Vikings, Minoans, and who knows who else—were also visiting at that time, probably taking boatloads of copper back overseas.

Perhaps the biggest wonder of all, though, is how Michiganders manage to get their mundane daily work done with so many conundrums of the ages begging for solutions. Michigan is, simply, the Rubik's Cube of prehistoric wonders, each colored square a mystery that interacts with all the others. We dare you to twist away at it, but be warned: Delving into the dark secrets of the past is weirdly addictive!

The Dolmen of Huron Mountain

Dolmens are prehistoric stone monuments often depicted as convenient altars for bloody human sacrifice. (They actually had other uses, such as marking a grave or ceremonial center.) Dolmens consist of one large, flat piece of stone resting on several smaller boulders, sort of like a Flintstones' table.

So what is a European-style dolmen doing in Michigan's Upper Peninsula? Writer and former teacher Fred Rydholm has been after that answer since he first laid eyes on the boulder.

In 1939, Rydholm had a job washing dishes for a camp in nearby Big Bay. One day he and some other employees were sent out to search for some lost hikers, including a geology professor. The group was found, but everyone had to stay on the mountain overnight. Around the campfire, the professor told tales of a rock he heard had been placed on top of Huron Mountain in ancient times. He said that the rock, mounted on three smaller boulders, could be a Norse altar rock put there by Viking explorers.

The story excited young Rydholm's imagination, and he never forgot it. Nonetheless, it was two years before he was able to climb the granite mountain to see the dolmen for himself. Once he had found it, he started researching it in earnest and began to believe that perhaps the dolmen was erected by prehistoric Native Americans. Still, it looked exactly like many European dolmens.

One hallmark of a true dolmen is that it will be situated at as high an elevation as possible. The Huron Mountain dolmen was placed on solid rock at about sixteen hundred feet up the mountain. The large, top boulder is about forty inches long and two feet thick and weighs about nine hundred pounds.

Strangely, it may have a twin—or a quadruplet—on this continent. "There is almost an identical dolmen on Tip Top Mountain on the northern shore of Lake Superior," said Rydholm. "There is another in Minnesota, and one in Wisconsin, near Colfax. A farmer sent me a picture of it." All were discovered at high elevations.

Are these rock formations the work of ancient seafarers or monuments built by some forgotten tribe of Native Americans who happened to stumble upon the exact same idea of dolmen construction as people in the Middle East and Europe? All that the citizens who live in the area are sure of is that a glacier didn't do it. If you decide to take a look for yourself, remember that the stone is on land that is now the private property of the Huron Mountain Club.

Gun Lake: Devil's Soup Bowl

The Devil's Soup Bowl is part of the Yankee Springs Recreational Area near Gun Lake and is a must-see for seekers of weird and unexplained natural land formations. Located off Briggs Road, the Soup Bowl is a massive pit in the middle of the woods that is several hundred feet deep and said to have been created by glaciers during the Ice Age. I found out about it from my dad, who, along with his buddies, used to ride their snowmobiles to the bottom of it back in the early '70s. It is very accessible during the summer months. Just park your car near the trailhead and enjoy a short walk to the Soup Bowl and a nearby scenic overlook, Graves Hill.

On the day my fiancée and I visited, I made the steep journey down the hard way. When you reach bottom and look around, it becomes very clear just how far down you are! Plan ahead for the hike back up, though. Supposedly there is a trail that leads all the way to the bottom, but I couldn't find it and ended up using my inhaler about seven times on my way back to the top.—*Marc Sebright*

The Legend of the Petoskey Stones

A quick glance at a Petoskey Stone is all it takes to see that this is no ordinary rock. The stones appear to be covered with hundreds of tiny, radiating suns. Do the circular designs on Michigan's state rock represent the ancient symbol of the mystical "third eye," as some New Agers claim? Of course, most geologists would call the markings a happy accident of nature.

The "stones" are actually a type of fossilized coral. They're named *Hexagonaria percarinata*, because the outer edges of the "suns" or "eyes" are six-sided in shape. The particular type of *Hexagonaria* called the Petoskey Stone, however, is found only in northern Michigan. The coral lived during the Devonian period, 350 million years ago, when Michigan's land mass was located much farther south and was, although this may be hard to believe, covered with a tropical sea.

The coral remains received the name Petoskey much more recently. Legend has it that in the 1700s, a French nobleman traveled to the New World to dabble in the fur trade. Antoine Carre did far more than dabble, however. He married an Ottawa chieftain's daughter and eventually became a chieftain himself. His Ottawa name was Neatooshing.

In 1787, the story goes, Neatooshing decided to winter with his family in northern Illinois. As the temperatures warmed with the return of spring, they headed northeast to the Kalamazoo River area, where Neatooshing's wife bore him a son. As they admired the infant, the morning sun shone on the babe's face, inspiring them to name the child Petosegay, which meant rising sun or sunbeams of promise. The child grew to be a handsome, shrewd businessman. He married another Ottawa chieftain's daughter and raised his own large family.

Petosegay owned much land, including a field where the city of Petoskey now stands. The settlers who erected the first buildings there decided to name it after the French-Ottawa chieftain, spelling his name as Petoskey. This also happened to be precisely where the lion's share of the ancient coral fossils has been found. Could it be mere coincidence that the only place in the world where these sun-patterned "stones" were found turned out to be the namesake of the young child named after the rays of the sun?

Lake Superior Water Gods: Guardians of the Copper

Mishipeshu

Two things are inextricably woven together in the lore of the woodland tribes who lived along Lake Superior: the mystical, shiny material the white men called copper and the fearsome spirits who ruled the lake waters. Foremost among the latter was *Mishipeshu,* the water panther. Michipicoten Island was its home. With curved horns on its head, a serpentlike tail, and dagger-shaped spines on its back, *Mishipeshu* guarded not only the turbulent Great Lakes waters but also the chunks of nearly pure copper moved into the area by glaciers. Although there is ample evidence that very ancient, unknown people mined this copper and moved much of it to some undetermined location, by the time the Jesuit missionaries arrived in the 1600s, taking the copper was considered strictly taboo by the local Ojibwa. Copper-napping was an especially bad

thing to do on Michipicoten Island—to remove that copper was to steal from *Mishipeshu* himself.

A Jesuit missionary named Claude Dablon told the story of four Ojibwa who made a trip to Michipicoten Island to carry home chunks of copper to use to heat water. The minute they shoved off from the island, their canoe heaped with chunks of metal, they heard the eerie voice of the water panther screaming after them, accusing them of stealing the playthings of his children. All four men died mysteriously and painfully while en route to their village, the last one surviving just long enough to gasp out the tale in his final moments of agony.

When more white settlers and adventurers pushed westward into Michigan in the 1840s, a copper rush started as people realized the value of the metal lying there for the taking around Isle Royale and the Keweenaw Peninsula. But *Mishipeshu* had evidently not forsaken his guardian duties. Great woe and accidents befell many of the key people and vessels in the nineteenth-century copper trade. In 1877, the steamer *Cumberland* was lost at Rock of Ages Reef on Isle Royale. Another ship, the *Algoma,* was caught in a storm in 1885, and forty-five people went to eternal graves in the water panther's lair. The little island of Isle Royale built four lighthouses intended to help avoid *Mishipeshu's* growl, but nine or ten ships were lost around Isle Royale alone, and many more suffered serious accidents nearby.

Mishi Ginabig

Mishipeshu is not the only spirit creature said to inhabit Superior's copper region. There is the horned serpent the Ojibwa call *Mishi*

Ginabig, which, according to the book *Ojibwa Narratives*, "had immense antlers and was as big as the largest pines." There may be some confusion between it and *Mishipeshu* in translations of various tales, but *Mishi Ginabig* is generally considered to be a huge sea serpent while *Mishipeshu* is portrayed with legs. *Mishi Ginabig* was reportedly seen by a group of Ojibwa in the early 1800s. But when a flash of lightning hit the lake on its west shore, an unseen force the people presumed to be *Mishi Ginabig*'s enemy, the Thunderbird, pulled the creature out of the water and up into the sky, where it disappeared from view.

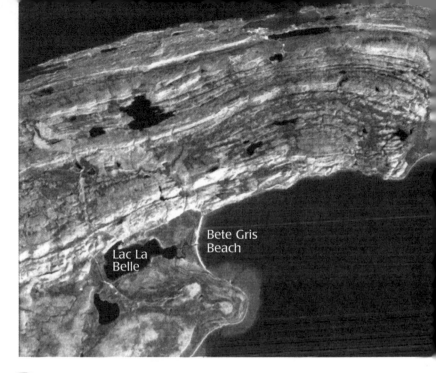

Lac La Belle

Bete Gris Beach

Mermaids and Mermen

The *Narratives* also reveal that the lake contains the equivalent of European mermaids or mermen, called *Nibawnawbe´*. These creatures sported waist-length hair and inhabited the shores of Michipicoten Island long before Europeans tainted native lore with fairy tales of similar creatures. Claude Dablon, in his report "Jesuit Relations," called them "sirens" and documented the Ojibwa belief that seeing a *Nibawnawbe´* meant someone in the family was about to die.

Still Guarding the Copper?

The copper rush around Lake Superior is mostly just a memory now, and the great disasters seem to have stopped as well. Only those who occasionally find and pocket a pebble of "red metal" can tell us if the spirits still seek and punish them for their deed. But those who stand on these shores to watch a sudden squall roil Superior's deep waters may be forgiven if they claim to glimpse a horned head or lashing tail amid the spray. After all, there is still unknown bounty on the lakebed from all those sinkings over the years. Who's to say that *Mishipeshu* has truly given up the playthings of his children?

Singing Sands of Bete Gris

It isn't clear whether they're warbling a Mozart aria or a tune from some aging rocker's greatest hits list. But the sands at Bete Gris Beach at Lac La Belle on the Keweenaw Peninsula do sing. However, they lift their gritty voices only when lying in place on their own patch of peninsula. Export them, and they lose their song. And they perform only when someone lays a human palm on them and twists downward. Local legend says their collective voice is actually that of a Native American maid who, in ages past, was separated from her lover when he was sent to the other side of the lake. She still calls to him with the aid of visitors to the beach. There are other beaches in the area, but only the maiden's sand sings.

The other legend of Bete Gris concerns its name, which in French means "gray beast." Some say the name came from sightings of a mysterious gray creature along the misty shores. Perhaps it is the sand's siren song that lures the gray beast. Whatever the source of the mysteries, the sandy sound can be tested by taking a drive up U.S. 41 and turning off at Lac La Belle.

Who Built the Ontonagon Pyramids?

Pyramidal mounds are not uncommon in North America. The Mississippian culture built them in population centers such as Cahokia in Illinois and Aztalan in Wisconsin. And the stepped pyramids of the Aztecs and Mayans in Mexico and South America are world-famous.

But pyramids in the forests of the Upper Peninsula of Michigan? Well, they do exist—at least two of them, and possibly more. The only problem is that we don't know who built them, Mother Nature or ancient fathers.

In the middle of the nineteenth century, the infamous surveyor and cusser Sam Hill (of the phrase "What in Sam Hill?" fame) wrote about two unusual "hills" or "tumuli" that he found. One, he said, "had the appearance of a work of art, and formed a square, flattened pyramid about ten feet high with 15-foot sides that 'sloped regularly' to the base." He found another, perfectly circular, mound forty feet high on a bank of the Ontonogan River, and discovered a line of old mine pits and ancient hammers nearby.

However, a book called *Michigan Prehistory Mysteries* by Betty Sodders claims that the tumuli surveyed by Hill were not the Ontonagon pyramids. Sodders interviewed Ontonagon resident Rudy Saari, who told her the real pyramids were located one hundred yards from the Ontonagon River, a mile and a half from the village. He said these mounds measured fifty-six and sixty-seven feet high, respectively, and that they were investigated by Professor James Scherz of the University of Wisconsin as well as by professors from Michigan Tech. All except Professor Scherz declared these two formations to be natural.

Bruce Johanson of the Ontonagon Historical Society, a former high school teacher, has personally made the trek to the remote area where at least one of the pyramids, a three-sided one, stands. "I have spent some time on one of those mounds," he told *Weird Michigan*. "It is a three-sided pyramid, flat on top, and one side is in a perfect alignment with the North Star. The slope of the sides matches the slant of the sun's rays at the times of the equinoxes, which suggests that this is a calendar mound which was also an observation platform. The top is fully seventy-two feet above the Ontonagon River." He feels that although these mounds have been dismissed as "natural" formations by archaeologists, there are too many indications that they were man-made for that to be true.

The bottom line is that there are structures that look like man-made pyramids in the forests near Ontonagon. Only Mother Nature knows if she made them or not, and she's not talking.

Rivet Punch of the Vikings

Lying in a glass case at the Ontonagon Historical Museum is an article that causes acute embarrassment to anyone insistent that no Europeans reached the Americas before Columbus. In 1964, the Ontonagon County mining inspector discovered an odd metal object while out on his rounds and brought it to the historical society to see if anyone knew what it was. The piece was sent to the Museum of Antiquities in Oslo, Norway, for study, where it was positively identified as a rivet punch meant to "squish" copper rivets used in the construction of oceangoing vessels of the eleventh and twelfth centuries. There is no doubt the item is genuine, and no one believes the mining inspector would have had any reason to plant it in an ancient mining area for hoaxing purposes.

How did it get to Lake Superior? That's just one more of the unsolved puzzles surrounding the abandoned copper mines of Michigan's Upper Peninsula.

The Michigan Relics: Great Hoax or Noah's Lost Diary?

Hundreds and hundreds of alleged "biblical" clay and copper artifacts unearthed in sixteen Michigan counties, primarily between 1890 and 1907, have been labeled the most monstrous hoax ever perpetrated on American soil. And yet some still believe that the strange objects, known as the Michigan relics, prove that people from the Middle East walked this land millennia before Columbus ever set sail.

The objects range from copper tools, coins, and implements to engraved slate tablets with pictograms and writing that appears to be ancient cuneiform in several languages. One tablet shows many scenes from the biblical flood along with a drawing of the ark, so its finders called it Noah's Diary. Another strangely shows the crucifixion of Jesus Christ mixed in with Old Testament scenes of ancient Israeli history. Most of the articles are stamped or engraved with what has come to be known as the "mystic symbol," a series of three characters usually presumed to mimic the (somewhat misunderstood) Greek letters IHS, which are widely accepted elsewhere as a symbol for Jesus Christ.

Three Michigan men, all of whose last names begin with the letter S, have come to be identified with the relics. The first was a former traveling magician named James

Scotford, who supposedly found the first relic, an unfired clay cup, in 1890 while digging postholes for a fence north of Edmore in Montcalm County. Scotford began exploring burial mounds and kept unearthing more and more relics, selling postcards of their photos.

The articles were denounced as fakes as early as 1891 by a Chicago expert, Dr. Alfred Emerson of Lake Forest College, who called them "humbugs of the first water." Other scholars agreed. But Scotford kept on digging . . . and finding. He might have remained simply a desecrator of Michigan Indian mounds had he not met up with the second S man, Daniel Soper.

Soper was a former Michigan secretary of state who lost his job after it was found out he had demanded $500

of his assistant's yearly $2,000 salary in return for the job. Soper saw dollar signs in Scotford's crude relics, and the two went into the business of artifact hawking. Besides Noah's Diary, they advertised that they had a copy of the blueprints for the Tower of Babel!

One of their luckiest finds was not a relic, but a highly respected man of the cloth and the third S, Father James Savage of Most Holy Trinity Church in Detroit. The Reverend Mr. Savage became entranced with the articles and began not only purchasing large quantities of them, but participating in digs with Scotford and Soper. Savage's sterling reputation lent much-needed credibility to the relics, and garnered both continuing publicity and growing sales for Scotford and Soper. It was said that Savage believed in the authenticity of the finds for as long as he lived.

Amazingly, of the huge number of objects discovered in mounds, a very high proportion happened to be uncovered while Scotford, who you'll recall was an adept stage magician, was present. Debunkers theorized that Scotford hid the objects on his person, then slipped them into the mounds after the excavation had begun.

It seems that Scotford, who was also a former sign painter and therefore had at least a modicum of artistic ability, would hardly have had time to manufacture so many artifacts, but he probably was not creating them all himself. He had two handy sons who, their landlady testified, spent all their time manufacturing mysterious *objets d'art*, hammering and sawing at all hours of the day and night. Soper and the Scotfords, unwittingly abetted by Savage, literally had a field day with relic sales from 1907 until 1911, when two more scholars weighed in with opinions that the artifacts were forged and the facts about the younger Scotfords' activities

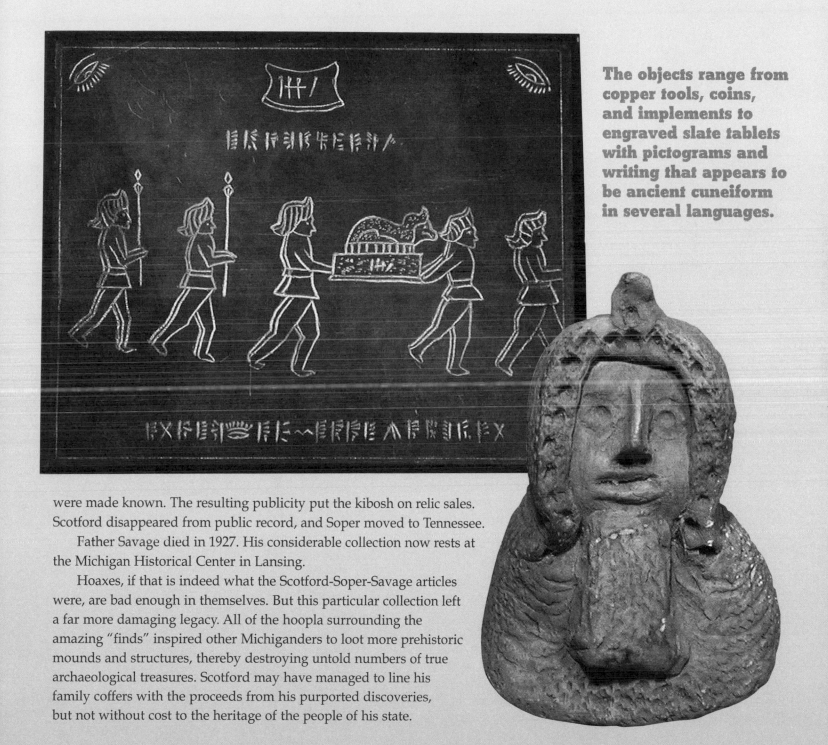

The objects range from copper tools, coins, and implements to engraved slate tablets with pictograms and writing that appears to be ancient cuneiform in several languages.

were made known. The resulting publicity put the kibosh on relic sales. Scotford disappeared from public record, and Soper moved to Tennessee.

Father Savage died in 1927. His considerable collection now rests at the Michigan Historical Center in Lansing.

Hoaxes, if that is indeed what the Scotford-Soper-Savage articles were, are bad enough in themselves. But this particular collection left a far more damaging legacy. All of the hoopla surrounding the amazing "finds" inspired other Michiganders to loot more prehistoric mounds and structures, thereby destroying untold numbers of true archaeological treasures. Scotford may have managed to line his family coffers with the proceeds from his purported discoveries, but not without cost to the heritage of the people of his state.

Ancient Twin Grins?

In the spring of 2002, Bessie Kmiecik entered the wilderness of central Wisconsin, near the Lemon Rind, to search for a historical legend—an ancient behemoth carved in stone. After a battle with briars and verdant undergrowth, Kmiecik managed to overcome sentinels that for centuries had enfolded the boulder in nature's arms along the upper reaches of the Black River. At last she reached the object of her quest: a carved boulder about ten feet around and three feet high. Some cursory cleaning gradually uncovered an ancient face incised in ages past.

Using a tape measure, Kmiecik found that each almond-shaped eye measured roughly six inches across, with a little more than a foot separating the set. The image's most distinctive feature, its silly-looking grin, etched as deeply as an inch and a half and as wide as two, stretched twenty-one inches across the stone. Kmiecik measured each side of the triangular nose to be more than a foot.

Expert opinion on the giant stone face has varied. Dr. James Scherz, emeritus professor at the University of Wisconsin-Madison, examined Kmiecik's photographs and posited that the object most likely served as an ancient calendar stone. Noting that the image faced east, Scherz observed that the lines extending from the nose may indicate the position of the sun on the horizon during planting season.

Further clues concerning the provenance of Wisconsin's Black River boulder might be found across the lake, in Michigan. There, in the 1980s, workers unearthed a similar boulder while excavating in the

Michigan's smiling boulder

Saginaw Valley, in the area between Saginaw and Tuscola counties. A comparison of the boulders appears to establish a kinship between the images: Both share shell-like eyes, triangular noses, and—yes—that odd smile.

An anthropologist from Michigan State University examined the carving and estimated its age at around five hundred years, making it contemporary with the Sanilac Petroglyphs, a series of carvings found to the northeast, in Michigan's Thumb.

Did the same culture produce the grinning heads and the glyphs? Referencing the points of similarity between the Wisconsin and Michigan boulders also suggests the possibility that an as yet unknown culture once ranged the Great Lakes before the arrival of our current Algonquian groups. –*Daniel J. Wood*

Wisconsin's Black River boulder

Ancient Circles of Water

Deep in the forests of Missaukee County in northern Michigan are a series of ancient earthworks that harbor many secrets. Over the years, I have visited these earthworks, and little by little, I began to pierce the dark cloak of time that has obscured so much of the life lived by those who came before us.

The Missaukee Earthwork Enclosures were built by the mysterious Hopewell Indians. Most archaeologists concur that they were built for a ceremonial purpose. The method of construction was to dig a circular ditch at the edge of a marsh and to make it deep enough to allow the marsh water to flow in. The dirt that was excavated in forming the circular ditch was placed on the inside of the circle, thus creating a mound with a circle of water. Gateways were formed by simply skipping a twelve-foot section in the digging effort. This same kind of construction was used for the circular earthwork surrounding Stonehenge.

This form of construction fits in with the well-documented ancient Indian belief that water is a spirit barrier. The water-filled circular ditch would provide an isolated, protected ceremonial space. Perhaps other spirit barrier substances, such as fire, hot ashes, or red sand, were laid across or removed from the gateways to bar or allow access of spirit entities into the inner ring.

By using a compass and a handheld GPS (Global Positioning System), I have laid out the pattern of all the existing earthworks in the Missaukee County area. Circles 1 and 2 are called the Twins because they are very close together and duplicate each other. They both have gateways at 340 degrees northwest and at 250 degrees southwest. The extra gateway in Circle 2 lines up perfectly with the southwest gateway of Circle 1, thus linking the Twins together.

I also used the GPS to calculate the directional bearings among the circles. The southwest gateways of the Twins are aimed directly at Circle 3, and their north gateways aim directly at the burial mounds. The distance between Circles 2 and 3, and between 2 and 4, is exactly 6.21 miles in each case. Finally, just as with the Twins, the north gateway of Circle 3 is also aimed directly at something—namely Circle 5—which is 24.8 miles away.

How did the ancient builders keep all these things lined up? They would have had to contend with a dense forest canopy as well as swamps, rivers, and streams in setting out these alignments over such distances. Could these earthworks be sacred points of destination for the magical linear flight of ancient shamans? Perhaps to understand this better, we need to envision a worldview in which there was a spiritual version of the terrestrial environment, the Land of the Dead, that can be journeyed to and through only in a state of ecstatic trance or at death. In this worldview, the flight of the shaman is the straight way over land. Could the aligned gateways of these circles be entry and exit points for out-of-body flight? Did a circle of water play a part in this? These are some of the questions posed by the simple use of a compass and handheld GPS, which may someday prove the key to these and other ancient sites.

—*Doug Masselink*

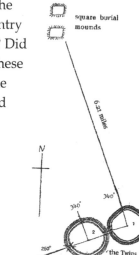

square burial mounds

6.21 miles

N

340°

340°

6.21 miles

24.8 miles

250°

2

1

the Twins

305°

3

250 SW

?

The Newberry Discovery

On a remote farm on the Upper Peninsula, near the small town of Newberry, a reclusive old farmer named McGruer hired two reportedly slow-witted woodsmen to cut up some firewood on his property in 1897. Their minds not entirely on their work, evidently, the pair spotted a mink and chased it to a cavity underneath the roots of a fallen cedar or hemlock tree. As they probed the ground for the animal, they felt something hard and stony, and cleared away the lingering root tendrils to pull out three ancient-looking statues and a tablet covered with undecipherable writing. The mink was immediately forgotten. The two men were convinced they'd hit the sideshow jackpot of the year and, with considerable difficulty, hauled the booty back to McGruer's farm, where they reluctantly allowed a few people to have a peep.

Excited neighbors convinced the men to exhibit the strange objects in a store in Newberry, and people came from all over to have a look. The Newberry newspaper described the figures as sandstone, although later descriptions claimed they were of unfired clay. There was a male, a smaller female, and an even smaller child figure, plus a tablet with incised cuneiform arranged in even rows horizontally and vertically. Nobody knew what to make of it, but everyone agreed it did not look like any Native American artifacts they had ever seen.

Weird Michigan caught up to the remaining fragments of the find at the Fort de Buade Museum in St. Ignace, where they rest in an old glass cabinet. All that is left to see now is the largest statue's head and upper body, the

"woman's" head, and fragments of the tablet. The face of the "man" is eroded and hard to make out, but framed newspaper accounts from the late 1800s relate the story.

It's been a long, strange trip for the Newberry items. Michigan author Betty Sodders has written extensively about them in her book *Michigan Prehistory Mysteries*, and the tablet in particular has been discussed in many publications, including Roger L. Jewell's *Ancient Mines of Kitchi-Gummi, Cypriot/Minoan Traders in North America*. At least one noted translator has identified the symbols on the tablet as from the Hittite-Minoan language . . . circa 2000 B.C.!

Moreover, scholar Dr. Barry Fell was able to translate the message. It's advice on how to tell the future by observing the way birds eat grain scattered on the ground. It seems extremely unlikely that old Farmer McGruer or his illiterate hired hands would have had access to any kind of Hittite-Minoan original to copy. And strangest of all is that the Minoans, from the island of Crete, are exactly the people suspected by many researchers as a major impetus behind the mysterious prehistoric copper mining that went on around Lake Superior several millennia ago.

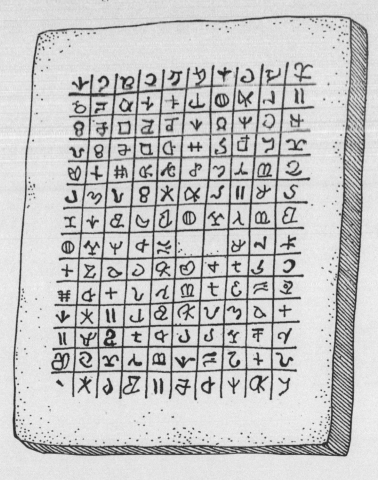

Back in the 1890s, however, few researchers were equipped to recognize ancient Hittite-Minoan when they saw it. The photographs of the items sent to the Smithsonian were dropped in a folder labeled MICHIGAN FAKES and left to languish. McGruer, somewhat embittered, stashed the items in an old horse barn that was partially open to the elements, and the statues and tablet became little more than a curiosity for daring teenagers to sneak up on and occasionally vandalize at night. Most of the study done on them in recent times was enabled by early newspaper articles and by those old photographs sent to the Smithsonian, taken when the statues and tablet were relatively whole.

Of course, there has been no end of conjecture as to which culture the statues may have come from. It is a fact that up to fifty million pounds of copper were taken from the Lake Superior area between 2400 and 1200 B.C. (roughly the same time frame the Hittite-Minoan language found on the Newberry tablet was in use). The mined copper was taken away; it simply doesn't exist on the North American continent anymore. As Jewell put it, "What would the hunting and fishing native groups who are found in the Lake Superior region do with 50,000,000 pounds of copper? Especially since it is in large chunks, many weighing 20 to 100 pounds, and some as heavy as several thousand pounds. This is the root question, because if they did anything but trade, the copper would still be here."

Were the Newberry statues and tablet stashed by some ancient seafaring people to use again on their next trip back to the New World? Or was Farmer McGruer more clever and devious than his townspeople gave him credit for? Perhaps future progress in archaeological technology will find the true answer to the origin of those enigmatic clay artifacts.

The Sanilac Petroglyphs: Site of the Shamans

Enchanting, and unfortunately, eroding, the famed rock in Michigan's Thumb that contains the state's only known ancient pictorial carvings, or petroglyphs, is still considered sacred by the Chippewa, who say it was left for them by their ancestors. The carvings of animals, spirals, mythic creatures, a warrior-hunter bending his bow, and other markings on the rock's surface continue to instruct them, as the artworks were originally designed to do, they say.

For the general public, however, the petroglyph area is now usually closed—both for the rock's protection and because of lack of funds for supervision. And because the rock is made from soft sandstone, easily worn away by the elements, park officials have erected a shelter over it. *Weird Michigan* found all this out the hard way when we stopped to visit. The rockface lies flat to the ground—not vertically, as people are accustomed to seeing petroglyphs in other places. Over the years, visitors have walked on it, chipped out some of the figures, and even vandalized it with their own carvings. And yet, the rock symbols remain as powerful as ever, drawing people from around the world to try their hand at deciphering the assortment of carved figures. So far, no magical key has been found to unlock the mystery.

The rock, which is about forty feet long by fifteen feet wide, was first discovered by farmers when major forest fires in 1871 and 1881 burned off years of growth and vegetation, exposing the long-covered surface. Archaeologists have had a difficult time dating the glyphs. Estimates of their age run from four hundred to one thousand years or older, but no one is really sure.

Neither does anyone know exactly which tribe made them, since more than one group lived in that area during the time. Because the rock is in such an isolated place near the fork of the Cass River, anthropologists have speculated that this was a ceremonial site visited mostly by holy men or shamans. In that case, it wasn't meant for the general population to see or use.

What sort of rituals might have been enacted while carving the petroglyphs? Archaeologist John Halsey told a *Detroit News* reporter in 2005 that he believed the place may have been a destination for holy men or hunters to go on "vision quests," which involved fasting and ceremonies

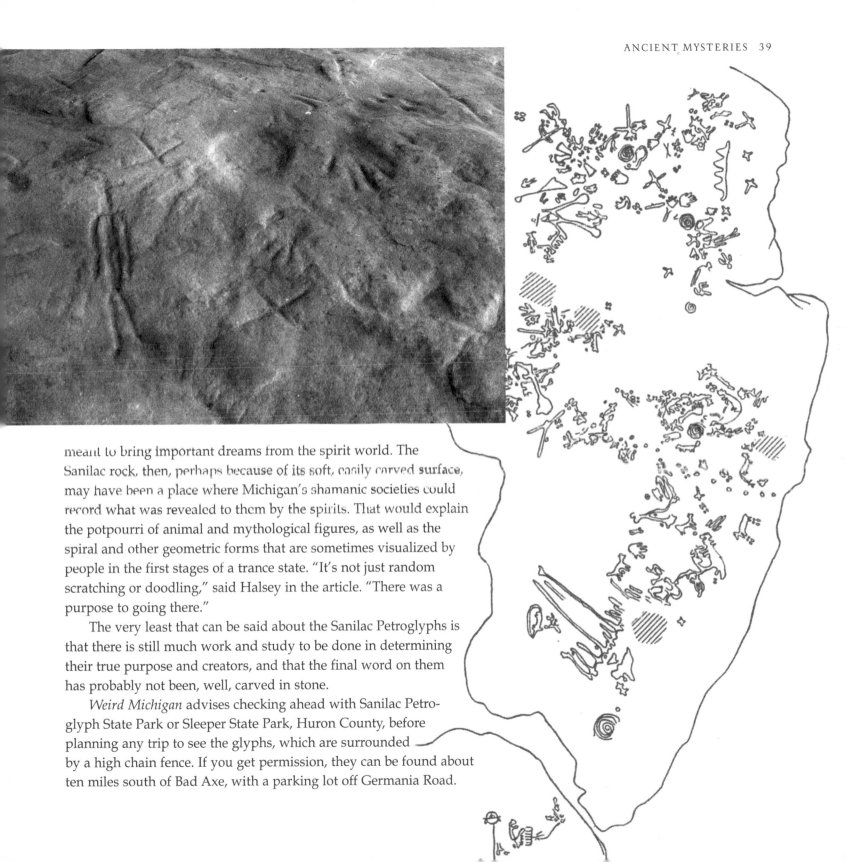

meant to bring important dreams from the spirit world. The Sanilac rock, then, perhaps because of its soft, easily carved surface, may have been a place where Michigan's shamanic societies could record what was revealed to them by the spirits. That would explain the potpourri of animal and mythological figures, as well as the spiral and other geometric forms that are sometimes visualized by people in the first stages of a trance state. "It's not just random scratching or doodling," said Halsey in the article. "There was a purpose to going there."

The very least that can be said about the Sanilac Petroglyphs is that there is still much work and study to be done in determining their true purpose and creators, and that the final word on them has probably not been, well, carved in stone.

Weird Michigan advises checking ahead with Sanilac Petroglyph State Park or Sleeper State Park, Huron County, before planning any trip to see the glyphs, which are surrounded by a high chain fence. If you get permission, they can be found about ten miles south of Bad Axe, with a parking lot off Germania Road.

Isle Royale's Mystery Disk

It has been handed down through his family for generations, but it's still a mystery to him, Paul Tolonen, now of New Mexico, says. "It" is a strange metal medallion covered on both sides with Far Eastern imagery. Not so strange in itself, except for the fact that it was dug up accidentally in 1929 by Tolonen's great-uncle, Sam Hattala, as he was excavating pier foundations on the shore of Isle Royale. Hattala found the medallion a good twenty-four inches below the soil surface on the rugged snippet of land surrounded by Lake Superior. It shows a figure resembling Buddha sitting in what looks like the entrance of a stepped pyramid. The medallion also shows palm trees, and one side bears carved letters around a heart-and-wishbone symbol with a tiny lion inside.

Isle Royale has often been thought to have hosted ancient traders, perhaps even from the Old Country before Columbus. Whether Tolonen's great-uncle knew that or not, he realized the medallion was an unusual thing to find in this northern island soil. Professor James Scherz at the University of Wisconsin in Madison has examined the medallion and shown it to other experts. Originally, scholars told Scherz the medallion was Masonic in origin, but Masonic experts insisted that was not true. In 1989, some Tibetan monks visited Madison and told Scherz the medallion was an image of a pyramidal temple in Borobudur, Java! The wishbone and heart indicate devotion to Java's royal family, signified by the lion. The medallion was probably a keepsake for some supporter of the temple, the monks believed. Scherz's subsequent investigations finally convinced him that the medallion was probably left on Isle Royale in the early 900s, perhaps by a Buddhist missionary from the Javan temple. It's only a theory, of course, but other explanations are scant to nonexistent. Weirdly, this artifact that may have traveled from Java to Isle Royale is now in New Mexico, making it a relic road-trip champion. And the medallion remains as inscrutable as the Buddha that sits upon it.

Humongous Fungus

One of Michigan's most popular tourist attractions is literally nowhere to be seen. The giant fungus of Crystal Falls, in Iron County, is an underground phenomenon that could never be viewed in its entirety without destroying a forest. But as the largest known living organism in the world, the thirty-eight-acre subsoil mushroom brings visitors from around the globe. It has even inspired an annual festival, the Humongous Fungus Fest. The highlight of the festival is the Largest Mushroom Pizza in the World, baked on a ten-foot-square pan. But since there are no ovens that size, the town has to improvise.

Jeff and Staria Syrjanen, owners of the Crystal Falls Ben Franklin Store and founding members of Fungus Fest, explain that every year, the town builds its own outdoor oven by stacking concrete blocks in a big square, then lining the inside with charcoal. A crane lifts the pizza pan atop the charcoal, and then the pizza is built layer by layer and covered with foil to bake. The Syrjanens do a brisk business in Fungus Fest T-shirts and mushroom-shaped refrigerator magnets.

Eager tourists will not find billboards pointing to the giant fungus, however. Its exact location is unmarked. Lying east of Crystal Falls, off Highway 2, very close to the Wisconsin border, the one-hundred-ton fungus is believed to be thousands of years old and very important to the ecosystem. The fungus breaks down decaying wood and is a factory for the carbon dioxide that plants require to generate oxygen.

Weird Michigan took a gander at the quiet woods where the fungus makes its home in the basement level and had to agree, it takes imagination to "see" it. If we did have X-ray eyes, most of the organism would look like a tangle of tendrils. Only a few tiny "button" mushrooms, the big plant's fruit, poke through the forest floor here and there, giving no hint of the twisty behemoth below.

The record-breaking *Armillaria bulbosa* was discovered by researchers hired by the navy to study the ecological effects of their low-frequency electromagnetic field system, which was formerly used for submarine communication. It took the science team three years to poke enough sample holes in the forest floor to figure out exactly how big the fungus actually was. We have to take their word for it that it was indeed—humongous.

Some people believe that within every human being lies a tiny spark of divine eccentricity. Most of us crush it out early or allow it to be doused by the disapproval of others. But a few people tend it and allow it to take flame, thereby setting themselves apart from the mass of ordinary humanity.

We all recognize that there is something unique about those individuals who allow their "freak flag" to fly. Some of these strange souls are larger than life (a few, literally), so that anything they do is accomplished with a grandness of gesture that earns them instant celebrity. Still others have lived—or died—so that their very names became symbolic of mystery, eternal puzzles whose tales take on new layers as each succeeding generation rolls them out for inspection.

Weird Michigan sought out the most unusual of this elite group in the Wolverine State. All of these legendary people are over the top somehow, and we mean that in a wicked good way. If these stories encourage any of our readers to fan the flames of their own hidden eccentricity of spirit, we cannot be responsible. But we will salute you.

Fabled People and Places

LIZZIE
WHITLOCK

1853 — 1899

FAT LADY OF CIRCUS

Big Louie, Giant of the Keweenaw

He was a miner, a sideshow giant, a bartender, and an elected justice of the peace during his relatively short life. But whatever his occupation at any given time, gentle Louie Moilanen was always guaranteed to be the tallest person in the room. The Ringling Brothers Circus billed him as the Tallest Man on Earth, but at eight feet four, Louie probably fell a few inches short of that honor. Still, he was probably very tired of being asked about the quality of the air up there.

Born in 1885, Louie emigrated from Finland at the age of four. His family made their home in Salo (a town later destroyed by fire), a tiny Finnish community on the Keweenaw Peninsula, where the Great Lakes air evidently agreed with the growing boy. At the age of eighteen, he already stood eight feet one. People were doubly shocked at his height because his mother measured barely a few inches over four feet tall and his father was considered of average height.

His family's farm was close to the Franklin Copper Mine, where Louie proved his worth by his ability to shoulder the same timber load as six normal-sized men. But the mines weren't designed to accommodate giants, so Louie found himself an easier job with Ringling Brothers. By then, he stood eight feet four, weighed four hundred and fifty pounds, and wore size 19 shoes. The circus billed him as Big Louie, the Copper Country Giant. He lasted only two years, though, finally becoming tired of people staring at him and homesick for his Keweenaw.

Back in Michigan, Louie became a popular bartender in Hancock. According to historian Wilbert Maki in a 2001 issue of *Michigan History Magazine,* his arms were so long he could simultaneously hand beers to customers at each end of the bar. He eventually became so well known that the town elected him justice of the peace.

Unfortunately, like many people of his time, Louie came down with tuberculosis and died, at the young age of twenty-eight. His custom casket, which measured almost nine feet in length and weighed three hundred pounds, had to be taken to Wasa Cemetery near Hancock on a flat wagon rather than the customary hearse. But Louie wasn't allowed to rest easy in his grave. After his burial, rumors flew that grave robbers had stolen his body for his giant skeleton. The grave was duly excavated to prove that Louie was still down there. A museum in Calumet still displays one of his massive suits, and the little Upper Peninsula town of Boston, near the lost village of Salo, now claims to be the hometown of Big Louie.

Lizzie Whitlock, Circus Fat Lady

Lying in Batavia Township Cemetery, in one of the largest graves in southern Michigan, are the remains of what some have called the "original circus fat lady." Whether or not Lizzie Whitlock was THE original, she was certainly one of the earliest "large people" in American circus history. Born Elizabeth Charlotte Stice in 1853 in either Iowa or Missouri, Lizzie went by the stage alias of Lottie Grant. She must have glimpsed her future early on, because she ran away as a teenager to join a variety of traveling sideshows. Some accounts say she left as young as age fourteen, others say sixteen. What's known for sure is that at age eighteen, she already tipped the scale at five hundred pounds.

Lizzie eventually made it to the big time in the freak world, signing on with Ringling Bros. and Barnum & Bailey Circus. Not content to merely sit and show off her poundage, she trained as a snake charmer and reportedly wowed the crowds with her skillful handling of rattlesnakes. She had a rich personal life as well, marrying three men and bearing four children over her lifetime. Her first husband, George Parker, died harpooning a seal, according to some of his relatives. Her second husband was a trapeze artist killed when he plunged to his death, and her third marriage was to Frank Whitlock, a barker and ticket agent. One relative has speculated she may also have had a fourth husband named Charles Love, known as the Skeleton Man. They would have made an unusual pair.

According to a Michigan newspaper article, Lizzie was proud to be known as the "fat lady," which is consistent with the attitudes of most sideshow people of the day. Many of them made good livings and were treated well by their circus employers because of the large crowds they drew. Lizzie, although not a wealthy woman, seemed to have been content with her life.

When she left the circus, Lizzie retired to Batavia, where she suffered from an unknown ailment the last two years of her life. The Beehive Shoe Store in nearby Coldwater hand-made her custom, size 24 shoes. She had a new pair on order when she died in 1899 at the age of forty-five. Since no one else in the county could wear the huge high-tops (the right shoe was nineteen inches long, two inches longer than the left), the shoes were saved; they now rest on display in that town's Wing Museum.

Lizzie weighed over six hundred and fifty pounds at her death from "dropsy" or heart failure. One of the six pallbearers crashed through the porch floorboards as they carried her casket out of her house. Her grave was unmarked until 1996, when the Branch County Historical Society donated a graceful headstone. By that time, Lizzie's exact location had been lost and the cemetery association had to hire a "body-witcher" named Carman McNitt to find her with the use of a dowsing, or divining, rod. McNitt told one local reporter he had no trouble locating the body because of "its extra large size," and that her head lay to the west. When *Weird Michigan* visited, Lizzie's grave was decorated with a lone whimsical doll and a basket of plastic flowers.

Paw Paw Fire Breather

Old legends of fire-breathing dragons may not be so far-fetched after all, since there was once a Michigan man from the little town of Paw Paw who could set fires merely by breathing. His feats were documented in no less an authoritative journal than the *Michigan Medical News,* and Dr. L. C. Woodman of Paw Paw told the unusual story in *Scientific American.*

Woodman had been amazed when a man named A. W. Underwood stopped by his office one day, looking for medical treatment for a weird malady. Underwood evidently didn't enjoy life as a pyromaniac, and was hoping there might be some logical explanation and cure for his strange ability.

There wasn't. At least, none that medical science of the time could discover.

Dr. Woodman learned to his astonishment that Underwood could ignite items such as handkerchiefs by breathing on them while rubbing them in his hands. And the fire breather emitted more than just a spark. The handkerchief, paper, dry leaf, or whatever else he aimed at would be fully enflamed and burn to cinders.

Woodman subjected Underwood, a twenty-four-year-old African American, to various experiments to make sure he wasn't being fooled by some sort of legerdemain. He tried making Underwood rinse his mouth with various concoctions and put gloves on his hands, and he brought other witnesses to examine the process. Nothing stopped Underwood from setting fire to his intended target. Those who pay attention to strange name associations might already have noted that the two principal characters in this story, Underwood and Woodman, both have names related to humanity's number one choice of fire material. But as far as anyone knows, no reason or cure was ever discovered for Underwood's strange talent, and he lived out his life exhibiting it and trying not to burn down the town.

The Eyeball Smoker

There's a great old song entitled "Smoke Gets in Your Eyes." But a Michigan man from the early 1900s could have sung the ditty truthfully as "Smoke Comes out My Eyes."

Alfred Langeiven (or Langeven) had the unusual ability of being able to force air outward from behind his eyeballs. Not shy about his strange talent, Alfred developed a repertoire of tricks to show it off. He would ask witnesses to place a hand close to his eye and then would blow air forcibly enough so that the person could feel a draft. He also liked to blow out candles in this way, and for a grand finale, he would inhale a cigarette and let the smoke come curling out around his eyeballs. He worked for a variety of sideshows around the United States, including New York's famous Hubert's Dime Museum, a vaudeville flea circus that closed in 1957.

Racing with Outhouses—Not to Them

A few hardy old-timers can remember when outhouse-pushing was a sport confined mainly to Halloween. The little wooden buildings were usually nudged only a few feet, so that the next person to come stumbling out in the darkness for some midnight relief would accidentally plunge into a smelly abyss. In the Upper Peninsula town of Trenary, this grand tradition has been cleaned up a little and turned into an annual event where outhouses are pushed not five but five hundred feet as they are raced to a thrilling finish. Diabolically, the event is held the last weekend in February, the most dreaded month for any outhouse owner.

The Outhouse Classic keeps its rules simple. The outhouse must be built of wood or cardboard, and contain at least one toilet seat and a roll of toilet paper. Mounted on skis, it must be moved by two stalwart pushers. Each contestant receives a free outhouse-adorned T-shirt. The entrants are free to design whatever kind of shelter they like, and the creativity of the average Trenarian appears to know no bounds. They build outhouses resembling everything from a tiki hut to Paul Bunyan. The tiki hut's racers reportedly dressed as cannibals—Upper Peninsula–style—with bones hanging from their noses and other strategic parts of their bodies (imagine the worst). Their racing cry was, "Yum-yum, eat 'em up."

Heading into its second decade, the event also boasts snow volleyball and an outhouse parade. And the race has attracted national media attention; even *The Wall Street Journal* sent a reporter in recent years. That doesn't stop the Trenarians from being themselves, however. At least one online account of the event has noted that the liquid you may see passed around in Mason jars to beat the chill is nothing less than good old Yooper moonshine.

Trenary, when not completely buried in snow, can be found about nineteen miles north of Gladstone.

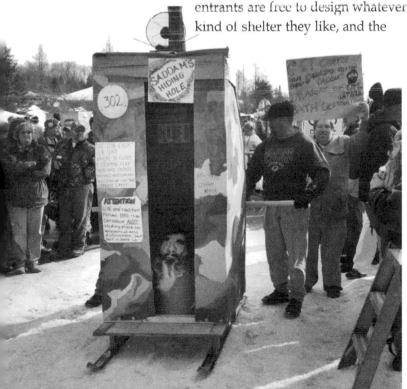

James Strang: King of Beaver Island

"I am eager, and mankind is frail. I shall act in time to come for my own benefit."

These are probably not words any kingdom's inhabitants would want to hear from their ruler. And of course, they were not words James Jesse Strang, the only man crowned king within the continental United States, ever uttered out loud to his people. He jotted them in his private diary before embarking on the grand adventure that would end, finally, in his assassination on Michigan's remote Beaver Island.

The strange Kingdom of Strang began just outside Burlington, Wisconsin. Next to a cow pasture, where Highway 11

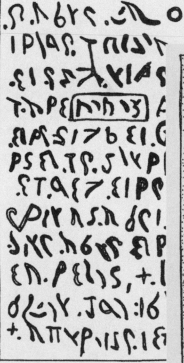

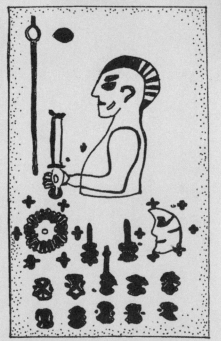

crosses the White River, stands a stone marker with a bronze map of a town called Voree. It's one of the few remaining testaments to Strang's bizarre vision of heaven on earth.

Strang didn't seem a likely glory hound. Born in New York State in 1813, he was a lawyer and postmaster who moved to the Burlington area with his wife in 1843. But the tide of Strang's life turned when he met Joseph Smith, the head of the booming new Church of Jesus Christ of Latter-day Saints, in Nauvoo, Illinois. Strang was a man short on physical stature but tall on natural charisma, and Smith took a liking to the red-haired young lawyer, baptizing him into the church personally and conferring elder status upon him.

After Smith was killed by a mob in Illinois, Strang surprised his local congregation with a purported letter from Smith naming Strang as his successor and instructing him to found a community called Voree, which was supposed to mean "Garden of Peace." Suspicion about the letter's true origins ran rampant, but it did appear to be signed by Smith. Strang soon received a revelation that he was to dig on a rise he dubbed the Hill of Promise, near the White River, and he took a group of elders along as eyewitnesses. Sure enough, there was a blue clay box filled with three tablets, six inches wide and twelve inches tall. The copper plates bore mysterious markings and figures that only Strang was able to decipher, despite having no training as a linguist.

Although some Mormons in other places had multiple wives, the practice wasn't openly admitted at the time. So when Strang decided to take a young woman as a second wife, he dressed the buxom girl in men's clothing and introduced her as his nephew and secretary. Later, he would openly declare polygamy legal and marry three other young women, prompting his original wife to move back to New York. And just in case anyone wanted to argue with the polygamy edict, the earth later coughed forth eighteen more plates from God condoning the new law.

Something prompted Strang to move from Voree. He chose Beaver Island in northern Lake Michigan and sailed out of Racine with his wives and followers in an exodus that continued from 1847 to 1849. On the island, which he renamed Saint James, Strang proclaimed himself king during a ceremony in which he was draped in a red robe and wore a star-studded crown borrowed from a theater company.

Strang's weird and stringent laws such as requiring all women to wear bloomers and instituting the death penalty for adultery soon caused dissension among his own ranks.

Strang was ambushed on June 16, 1856—shot in the back by a follower he had sentenced to be horsewhipped. He languished for several weeks, enough time for two of his wives (all four were pregnant) to cart him home to Wisconsin to die. The King of Whatever expired in his parents' home along the White River on July 9, 1856. His followers all either left the church or were absorbed into other branches of the sect. Mankind turned out to be not quite as frail as Strang had supposed.

The Dog Lady Island Legend

Just south of Monroe in Macomb County, the Plum Creek reveals an overgrown little island boasting little but a rusted-out school bus and the ruins of an old mansion. The 8-acre slip of land has been called Dog Lady Island since the 1960s, when teenagers began to party there. But sometimes, a pair of deep-set eyes would peer from the bushes at them. Occasionally they glimpsed the old woman the eyes belonged to…in rags, and accompanied by snarling hounds. They called her The Dog Lady.

She lived alone in a shack, they said, and crawled on all fours. Some swore she growled and licked her chops. Until she lost her tongue. Seems one of her dogs chewed it out of her mouth over a morsel of raccoon.

The island had been purchased in the late 1800s by a family who took over the large home built as part of a women's religious school. Sometime in the 1930s a couple was hired to watch the mansion, which burned to the ground in 1961. The husband soon died, leaving his elderly wife with her dogs.

While there is no evidence that the lady went feral, a rumor that she slept in a coffin left by the Iron Coffin motorcycle gang in the '70s might be true, although it's doubtful any teens were caught, tortured, and murdered by the gang as alleged. But some teens claimed she leaped to the roofs of their cars to scratch the windows with her claws, spittle flying from her curled lips.

Developers tried unsuccessfully to rezone the island for entertainment purposes, naming it first "Utopia" and then "Croakie's." We couldn't find anyone who knew the true fate of the Dog Lady, but many have claimed to still feel her watchful presence on Dunbar Road, near the old island causeway, and hear eerie howling from the desolate island when the moon is full.

Beards, Baseball, and the Second Coming

Bearded baseball teams and jazzy pop orchestras were not the typical trappings of early-twentieth-century religious groups. But Benton Harbor's Israelite House of David, which incorporated both, and much more, was not average in any way. The group was co-founded by the charismatic Benjamin Franklin Purnell and his wife, Mary, who arrived in town on St. Patrick's Day, 1903, penniless but bursting with enthusiasm. Starting with nothing, the colony eventually ran farms, businesses, and an amusement park that rivaled Coney Island. But as often happens in human enterprise, things eventually began to go awry.

Benjamin grew up in Kentucky hill country, and he and Mary had moved around the Midwest quite a bit before settling in Benton Harbor. He worked in a broom factory, among  other places, while developing his teachings, which had their foundation in the beliefs of the Philadelphians of 1650s England. Several of his main ideas involved what Benjamin called "the eternal life of the body" and the idea that he and Mary were the messengers of the Second Coming of Christ. It was during this time that he began letting his hair grow long in imitation of Jesus. (Later all of his converts would do likewise, also growing long beards in accordance with biblical Judaic custom.)

Finally, Brother Benjamin and Mary were inspired to begin their own colony in Benton Harbor. Underwritten by some well-to-do Benton Harbor business owners, including two brothers, Lewis and Albert Bauschke, who built one of the first gasoline-powered automobiles, Brother Benjamin began attracting followers, fame, and fortune. As the converts and money poured in, the colony expanded. Benjamin purchased farms and tracts of land and erected more buildings, adding an aviary, monkey cage, and ice-cream parlor. So many people started visiting to gawk at the strangely dressed Israelites that he figured he might as well give them a place to spend their money and help support the needs of the colony, which had grown to over seven hundred members. In 1908, he began construction on Eden Springs Amusement Park, complete with a zoo, game arcade, and free entertainment.

Once the amusement park became a going concern, some of the Israelite members organized a baseball team and began to play local teams. Brother Ben had a 3,500-seat stadium built next to the amusement park and organized a traveling team that played at a professional level all over the United States and Europe. Crowds everywhere turned out to see the long-haired, bearded men run the bases and play clownish tricks such as hiding the ball under their beards. The colony considered these travels a form of missionary work.

House of David Band, Benton Harbor, Mich.

There was no evidence for most of these accusations, but Brother Benjamin and his long-haired colony became regular fodder for sensationalistic newspaper stories. Perhaps as a result of all the publicity, the state of Michigan brought a variety of charges against Benjamin in 1923, including religious fraud and statutory rape. The House of David was charged with teaching and practicing immorality, among other things. Benjamin went into hiding, mostly by staying secluded on the second floor of his sparkly Diamond House on the colony grounds. He was finally taken in a showy raid after state troopers splintered the house's unlocked front doors with firemen's axes.

The trial and appeals dragged on for four years, and eventually many of the charges were dismissed. In 1927,

The group also found a way to utilize its musically talented members by forming several bands, which would often begin by standing with their backs to the audience to dramatize their long hair before whirling around and bursting into a ragtime tune.

Benjamin was reputed to be a brilliant leader, well liked by most of his followers. But as time went on, some members became disgruntled and left the group. Benjamin called them "scorpions." He had earlier purchased a large tract of land in northern Michigan named High Island, and rumors began spreading that colony members who broke ranks were sent there for punishment. More sinister rumors developed. The island was said to be filled with the skeletons of dissidents, lying in unmarked graves. Benjamin was also reputed to keep a group of women there in a harem hut for his pleasure.

First Prize, Blossom Parade, 1928

weakened by poor health and probably disheartened by the long legal battles, Benjamin died. Contrary to original colony beliefs, his body did not appear to possess eternal life.

After that, the colony split into two groups. One faction still believed Brother Benjamin was the rightful leader and kept the name House of David. The other group insisted that leadership had passed to Benjamin's wife, Mary, since she had been co-founder, and called itself Mary's City of David. Today almost nothing is left of the amusement park or other attractions. And yet a handful of believers continue in both factions of the colony, living quietly in separate little communities and concentrating on their religious studies and ways to perpetuate their faith and practices.

The members of Mary's City of David still serve vegetarian luncheons and host vintage baseball matches. They also offer tours of their museum and considerable grounds in Benton Harbor. They maintain a well-illustrated Web site at maryscityofdavid.org.

Brother Benjamin Purnell did leave something else to the world, however, despite the dissolution of his material kingdom. He is considered by many to have been the first of the modern evangelists, precursor of the likes of Jerry Falwell and Jim and Tammy Faye Bakker. Jim Bakker, by the way, was also a Michigander, from Muskegon.

Israelite House of David Lives On

The House of David's history goes back to late 1700s England when Joanna Southcott went into a trance and had a vision. This vision was that she was the first of seven messengers sent by God to prepare for the second coming. Further messengers followed, and eventually the faith made its way to the United States. It was embraced by Benjamin Franklin Purnell. He and his wife Mary arrived in Benton Harbor on St. Patrick's Day 1903 with a small group of followers. They had just been run out of Fostoria, Ohio. They quickly began setting up a settlement on the outskirts of town.

The Israelites were celibate, vegetarians, and they never shaved or cut their hair. They turned over all their worldly goods to the Purnells. The group built several magnificent buildings that survive to this day. Tourists began flocking to the colony grounds on the weekends. To accommodate the throngs, the colonists built a world famous amusement park. This park featured a miniature railway with little steam engines and cars built in the House of David's own machine shop. In addition, they ran a toy factory, hotel, vegetarian restaurant, ice cream parlor and several other enterprises.

From the start, there had been rumors about Benjamin's relations with the young girls in the colony and other questionable practices. It was disgruntled ex-member John Hansel and his lawsuit against the colony that drove the prophet underground. He hid on the grounds until a spectacular late-night raid in 1926. He was arrested and put on trial in 1927. He was dying and he spent the trial on a cot. He was found guilty and ordered exiled from the colony, but he died before this happened. He told his followers he would be back in three days. The devoted kept up a day and night vigil for three days, and they are still waiting. They preserved his body and you could see it in the chapel of Diamond House, his last home, until the early 1960s. One can assume he is still there.

After his death, the colony split into two colonies next door to each other. Today, there are only a handful of elderly members left, but the two sites have potential as historic sites worthy of preservation. In fact, Mary's City of David is open to tours and even has a museum. *–Kevin Clutter*

The Miraculous Shrine of the Snowshoe Priest

A nineteenth-century priest who visited most of his parishioners on snowshoes, Bishop Frederic Baraga inspired one of the largest and most unusual shrine sculptures anywhere. Towering over a bluff on Keweenaw Bay in the Upper Peninsula, just south of L'Anse, is the massive metal statue of the Apostle of the Great Lakes. The statue itself is thirty-five feet high and holds a seven-foot-long cross. The priest's famed snowshoes measure twenty-six feet long from tip to tip. The whole thing weighs four tons and is supported by five laminated wooden beams with teepees at each base that represent Baraga's major mission sites. The statue stands on a stainless steel cloud.

Baraga was born in Slovenia, with the proverbial silver spoon in his mouth, but voluntarily replaced silver utensils with crude wooden ones when he joined the Catholic mission fields in the Great Lakes area in 1830. The first bishop of the Upper Peninsula, Baraga traveled seven hundred miles or more in deep snow every winter to reach all his mission churches. Rather than simply trying to Europeanize the indigenous people who lived in northern Michigan, Baraga learned their languages and produced an Ojibwa dictionary that is still in use.

Baraga has not yet been pronounced a saint, but tiny shreds of his stockings and splinters of wood from his casket have been preserved and used as holy relics among some of the faithful. His body was also said to be close to incorruptible. He died in 1868 and was buried in a brick vault under St. Peter Cathedral in Marquette. In 1936, his casket was opened and the body examined. After sixty-eight years, Baraga was still in a remarkable state of preservation, said observers. Even his face was still recognizable, although wrinkled and "nut-brown."

Satan Always on Holiday in Hell

Weird Michigan can honestly say that we went to Hell and back for this book. And yeah, it was hot as blazes there, but it WAS the middle of July.

The strange little burg named Hell is a bit off the good intentions path, but enough people manage to find it every year to support a restaurant, an ice-cream shop called Screams that also sells Halloween costumes and paraphernalia, and the Hell Country Store and Spirits with Hell's postal substation inside. Hell's postmark is very popular, said the postmistress from Hell, Kelly Stowe.

Activities are somewhat limited, but all inferno-related. The Dam Site Inn sells a fiery Caesar cocktail called a Bloody Smitty, or you can escape some of Hell's sizzle with an ice-cream cone from Screams' Creamatory. Wander out in back for free photo ops created with your face inserted into plywood paintings of assorted witches, devils, and imps. And once a year the town hosts a classic car show and parade, "Helluva Cruise."

What most people want to know is how this rather scenic little area became known as the abode of Beelzebub, since there isn't a sulfurous flame in sight.

Just off Highway M-36 in southwest Livingston County, the site was selected by settlers in the early 1840s because of its rolling hills and pleasant stream. Never mind that the stream was called Hell's Creek, even then. An industrious New Yorker named George Reeves liked what he saw there and built a dam, gristmill, sawmill, whiskey distillery, and a general store, attracting workers and customers until a sizable little community had sprung up.

Somehow Reeves had failed to give his pioneer metropolis an official name, however, and residents began to clamor for an identity. The most popular legend says that Reeves and some townspeople were sitting around the stove in the general store one day, and someone started urging Reeves to choose a name. Supposedly, he shot back that he didn't care and they could call it Hell if they wanted to. So they did.

Ironically, the name was probably based on a German phrase that means exactly the opposite of Hell. According to a 1965 article in the *Detroit Free Press*, Reeves once played host to a German traveler who ended up stranded in the town on his way to Chicago. When Reeves showed him the hilly property crowned with the lake he had dammed (now known as Hi-Land Lake), the traveler exclaimed in German, *"So schön hell!"* In German, *schön* means beautiful and *hell* means bright. Thus, when the residents asked Reeves what they should name their town, his reply that they should call it Hell was an understandable jest.

Until recently, Hell's highest visibility has probably come through the tendency of Michigan weathermen to use the town's name as comic relief in their broadcasts, as in, "Hell froze over today." But the place made national headlines in 2005 when a cartoonist decided to create a comic book titled "Hell, Michigan." The horror-themed comic deals with axe murders and people boiled alive in

OFFICIAL HELL WEATHER

IF TAIL IS...

COLD - IT'S COLD AS **HELL**
HOT - IT'S HOTTER N **HELL**
WET - IT'S RAINY LIKE **HELL**
MOVING - IT'S WINDY AS **HELL**
GONE - RUN LIKE **HELL!**

EXIT VISA
ENTITLES THE BEARER SAFE PASSAGE THROUGH
hell
michigan

Post Office from Hell
The local post office in Hell stays busy with mail routed this way for the postmark. The Hell stamp is especially popular with people paying taxes and alimony!

HELL →

swimming pools—completely fictional events that never occurred in the real Hell (yet!).

The residents of Hell have taken a devil-may-care attitude toward the comic and in fact, happily sell it in the souvenir section of the Country Store right next to the coffee from hell ceramic mugs. Sales have been hot.

One final note: It happens to be almost exactly 666 miles between Hell and another Michigan town—Paradise.

Hell Stuf
Ice Cream
Halloween

hell
michigan

Harry Houdini's Halloween Death

Famed magician and escape artist Harry Houdini may have grown up in Appleton, Wisconsin, but he died in Detroit, on Halloween, 1926, at the age of fifty-two.

Twenty years earlier Detroit had been the site of one of Houdini's most spectacular stunts, when he leaped off the Belle Isle Bridge with his hands cuffed together. After the plunge into the river, Houdini shucked his manacles while he was still underwater, then swam to a lifeboat and clambered aboard to bow to the cheering crowd.

The son of a Hungarian rabbi, Houdini changed his name from Erich Weiss sometime after he left home at the age of twelve. Besides inventing and perfecting illusions and escape techniques, Houdini was very interested in spiritualism, the popular movement that promoted séances to communicate with the dead. Much of his interest involved trying to disprove the practice.

Houdini traveled widely, and it was in Canada that an unwitting assassin caught up with him. Houdini had often boasted he was in such perfect shape that he could take any sort of blow to his middle. In Montreal, a college student tested Houdini's claim but caught the magician off guard, landing four hard punches to his abdomen. Houdini was injured, but, the consummate trouper, he managed to finish his Montreal tour. He then traveled to Detroit, where his wife, Bess, was waiting anxiously with a doctor. Houdini still insisted on making one more appearance, at Garrick Theater, so his last performance was in Detroit. Unfortunately, by then, it was too late for a physician's care to help him. His appendix had ruptured from the violence of the blows, and Houdini died at one twenty-six p.m.

It's well known that despite his desire to disprove Spiritualism, he and Bess had arranged a secret code by which they would communicate if possible after death. She began holding séances to see if Harry's spirit would come through. Despite one incident that Bess later claimed was a false alarm, she never did hear from her departed husband and finally gave up after ten years of trying. Houdini's fans still hold séances on Halloween to try to bring up the spirit of the great magician, although none have been known to be successful.

Where in the World Is Jimmy Hoffa?

Everyone knows the name of Jimmy Hoffa, Detroit Teamsters Union president most famous for suddenly disappearing on July 30, 1975. Most people don't know, however, that Hoffa's middle name was Riddle, a moniker that neatly sums up what Hoffa's death would become.

Hoffa, a freight handler from Brazil, Indiana, worked his way up the Teamsters ladder after precociously leading a grocery store strike at the age of seventeen. The five-foot-five Hoffa made some unfortunate enemies, however, including U.S. Attorney General Robert F. Kennedy, whose investigations eventually landed Hoffa in the slammer. After his parole, Hoffa returned to his quiet family life and was last seen in the parking lot of a restaurant just outside Detroit, in Bloomfield Township, after having announced his intentions to run for a Teamsters office again.

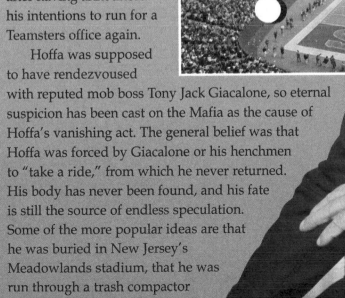

Hoffa was supposed to have rendezvoused with reputed mob boss Tony Jack Giacalone, so eternal suspicion has been cast on the Mafia as the cause of Hoffa's vanishing act. The general belief was that Hoffa was forced by Giacalone or his henchmen to "take a ride," from which he never returned. His body has never been found, and his fate is still the source of endless speculation. Some of the more popular ideas are that he was buried in New Jersey's Meadowlands stadium, that he was run through a trash compactor

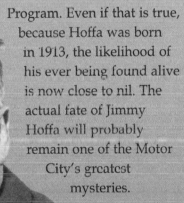

and dumped in a landfill, or that he sleeps with the Lake Michigan, Superior, Huron, or Erie fish. In 2003, the FBI acted on a tip and searched the yard of a Munger Township home and also dug under the swimming pool of a home in Hampton Township, both times to no avail.

A 2004 book titled *I Heard You Paint Houses* suggests an Irish mob member named Frank Sheeran confessed to the dirty deed, but that remains to be proved. Still others speculate that Hoffa's death was faked and that he lives on somewhere under the federal Witness Protection Program. Even if that is true, because Hoffa was born in 1913, the likelihood of his ever being found alive is now close to nil. The actual fate of Jimmy Hoffa will probably remain one of the Motor City's greatest mysteries.

Unexplained Phenomena

S*ome people think* they have UFOs all figured out. Others are positive all crop circles are faked and that strange lights are only marsh gas. *Weird Michigan*, however, knows better. These and other anomalous phenomena have never truly been explained to anyone's total satisfaction.

We suspect that even the most hard-core skeptics cherish some secret hope that there really are little men in green elf suits hiding out in our state, or mysterious lights that appear night after night over an old railroad bed. It's good to think that in this overly technical world, science can't explain everything.

Maybe that's why when strange events present themselves, we converge like ants to a picnic and nibble away at the puzzle. But if we ever did unravel the mysteries of the universe, how boring life would be! Best to cherish the unknowable. It slaps us upside the head when we get too big for our britches and keeps us humble. May there always be something out there we just can't get our heads around.

The Paulding Light

Healthy debates on everything from politics to the Pistons' chances for the playoffs are a time-honored Yooper tradition. But if there's any one topic in the Upper Peninsula that is the focus of a raging, ongoing argument between skeptics and believers, it's the strange phenomenon of the glowing orb between Watersmeet and Paulding off Highway 45. Known variously as the Paulding, Watersmeet, or Dog Meadow Light, it's a bright sphere that appears over the tree line nearly every clear night. It's a light of many talents. Some people say it changes colors, causes electrical disturbances, and even chases or plays games with people.

Ghost legends about the light's origin abound, but the most popular is that it's the ghostly lantern of an old railroad worker killed on the job, who still shows up faithfully to light the way. The swinging of the lantern as the ghost walks along causes the pendulum motion that is sometimes observed. But is the light a genuine mystery caused by supernatural

forces or mere illusion formed by distant car headlights? *Weird Michigan* decided to enter the fray to find out.

We arrived there one chilly evening in July, at the height of the light-watching season. We pulled off the highway onto Robins Wood Road and drove up the gravel drive toward the guardrail that blocks an old bridge that washed out about eight years ago. The road used to lead straight to Paulding, but now its first quarter mile or so serves mainly as a mecca for people of all stripes wanting to see the oddly reliable lights. This night the road was lined with assorted vehicles.

We joined about forty other hopefuls of every age, all swatting mosquitoes off legs, arms, and faces. People chatted among themselves, while keeping a watchful eye on the hilly area where the lights appear. Small children in pajamas dashed among the crowd, and a few frisky boys took turns sliding down a clay bank like squirming otters. The crowd's mood of nervous expectancy deepened as the sun inched out of sight and the first light appeared. Even the children quieted, and for a moment, everyone just stared.

It could have been headlights. But then it flared brighter and turned bright red. Would headlights do that? Could headlights do that? Everyone seemed to have an opinion. We turned on our tape recorder and captured the experiences of some of the folks who were there that night. . . .

Light Watchers at Watersmeet, July 5, 2005

I've been seeing this light now for, oh, I'd say the last ten to twelve years. Sometimes it'll be straight down the road; sometimes it'll look like it's coming close toward you; sometimes it will pendulum back and forth. Sometimes it'll be green; sometimes it'll be red, and all of a sudden it will just disappear. I'd say it never really played games, but I remember sitting in a vehicle where it was so dark we could hardly see each other, and it came so close that all of a sudden we could see our faces. It was probably half a mile down the road, but it was so bright.—*John Aimone*

Light Stalls Car

Someone we know of drove up to the guardrail there, turned off the car, and waited for the light. The light came closer and closer, up to the guardrail, and she went to start her car, but it wouldn't start. After the light went away, she finally got her car started, and she never came back again.—*Nancy from Tennessee*

The Brightest Light You Can Imagine

My niece was out here at the guardrail, and the light came right up by it—really bright. We've seen it through high-power binoculars, and it's just a really strong, bright light—the brightest light you can ever imagine seeing.
—*Woman from Lansing*

Looks Like a Car . . .

With two headlights coming over the ridge.
—*Man with binoculars*

Felt a Chill

We were standing right in front here, and there was no wind at all that night, and there were people standing behind us, and all of a sudden my daughter felt a cold chill. She asked if I was cold, and I said no. Then all of a sudden the wind just came up, and it blew from that side across the road to the other side, just for a little while, and it was done. When we turned around, the people behind us said they didn't feel any wind.—*Woman*

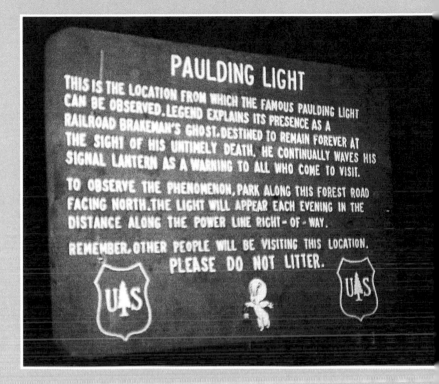

A Paulding Light Tale

In regard to ghosts, these images that you see are images from the past. They can be animals, things, or people. There has to be some reason for the appearance, something that triggers it, such as a disaster or an unfulfilled wish in life. With this in mind, I can talk to you about the Paulding Light.

The story goes that there was a derailment on the old Choate Branch Railroad and that the lights are caused by phantom images of the old railroad cars that used to rattle past.

If you look at the back of an old railroad caboose, one light is green and one light is red, so it's hypothesized that when you see the colored lights there, what you see is the rear of the train, not the front.

This is the story that I was told several years ago by a former pupil of mine. This fellow is reliable; he's now a member of the clergy. There was a businessman in Ewen (this would be about 1983) who had just bought a new Ford Escort, a little four-door sedan. He and his wife wanted to take a ride and put some miles on the new car. They invited another couple along and decided to see the Paulding Light. This was before the bridge was out and the barrier was installed on the Forest Service Road, so they drove right down to where the old Choate Branch Railroad crossed the former highway. You can still see where the tracks used to cross the road.

So they stopped right there and were enjoying the evening, when the wife saw a white light and a red light approaching. She got scared and asked to leave; her husband didn't want to, but finally agreed. But when he started to put the car in gear, everything went dead. The lights went out, the radio stopped, and as they sat in the car, a blinding flash passed right through the car and a light passed right overhead and went with lightning speed into the woods to the left. And then what struck this gentleman, because he runs a service station and he knows cars, was that all of a sudden everything was back on. The lights were back on, the radio was on, and the engine was running . . . without having turned the key to engage the starter! Now that's impossible! The wife was hysterical by the time they reached a friend's house to tell them the story at two a.m.—*B.H.J.*

A Chance Dance with the Ghost Light

My first encounter with a "ghost light" was by chance. While my wife and I were vacationing in the Upper Peninsula, we stopped in the small town of Watersmeet and heard about the mysterious light. Following directions, we found ourselves parked at dusk on a hill on a US Forest Road. Approximately one hundred to one hundred-fifty yards in front of us was another hill. A power line corridor ran to our right over the hills and through the valley below.

As it grew dark, a small amber light appeared on the hill in front of us. Suddenly it went out as if switched off. After a few minutes, it reappeared. This time it glowed to a bright white light. It seemed very similar to a gas lantern seen at a distance. We observed this same display several times before leaving.

Our next visit was in May of 1980. This time I had my 35-mm camera loaded with ASA 400 film. I set my camera on a tripod with a shutter release, and we waited. Once again the light appeared. It was amber glowing to a white light. The light disappeared for several minutes before returning. It remained "on" each time for about one minute and was approximately one hundred and fifty yards from us.

The light appeared to move. It flickered and swayed as it moved. Its light was reflected off the power lines and my jacket. Once, it appeared to split in two. This was the case, as the negative of the film showed two dark spots, one above another. The most startling display happened after the light "winked" out. Above some pine trees to the left of where the light appeared, I noticed a small red light. It began to drift upward in a zigzagging motion. It winked out. Another light appeared that made arcs above the trees. Then two red lights appeared. One followed the other in undulating movements.

Local people informed me that the lights go "out" when approached. They said they would also appear suddenly alongside cars or individuals. I was also told the light appeared in the area before the power lines were installed.

There are supposed to be over one hundred known "ghost" lights in the United States. There has been much folklore offered to explain these lights. Several involve the theme of a railroad worker killed on the job. Others include tales of lovers committing suicide because they were unable to wed. Some people believe they are beings from other worlds or other dimensions.

Some of the conventional explanations vary also. Will-o'-the-wisps are caused by spontaneous combustion of gas from decomposing organic material. Usually gas expands, though, and does not remain in a small, compact mass. The automobile headlight is another popular explanation. However, many ghost lights were seen in areas prior to the invention of the automobile, and it does not explain how these lights suddenly appear next to or overhead of observers.

The piezoelectric effect is probably the most logical "explanation" of many ghost lights. It occurs when crystalline materials in the earth's crust are suddenly stressed. This may result in a plasmalike, luminous display. This effect often is attributed to variously colored lights seen prior to earthquakes. Many ghost lights do appear over fault lines such as the San Andreas in California.

No one explanation covering the many lights has been put forth. This intriguing and awesome phenomenon continues to be a part of our folklore and legend.—*William Kingsley*

Disappearing Lights on the Lake

In the summer of 1998 or 1999, I was in high school and had just returned from a trip with my father to Alaska. For reference, this was in northern Michigan, as my father lives a few miles outside Traverse City. Anyway, my uncle decided to take two of my cousins and me fishing on a lake (I'm still not sure of the name). It must have been about seven or eight p.m., and we were just sitting in the boat when I looked up and saw the weirdest thing I've ever seen in my life. I actually said something I shouldn't have, causing my uncle to say, "Josh! Don't speak like that!" at which point he looked up and saw what I was talking about!

About 100–200 feet above us was a light. It was about 100 yards in diameter, kind of shaped like the oval of a track around a high-school football field. It looked like the sun, but wasn't too bright to stare into directly. We all watched it for about five minutes as it just sat there "hovering," and then it disappeared. In about a two-second period it just shrunk to a small point in the middle and was gone. About five minutes later a smaller light appeared over a hill across the lake, only this one moved a little, then it disappeared too. I've looked up all kinds of things from ball lightning to St. Elmo's fire and have never been able to figure out what this was. Also, this is weird, but none of us ever talked about it again until I brought it up a few years later. It was like I pushed it to the back of my mind, and I had to actually ask if it was a dream or if it were real. According to my uncle, it was quite real.
—*Josh DeBusschere*

Michigan UFOs

Green Elves and More

The 1950s were a good decade for well-dressed humanoids in Michigan, especially in the general vicinity of Detroit. Somewhere near Ann Arbor, according to Albert Rosales's online *Humanoid Sightings Database,* one Richard Miller was instructed by aliens over his shortwave radio to meet them in an isolated area. Miller obeyed and was rewarded by the sight of a disk-shaped craft landing near him. What appeared to be a young human male wearing a dark brown suit greeted Miller and introduced him to his "commander," an undescribed fellow by the name of Soltec. The usual messages of peace and love were then communicated to Miller, who faithfully reported his experience for the good of humankind.

And according to Harold T. Wilkins in his 1956 opus *Flying Saucers Uncensored* a forty-one-year-old Dearborn man named Lawrence Cardenas glimpsed not one but fifteen men dressed in something like dark green elf suits, including the peaked caps. They wore heavy goggles and stood about medium height. As Cardenas drove by this spectacle on his way to work at a laundromat, he noted that a slightly larger man appeared to be the boss of the odd group. For Cardenas, the other-worldly aspect of the sighting was clinched when he spotted a strange craft with colored flashing lights parked nearby. Evidently, he just continued on his way to work, leaving the greensuits to their mysterious business.

Another early sighting, reported on the michiganufos.com Web site, happened in August 1951, when a counselor at Camp Big Silver on Silver Lake, just south of Pinkney, was giving an astronomy demonstration to two campers using a telescope. The counselor, Walter Webb, just happened to be the chief lecturer on astronomy at Boston's Charles Hayden Planetarium—someone who knew his way around the night sky. Suddenly he and the two boys noticed a yellowish red light moving westward in an "undulating fashion" south of the lake. Webb thought it was an airplane until he remembered that planes fly in straight lines. By that time, the light had disappeared. He could not come up with a scientific explanation for what the three of them had seen.

Brown-Quilted Swamp Gas or UFOs?

Renowned UFO investigator J. Allen Hynek probably wished he had never heard of Michigan. For months after he arrived in Washtenaw and Livingston counties in 1966 to investigate one of the best-publicized UFO flaps in American history, he couldn't open a newspaper or a magazine without seeing himself ridiculed in cartoons and editorials for declaring it was all a case of "swamp gas." Even hard-core skeptics thought that explanation a little ridiculous, given the facts.

After all, several witnesses had drawn sketches of a very solid object that looked like a classic flying saucer. How could swamp gas assume such a definite shape? Even the saucer's exterior was described in detail: brown and looking almost like quilted material. In all, over one hundred witnesses reported seeing UFOs, including police officers, sheriff's deputies, and a civil defense director. On March 18, the *Detroit News* ran the story of how four different Washtenaw deputies followed several circular objects that "oscillated" and glowed red, white, and green. It also featured a drawing made by the deputies of a craft shaped like a football with a crosshatched texture, a round dome on top, lights on either end, and antennas sticking out below.

In Dexter, one patrolman's report of an unidentified object whizzing over Brand and Quigley roads prompted Washtenaw's sheriff, Douglas Harvey, to send six two-man patrols and three separate detectives to chase the object at speeds up to 70 miles per hour in their squad cars. They didn't catch it.

A farm family probably came the closest to the object. Frank Mannor, his wife, and teenage son all watched the strangely lighted object from their home on McGuinness Road. Mannor said he approached it to within five hundred yards and described it as pyramid-shaped, with a coral-like surface. The object hovered over a field, rising to treetop level periodically, then descending close to the earth again, changing colors as it moved. Mannor's wife called the police, who arrived in time to observe the spectacle and listen to its high-pitched whining sound. FLYING SAUCER FORMATION SPOTTED OVER WASHTENAW read the *Detroit Free Press* headline on March 21; the article noted that officers claimed to see between six and twelve saucers, one of them insolently buzzing a patrol car. Two weeks later, on April Fool's Day, *LIFE* Magazine ran a piece on the whole episode, quoting Mannor's statement, "It wasn't no hullabillusion."

Hynek, who worked on the government's UFO investigation group called Project Blue Book, was sent in by the air force to try to make some sense of the sightings. Pushed by eager reporters for his take on the situation, he offered the swamp gas theory, explaining that various colored lights can be created by gases from decomposing vegetation. Hynek also blamed pranksters shooting off flares and the planet Venus as other possible sources of the lights. One Oakland County sheriff's deputy, Keith Lester, was outraged. The *Springfield Main Union* quoted him as saying what he had seen was "definitely an object," adding that "the Air Force is going to get into trouble going on this way. It seems like a whitewash."

Reporters attempting to contact the Mannor family have found that the farm and farmhouse no longer exist, and even the configuration of the roads has been changed due to housing development. The elder Mannor is deceased, and it appears all traces of the 1966 sightings have been effectively wiped off the map. Natural progress or more government whitewash?

—William Kingsley and Dr. Harry Willnus both contributed material to this story.

CON'T:

n returning to the patrol vehicle, the undersigned officers returned
to the McGinnis Road address, where the MANNERS were talked to.

TALK WITH FRANK MANNER: FRANK MANNER stated that he
lights coming from the swamp, and had awakened his son
MANNERS then proceeded into the swamps in an attempt to
which was producing that thing". Upon entering the lower
RONALD stated "what is that thing", and as FRANK MANNER
direction indicated, the object was observed.   At the
the small lights went out, and in just an instant, re
swamp, a distance of about 500 Yards.   At this time,
illuminated from a brilliant source of light, which fl
the two (2) small lights.   After watching the object f
the rays of light from two fleshlights were observed fr
the object.   The light from the object intensified, t
whistle simular to the sound of a Rifle bullet Ricochet
object passed directly over the MANNERS in just an inst

DESCRIPTION OF OBJECT: Object was observed to be of
appearing to be Quilted type outside surface. Object
flat upon the bottom, and cone shaped toward the top
low in height. Two small lights appeared to be at th
object, glowing in a bluish-green light, and intens
red in color. When the vehicle or object illuminate
was a yellow-white in color, and ran horisontal bet
lights, allowing some of the object to be viewed.
to be rough in texture.

PERSONS OBSERVING OBJECT:

FRANK MANNER, OF 10600 McGinnis Road, Dexter, Mich
RONALD MANNER, of 10600 McGinnis Road,
Several others, names unknown.

FURTER UFO SIGHTED: Shortly
CHELSEA POLICE DEPARTMENT,
Village of Chelsea. Ho
in a Westerly Direction

A further sighting o
woods and swamp
and Webster-To
Washtenaw Coun
get closer
Swaren e

WASHTENAW COUNTY SHERIFF'S DEPARTMENT   Comp. No.

Comp. Name   Bob Wagner   Nature of Comp.   UFO

Address   Dexter Body Shop   Location   Between McGinnis Rd. & N. Ter
          Dexter Mich.   Date Received   3-20-66   Time   8:30 ?
                              Date Occurred   3-20-66   Time   8:30 ?
Phone No.: Res.   Bus.   Dep. Kelly
Telephone XXXX Radio   Letter   in Per   · Received by
Officers Assigned   Dep. McFadden & Fitzpatrick and Car #34

Time Assigned   8:35 Pm

Details of Comp.   Comp. called and stated that there was a strange object in
                    the swamp at the end of McGinnis Rd. It was on the ground,
                    went up in air about 500' and came down making a lot of noi

INVESTIGATION: Dispatched to the above location, and made contact with
the complainaut at 10600 McGinnis Road. Complainant advised that an
un-identified object was presently located in the swamp, to the rear of
afore mentioned location, and had been so located for approximently (½)
one half hour.   approximently 500 Feet, and then to
                                          that lights were observed upon the
                                          a blus-green to a brilliant
                                          appeared to be having difficulty

                                                    had watched
                                                    ed swamp, in
                                                    MANNER'S
                                                    lights.

Close Encounter of the Detroit Kind

It was Friday evening, February 10, 1978, and Marc Avery, a well-known afternoon radio host on WMJ in Detroit, was headed to Metro Airport to catch a flight to Florida for a much needed ten-day vacation. Avery's wife was with him. It was exactly seven fifty-five p.m.

Heading down the newly opened I-275 freeway, Marc suddenly encountered two extremely bright lights coming toward him. "At first I thought it was a plane and it was going to land right on the freeway," he said. He went on to explain that he slowed his car to a crawl. Dozens of other cars did the same. What happened next shocked him.

The object continued to approach and then seemed to pause right over the freeway! When the glare of what he thought were landing lights wore off, Avery described "looking up into the belly of a craft." He told me, "It was like laying on one's back in a basement looking at the ceiling. Picture the ceiling being covered with Plexiglas with lights underneath. Some lights were on, some were off."

The whole event lasted forty to fifty seconds. The craft, Avery said, "then went west, directly west, no banking turn." He had never seen anything like it.

Avery got to the airport and called in live to the evening WJR host, Warren Pierce. The on-air call was heard by thousands of listeners, including this investigator, who managed to tape this first in UFO history (namely, an on-air discussion between two radio hosts, one of whom had just had a close encounter).

Avery was positive that what he saw was not a plane or a chopper. "It was something I've never seen before or since," he told me. I carried out an extensive investigation of this case, but was not able to pinpoint what Avery saw. However, there were numerous other reports that very night of strange lights in the sky over western Wayne County.

Avery passed away on February 8, 2004. Warren Pierce still broadcasts for WJR radio. –*Dr. Harry Willnus*

The Mud Lake Ice Circle

Mud Lake may not be Michigan's most imposing lake in the summer. Set near Horton, about fifteen miles south of Jackson, and less than a mile in diameter, the little body of water isn't exactly a tourism hot spot. Even its name isn't unique; there's another Mud Lake in the northern part of Jackson County that normally gets all the press. But in the winter of 2003, not only was Mud Lake a literal hot spot, it was making news around the world.

It all started when lake resident Vaughn Hobe saw the light. An unidentifiable, brilliant white light illuminated the area over the lake on a bitterly cold and windy night at about one thirty a.m. on December 18. He stared in disbelief for a while, then told himself it was simply the best moonrise ever and went to bed. Ten days later, on the twenty-eighth, he and his son were collecting firewood from a bluff near the lake when they looked over and saw the anomaly: a "three to four foot wide ring around forty feet across with white snow in the center," according to a report on michiganufos.com. Outside the ring was an additional pattern that radiated as far as the shore.

Something had melted the ice in a perfect circle while leaving the center of the circle intact. But what could do that? Hobe decided to call in some experts, who came from near and far, including Jeff Wilson, independent crop formation investigator; Todd Lemire, chief field investigator for the Michigan Mutual UFO Network; and later, Linda Moulton Howe, an internationally known author and researcher.

Besides the ice circle, Hobe told the investigators he and his son had been seeing illuminated orange spheres hovering over the lake for the past several years. Hobe even chased one on his snowmobile. Also he said that one neighbor had been followed by "objects" while driving and another saw three unidentified objects flying over their field. Hobe did tell the investigators that he had been a UFO buff all his life.

One expert concluded that the circle was formed by normal "hydrological processes." Another thought that wind might have been the culprit. But the investigators are at a loss to explain the brilliant white light and the orange orbs, and say they can't tell if there is a connection between those phenomena and the ice circle. One of the weirdest things was discovered by researcher W. C. Levengood, who found that plants grown with water from the ice circle's "splash pattern" grew 174 percent faster than plants grown with ordinary water!

Michigan Crop Circles

"He's a little green guy, but the prosecutor wouldn't let us bring him back from Jupiter."
—*Sheriff Charles L. Brown*, The Saginaw News, *December 11, 2002*

Sheriff Brown was referring to the suspected perpetrator of two crop circles, seventy-two and twenty feet in diameter, discovered by Saginaw County farmer Gordon G. Turner while harvesting his oats in October of that year. Over one thousand people stampeded to the Turner farm, near Hemlock, after the initial reports hit the papers, including a number of investigators who had varied opinions on whether the circles were created by the little green guy or by a few local boys with a board and a string.

Crop circles have captured the imaginations of people worldwide as they continue to appear suddenly in fields around the world in ever-increasing patterns of complexity. Some are clearly hoaxes; others are impossible to explain. They are often found near power sources and bodies of water and, in England, seem related to some of the country's oldest sacred spaces. People may report seeing strange lights or humming noises before the formation of a circle, but often there is no indication anything is amiss until a field owner accidentally stumbles across one of the massive earth decorations.

That was the case about a year after the Turner circles, in July 2003, when a subtle suite of circles was found by another farmer, Pat Espy, about fifty miles south of Hemlock, in Livingston County near Howell.

Espy was surprised when he came upon the circles, as there were no tracks or paths leading to them. The first one he found was only four feet across, but the second was about fifty feet in diameter and had two extensions leading off like spurs at the eastern and western points. The formation was unusual, said Michigan Mutual UFO Network member Todd Lemire in his official report,

because there were four additional circles, laid down at the north, south, east, and west points on the larger circle, layered UNDER the larger circle.

In addition, many of the checkpoints associated with crop circles considered genuine by experts were present, such as intricate weaving and braiding of the grain stalks, and something called a "blown node collar" on the growth nodes of the stems. Crop circle expert Jeff Wilson explained in an *Ann Arbor News* story that the nodes explode when whatever energy used to bend the stems superheats the water in the plant until it expands and bursts out. Wilson, director of the Independent Crop Circle Researchers' Association, said hoaxers cannot duplicate this effect, and that he and Lemire found at least twenty such stems in the Espy event.

The circles got at least two Howell area radio personalities in some superheated water too. The on-air hosts at radio station WKQI told listeners that they had created the crop circles but later admitted that their statement was a hoax. An article in Mt. Pleasant's *Morning Sun* on August 9 implied the pair would face some consequences from their employer for the falsehood.

Other Michigan crop circles have appeared as early as 1932 in Washtenaw County, as well as Wayne (1966), Iosco (1982), Shiawassee (1989), Jackson (1993), Huron (1995), Livingston (1997), Eaton (2002), Calhoun (2002), Washtenaw again (2003), and Van Buren (2004).

There are almost as many theories on crop circle origins as there are researchers. The prevalent school of thought is that most, if not all, are hoaxes. On the other hand, some people believe the circles serve as geographical markers for ships from outer space; others

think they are formed by ships from inner space, inside the earth, or in other dimensions. Some say the circles are actually complex mathematical formulas couched in geometric shapes and that "someone" is trying to tell us something with them. Others suggest that the complex formations are just expressions of weird electromagnetic energies from the earth.

And a few ideas that have been thrown out there—way out there—hold that the circles are caused by a weather effect similar to ball lightning, by overgrown fungi, stampeding hedgehogs, or, naturally, the devil.

Michigan's Headless Chicken

The small town of Fruita, Colorado, holds a yearly festival dedicated to a bird that defied the laws of biology by staying alive after being decapitated for a farmer's dinner. In 1945, Mike the headless chicken lived for eighteen months with only a brain stem and one ear to guide him, and became the star of a national sideshow tour. But he wasn't the first chicken to survive the chopping block. Michigan's Sault Sainte Marie boasted a crowd-pleasing, headless black leghorn decades earlier, in 1903. This deprived pullet didn't live as long as Mike, nor did she match Mike's dizzying heights of fame and glory (Mike even has his own Web site, miketheheadlesschicken.org), but she caused plenty of amazement in her day.

The natural wonder was inadvertently created by one of the cooks at the Belvidere Hotel, who removed the hen's noggin and tossed her body into a barrel to be prepared for that night's roast chicken special. But when the cook pulled the hen's body out to be plucked, it flew away and began strolling around the hotel's basement floor.

Too amused to end the hen's life again, the hotel employees began feeding her oatmeal gruel from a syringe and claimed that she seemed to enjoy her meals, although, as the *Sault Ste. Marie Evening News* noted, "she has no brains and no tongue to taste it with." Some of the Belvidere workers, in fact, made a small fortune by betting patrons a dollar that they had a live, headless chicken in the basement, then escorting their dupes to the basement to prove their claim and collect. The stalwart hen made national newspaper headlines.

Unlike Colorado's Mike, however, Michigan's headless black leghorn was not awarded the dignity of a recorded name, and she lived only seventeen days before finally succumbing. Rumor around town has it she was stuffed not with bread-crumbs but with a taxidermist's form, and was displayed at various places. No one seems to know where she ended up. But she was seen by hundreds during those seventeen amazing days and is remembered now as a testimonial to life and its occasional ability to survive against all conceivable odds.

The Day Brown Goo Fell on Westland

The mysterious substance seemed to rain down from the heavens. It was a dark reddish brown with a strange texture, and it fell out of the sky and onto Ernestine Stange's white home and driveway in November 1998. And while the date may have been close to Thanksgiving, this wasn't gravy. The "mystery muck," as the *Detroit Free Press* called it, also covered parts of Ernestine's next-door neighbor's house. No other homes in the Detroit suburb of Westland were touched with the icky substance. Ernestine thought the mess was probably human feces dropped from an airplane, while her neighbor, Mariusz Boguszewski, blamed super-pooper birds.

Neither was right.

Ernestine picked up her phone and began making calls, first to airports, then to county health officials, and finally to the Michigan Department of Agriculture, which sent out a specialist. Test results showed, thankfully, that it was not human waste. That was only a small comfort to Ernestine, who had to endure endless jokes about it "hitting the fan" at her place. She still didn't know what "it" was and feared a health risk in trying to clean it up.

Strangely, the same sort of thing had happened earlier in the year near York, Pennsylvania. The official term for mystery sky goo is Unexplained Biologic Material, or X-Bios. The material in the York case looked a lot like what fell in Westland, and both substances turned out to contain bacteria, black mold, and algae. Not a pretty mix.

According to an article in the *South Texas Informer and Business Journal,* X-Bios have been occurring for at least twenty years. While the looks and textures may vary, they are always mysterious and unfailingly gross. In 1985, a woman's front porch in Washington was slimed with a milky jelly full of human white blood cells and bacteria. The source was never found.

Michigan's Brigadoon?

The musical Brigadoon is a retelling of an old Scottish legend about a town that materializes once every hundred years, then vanishes, to the disappointment of those who stumbled upon it during its brief appearance. Manton, a small town just off Highway 131 in Wexford County, has its own version of *Brigadoon,* a farmhouse that appears and disappears much more often.

Don Frosty, who has since moved to another town, remembers investigating the place as a teenager. "It was on the eastern part of the city, on the outskirts," he told *Weird Michigan.* "There were two old mining roads, and it was off one of those." Frosty, who never could get the place out of his mind, went there several times with a woman he dated at the time.

"We walked all through the two-story house," he said. "We had flashlights to see by. I don't recall any furniture in it; it was empty like an abandoned house with a wooden floor and no drapes on the windows. The windows were intact. But when we would go back there the next day, in the daylight, there was nothing. Just a field."

Frosty still can't explain it. But for his sake, it's probably better that the place now seems to have disappeared for good. In the tale of *Brigadoon,* the town miraculously comes to life one final time, and the hero stays in it . . . forever! Frosty and his exploring friend may have had a narrower escape than they ever realized.

Mirages: A Tale of Two Cities

Most people think mirages occur only in deserts, probably because of the billions of cartoons that show a parched character crawling through the sands toward some lush oasis. But a Michigan incident proves mirages can appear over water . . . and over great distances.

One of the farthest confirmed mirages ever known happened in Grand Haven on April 26, 1977. That night startled city residents could suddenly see what looked like the lights of another city shimmering weirdly over Lake Michigan. Had Atlantis finally risen—in Michigan? Eventually the onlookers noticed that one of the lights seemed to blink in a pattern, and that it glowed red like a signal light of some sort. Remembering that across Lake Michigan from Grand Haven is not Atlantis but Milwaukee, Wisconsin, someone contacted an acquaintance there. Sure enough, the flashing red light blinked in the exact pattern of Milwaukee harbor's beacon. The Michiganders were seeing Wisconsin's shore, seventy-five miles away, without so much as a spyglass!

While it seemed like a mystic miracle, mirages are really the result of a complicated process in our atmosphere called refraction. Or at least that's what the scientists say. Things from over the horizon, normally beyond our ability to see them, are brought into view. Conditions have to be perfect, however, and it's hard to believe there isn't at least a small bit of magic involved in seeing a city that is seventy-five miles away with the naked eye.

Another possible mirage happened in Manistique in 1904 when, according to the *Evening News,* on the evening of November 14, firemen in that city noticed a strange red glow on dark clouds, which could be seen until morning at two different points—in the northeast and northwest. They assumed the Northwestern Leather Company was on fire and set off running with their equipment. The Leather Company had not a lick of flame, however. The confused firefighters were left to puzzle over what the strange sky lights could have been. It was suggested that perhaps the clouds were a mirage of a forest fire many miles away, but no one ever solved the mystery.

Up in Flames in Pontiac

How does a twenty-seven-year-old man end up burned from the inside out, without so much as scorching his clothing, eyebrows, or hair? Some people think the only answer to the mysterious death of Billy T. Preston, an autoworker at Pontiac's General Motors plant, is the phenomenon known as spontaneous human combustion. According to some sources, there are only about two hundred known occurrences since 1673, when a French doctor described the case of a woman in Paris who was found almost completely burned. Strangely, her head and the tips of her fingers were left unsinged.

Preston had intended to die, anyway. Sick with kidney disease, he had set up his car with tubing that fed carbon monoxide into the vehicle. He then got into the car, closed the door, turned on the key, and sat there until he passed out from the fumes. But somehow, after he died, parts of his body inexplicably burned up. When his corpse was found on the evening of December 13, 1959, still sitting behind the steering wheel, not a shred of his clothing was charred. However, the lower part of his body was reduced to ashes, and his back, legs, and arms were deeply burned, as was his respiratory system.

The police were called in, but they ruled out foul play since no one could have unclothed the victim, burned him, and then reclothed him without disturbing his damaged flesh. The only damage to the car was a small smoldering area at the point where the fumes had been emitted into the vehicle. Evidently, some force or condition inside Billy himself led to his horrific funeral pyre.

The cause of spontaneous combustion has never been ascertained. Originally, people thought it must be caused by overconsumption of alcohol, but a person would have to drink so much booze that the alcohol would induce poisoning long before the body could be saturated enough to combust. Investigator Ivan T. Sanderson has suggested the phenomenon may be caused by metabolic changes in the body brought on by illness or negative moods, allowing certain compounds to build up that make the body subject to ignition. But if this is true, many more people should be going up in flames. Other theories have included being hit with ball lightning, producing too much static electricity, or the body using its own fats to act like a human candle after accidentally catching fire some other way.

Some people have survived the experience, briefly, but suffered strange internal burns. One of the scariest cases in history was that of a developmentally disabled woman in northern London who was sitting with her father in their living room in 1982 when her upper torso suddenly became consumed by fire. Her father and another relative said that flames were pouring out of her mouth, just as from a dragon in the movies, with a roaring sound. They were able to put out the fire, but she died later from her injuries.

As for Billy T. Preston, probably no one will ever know what lit his remains and performed, in effect, a partial cremation. But it's a case that the police detectives and doctors of Pontiac will never forget.

The Michigan Triangle

Many stories have been written of weird and unexplained happenings in an area off Florida known as the Bermuda Triangle, where, it is said, boats and planes have disappeared in good weather with no evidence ever found as to why they vanished. UFO sightings are supposedly frequent in this area. Many boats have also reported compass failures and other weird trouble inside the triangle.

But there's another mysterious triangle, right in our own state. It is known, fittingly enough, as the Michigan Triangle. The boundaries are said to be from Ludington to Benton Harbor, and then across the lake to Manitowoc [Wisconsin] and back to Ludington.

Numerous stories have been told of unexplained vanishings, weird happenings, periods when time seemed to slow down or speed up, and the appearance of strange creatures.

A well-documented case is the disappearance of Captain George R. Donner, of the lake freighter *O.M. McFarland,* from his cabin while the ship was under way on April 28, 1937. The *McFarland* had picked up 9,800 tons of coal in Erie, Pennsylvania, and then headed west through the lakes, bound for Port Washington [Wisconsin]. Because it was early in the season, the lakes and the locks in the upper part of the Great Lakes were still choked with ice, which slowed the *McFarland*'s progress.

Donner had remained on the bridge many hours, guiding his ship through the treacherous ice floes. When at last the vessel turned into Lake Michigan, the exhausted captain retired to his cabin, with instructions that he be called when the ship neared Port Washington. Some three hours later, as the *McFarland* neared her destination, the second mate went to the captain's cabin to awaken him as instructed, but the captain was not there. Thinking that Donner had gone to the galley for a late-night snack, the second mate checked the galley and learned that the captain had not been there. Strangely, the mate reported that the captain's cabin had been locked from the inside.

The crew began an exhaustive search of the vessel, but to no avail: The captain had disappeared. No clue as to what happened to Donner was ever found. Ironically, the day Donner disappeared was his fifty-eighth birthday. Believers in the Michigan Triangle point out that the *O.M. McFarland* was in the triangle when Donner vanished.

A more recent event took place on June 23, 1950, when Northwestern Airlines flight 2501 took off from New York with a crew of three and fifty-five passengers bound for Minneapolis. Later that night, at eleven thirty-seven p.m., the large, four-engine DC-4 reported that it was at 3,500 feet over Battle Creek, Michigan. Due to bad weather near Chicago, the plane changed its course to a northwesterly direction over Lake Michigan, with an estimated time of arrival over Milwaukee of eleven fifty-one p.m.

From there, the plane simply vanished—nothing of the plane or its fifty-eight occupants was ever seen again.

A massive Coast Guard search turned up only a blanket bearing the airline's logo. Triangle believers again note that the tragic loss of flight 2501 occurred near the center of the Lake Michigan Triangle.—*Excerpted from and printed with permission of* The Sheboygan Press, *April 2005, and of the writer, Bill Wangemann*

Michigan's state mascot, the wolverine, is so rare these days that catching a glimpse of one is almost a cosmic event. But people in this state have recorded dozens of sightings of other weird and fascinating creatures. Trouble is their existence is doubted by those unwilling to hop outside the bounds of orthodox biology. Bigfoot, Dog Man, several varieties of sea serpents and monsters: The woods and waters of Michigan fairly seethe with monstrous and mythic fauna, if many sober eyewitnesses from the UP to the Thumb are to be believed.

And why shouldn't we believe them? Just look at the ancient Native American legends about creatures that sound suspiciously like the ones being observed today; it's possible these beings have been here all along, even before Europeans arrived to gawk with their fancy spyglasses. And as elusive as they are, it's clear these creatures know the local turf and surf well enough to stay hidden. But some Michiganders say the

Bizarre Beasts

mystery beasts don't merely know the land, they are the land. To their way of thinking, these nebulous creatures might be thought of as embodiments of the earth spirits that shake down the pines on dark and windswept nights.

The conclusion is obvious, but disturbing. Like Woodie Guthrie almost said,

"This land is your land, this land is my land, this land is . . . gulp . . . *their* land!"

Bigfoot

Mark Twain once remarked, "The report of my death was an exaggeration." If Bigfoot (or Sasquatch, as he's known on the Pacific Coast) could talk, he might say the same. True, recent events have laid doubt on such icons of Bigfoot lore as the Patterson video of the striding female Bigfoot, and the big footprints "found" in California forests by admitted (and deceased) hoaxer Ray Wallace. But there are a lot of Michiganders who know what they've seen and swear it's the genuine article. And there do seem to be just too many sightings in too many places to put them all down to some jokester in a gorilla suit.

If state newspaper reports are any indication, the furry "apemen" have strutted their odoriferous stuff from Ishpeming to Kalamazoo. Crashing through deep woods in ungodly long strides, stinking like animal musk and offal stew, poking their shaggy, bullet-shaped craniums from behind trees all over the Upper and Lower peninsulas, there appear to be enough Bigfoots in Michigan to mistake the place for the planet of the Wookies. And the planet of the Wookies is as likely a source of origin as many of those proposed by various writers.

Some researchers claim Bigfoot, Sasquatch, Yeti, and the like are the remnant population of a supposedly extinct great ape called *Gigantopithecus*, who lived two million to ten thousand years ago. They posit that it may have migrated over the Bering Strait land bridge along with early humans also stricken with continental wanderlust. There are a few kinks in the theory, though.

Gigantopithecus was twice the size of today's gorillas, but it walked like them, dragging its knuckles. Bigfoot, in contrast, walks completely upright, according to all reports. Also, Bigfoot's footprints are shaped more like those of a flat-footed human than those of an ape. There are some old Cree stories about "hairy heart beings" that could interbreed with humans, suggesting that perhaps this creature is indeed more human than ape.

Some Native Americans have told *Weird Michigan* they believe Bigfoot is a spirit creature and that is why he will never be captured. Those with a bent for UFO-logy believe that Bigfoot is either a type of alien or an alien interbreeding experiment gone very wrong. Others think it is "demonic," and still others omnisciently declare it to be nonexistent.

Whatever you believe, when you're sitting in the pines a zillion miles from nowhere and you hear a giant branch snap behind you and suddenly feel some creature's hot, fetid breath wreathing the back of your neck, you're not likely to care much for theory. We wish you happy camping. . . .

Scared (Rhymes with) Witless

I have seen Bigfoot tracks, 16 x 9 inch tracks that look really strange, in Mason County. The Michigan county authorities checked them and said they are strange. Bigfoots eat out of garbage cans, and eat small dogs and cats. In the area are lots of swamps. The biggest one is seven miles wide by ten miles deep. My dogs won't stop smelling the tracks. They bark and get very edgy towards dark. I tried to get them on camera, but had no luck. It's like they know my brother and I are trying to film them. As soon as we go to bed or leave the house they get my garbage. Not any other animal walks on two big humanlike footprints. They do exist and it's scary to know something like that is out there.—*Tom*

TV Star: "I Saw . . . Thorny Man"

Michigan native and TV star Barry Watson, best known for his role as Matt on the WB's *Seventh Heaven,* says he saw Bigfoot as a child. Watson, raised in northern Michigan along the Canadian border, was quoted in a February 11, 2005, *Milwaukee Journal Sentinel* article as saying, "I did see Bigfoot when I was a kid, and I still believe it to this day. I saw a big, thorny man outside my window."

Sister Lakes' Hellzapoppin' Sasquatch

One of the biggest Bigfoot specimens ever reported had to be the one chronicled in *True* Magazine in June 1966. Its article, "The Hellzapoppin' Hunt for the Michigan Monster," was recounted by Elwood D. Baumann in his book *Bigfoot*. The sightings actually began around 1964 near Sister Lakes, when people began reporting seeing a hairy monster that stood nine feet tall and, by most estimates, tipped the scales at about five hundred pounds. Witnesses spoke of its wailing cry, the way its heavy footfalls shook the ground, and eyes that glowed eerily in the dark. As police began investigating, they discovered the now familiar giant footprints the creature had left behind. They measured seventeen inches long and six inches wide. The monster continued to be spotted, including one sighting by two young girls (some accounts say three girls) on a country

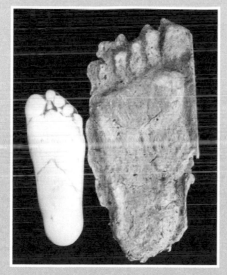

lane during broad daylight. The creature frightened them but did not try to hurt them. The women in the following story, which happened not much later and in the vicinity of the nearby town of Monroe, should have been so lucky!

Bigfoot Goes Berserk

It's bad enough when a giant ape steps out into the road in front of your car. It's even worse when he turns out to have a mean left hook. In one of Michigan's most famous cases, recorded by Bigfoot researcher Wayne King and told

to Jim Mencarelli of the *Ann Arbor News* in October 1979, a mother and daughter became instant—and bruised—believers in the Bigfoot phenomenon.

It was 1965 when Rose Owen and her daughter, seventeen-year-old Christine Van Acker, received the shock of their lives late one night along a rural road in Monroe County. A tall, hairy, manlike thing stepped right in front of their speeding vehicle and caused the screaming women to brake into a skid, just "grazing" the animal as it stopped in the middle of the road next to their now stalled car.

Enraged, the creature rushed at the women before they had time to roll up their windows. Reaching into the vehicle, it punched Christine in the jaw and slammed Rose's head against the car interior before loping off into the woods. Afterward, both women took lie detector tests. Christine failed, but Rose passed. Both of them were examined and found to have bruises and in Rose's case, two black eyes.

King, himself a Bigfoot eyewitness, also told Mencarelli that he took a photo of a Bigfoot's handprint on a farm near Dansville owned by John and Virginia Culham. The Culhams never saw the creature, but found other evidence such as a demolished grain shed, disappearing and disfigured livestock, and high-pitched, loud screams emanating from the nearby countryside. King said, "That, my friend, is the cry of a Sasquatch."

Oscoda's Foley Swamp Thing

Hunting season near Saginaw always brings some kind of story related to the woods. In October 1990, the *Saginaw News* had something a lot more exciting to report than the name of the hunter who bagged the biggest buck. People were coming out of the woods, especially in Foley Swamp in the Huron National Forest, saying they had seen Bigfoot.

The reports began even before the start of bow season, with two hikers who said they saw an eight-foot-tall "hairy beast." Two other people told the sheriff's department they saw the creature in the Foley Swamp on September 28.

The *Saginaw News* talked to the owners of a nearby motel and sports shop, and learned that other hunters had professed seeing something big and unusual in the Foley. One group had confided to motel owner Jim Stone that almost every year they saw what looked to them like Bigfoot in the swamp. And the previous year two shaken hunters had described to Stone how they shot a deer, but before they could get it out of the swamp, something else dragged it away and chomped off a big piece of its head. Whatever it was, they said, was strong enough to drag the big buck faster than the two men could run after it.

Mayville, in Tuscola County, made the news in 1992 when the *Saginaw News* reported that two truck drivers got a twofer in the sightings department, spotting two of the creatures on Pattison Road outside town in early April. The men said one was bigger, standing an estimated seven

to eight feet tall, while the other reached only about five feet in height. It occurred to the men that the bigger one could easily flip their truck over if it so desired. Instead, the hairy pair stared at the truck's headlights for a long moment, then began approaching the vehicle. The driver kept his head, kicked the gears into reverse and began slowly backing away. That was enough to make the Bigfoot couple skedaddle. The men were so unnerved by the incident that it took them several weeks to make the report.

Senior Citizen Bigfoot

If humans grow white hair, hunch over, and move creakily from arthritis when they get old, it's logical to assume Bigfoot probably does too. Perhaps that was what one woman saw—a geriatric Bigfoot—near Lexington in Sanilac County in the summer of 1987. According to a report in the Bigfoot Field Researchers Organization Web

site, the woman had been trying to sleep on a hot night in August, but her dog kept barking, along with all the neighbors' dogs within hearing range. When she heard a rustling sound outside her open bedroom window, she peeked out and saw "a monkey-type creature" step onto her front lawn from nearby trees. Hunched over, it stood about five feet tall, she said, and was covered with whitish fur and had "narrow shoulders like a human," with longer arms. Unlike the descriptions of most Bigfoots, this creature had no hair on its apelike face, and the woman was able to see it squint and wrinkle up its forehead as it walked into the light cast by a yard lamp. The forehead was slanted like a monkey's, she added, the "slant" comprising about half of its facial area.

The creature continued walking on two legs, holding its left hand higher, as if it were injured or hurting. The woman ran to alert her father, who grabbed a gun and flashlight and headed for the yard. By the time he got out there, the creature was gone and could not be found. "I became scared and believed that the creature could have easily climbed a tree," she said. If it did, it stayed there until the coast was clear and has not been reported since.

Blame It on Bigfoot

When you live in the Michigan countryside and your barn doors keep getting ripped off their hinges, there is one go-to suspect everyone thinks of first—Bigfoot. In a 1981 *Detroit News* story that was posted on the Bigfoot Field Researchers Organization Web site, the Barone family told a harrowing tale of strange encounters on the family farm. In the article, Cindy Barone said that the high-pitched screaming the family had to listen to at night didn't bother her so much—what did bother her was not knowing what Bigfoot really is.

It started that September when the family kept finding sections of fencing torn down and shredded into pieces. The neighbor's barn door was ripped off its hinges, and barrels of grain dumped over and devoured. The farm animals continually acted spooked.

But the final straw came the night the family's two daughters, Tina, thirteen, and Roxanne, twelve, headed for the barn to do their nightly chores. Roxanne had heard noises in the building earlier and refused to go in, so Tina cautiously reached inside for the light switch. "I felt fur," she said. But she was wearing a glove, which she pulled off to be sure of what she had felt. It was fur all right. And the fur was attached to something very tall with red eyes, standing on two legs and growling.

Tina yelled at Roxanne to run as she slowly backed away, but the creature began moving toward her, so she ran too. Happily, it didn't follow them.

The girls got their eighteen-year-old cousin David to chase the beast with a shotgun. The two had a stare-down. "When it stood there and looked at me, it didn't know what to do and I didn't either," said David. He added, "It's unbelievable. It's big."

David insisted it was some kind of animal, but he didn't know what. He shot into the air, and the animal ran screeching into the woods. It looked like something between a bear and an ape, he said. The family reported their scare to the local sheriff's department and said they planned to keep cameras handy in case it came back.

I Am Curious Bigfoot

Bigfoots everywhere display one characteristic in common: a keen interest in humans. Their curiosity about us is evident in the way they seem drawn to observe us — usually from a dense corner of the woods, but sometimes from as close as our front porch or sometimes more intimately than that!

In March of 2004, the *Mt. Pleasant Morning Sun* ran a story about a witness who called the Saginaw Chippewa Tribal Police to report seeing a "hairy figure without clothes" in his yard late at night. Evidently, the figure was taller and stranger than most people who might appear in the man's yard without clothing, so the article's headline called it a Bigfoot sighting.

But there's more. The same person was driving on Leaton Road later that night when the same (inasmuch as he could tell) Hairy One lunged at his car and crashed right into it. The car was not damaged and presumably neither

was the Bigfoot, whose inordinate interest in this man was never explained.

Much, much earlier, in May of 1956, two men near Gladwin learned of Bigfoot's penchant for personal human contact when they experienced a close encounter of the armpit kind. According to Jane and Colin Bord's *Bigfoot Casebook,* Otto Collins and Phillip Williams ran into a giant hairy creature with "green eyes as big as light bulbs." It emitted a rancid body odor, which must have powerfully enhanced what happened next. In seconds, it scooped them up, one under each arm, and held them tightly as if to make off with them.

It's interesting to ponder what the manimal's intentions may have been. Fortunately, the men never had to find out, since they had a third comrade, who was armed with a rifle. When the companion raised his gun, the Bigfoot dropped Collins and Williams and ran off into the woods empty-handed. Had the Bigfoot wanted to adopt the men, whose size could have looked childlike to the monster? Did he crave male companionship? Need a couple more hands for poker? Or perhaps the Bigfoot's missus had just asked him to pick up a couple of things for supper.

The Ferocious Black Squirrels

They are supposedly just like any other squirrels, but there is something about the all-black versions that seems to surprise and spook people. The Scary Squirrel World Web site calls them "maniacal black nutkins." Even otherwise intelligent college students are frightened of them. "They freak me out," said one Michigan State University sophomore in an article in the university's *State News*. "It's like they will just fall down from the trees in front of you and scare you."

Strangely, the black squirrel trail leads back to cornflakes wizard W. K. Kellogg. Kellogg is said to have had a vendetta against red squirrels in Battle Creek, so he had black squirrels imported to fight the red ones in an all-out Squirrelmageddon turf war. The black furs were so successful as tree warriors that Kellogg's brother later transported many of them to Gull Lake where, presumably, they became the ancestors of the squirrels now dropping out of the skies on the M.S.U. campus.

Another place in Michigan that claims a mega black squirrel herd is Diamond Lake Island, near Cassopolis, in the southwestern part of the state. Local legend has it that the squirrels got their color from eating the many black walnuts that grow on the island.

Actually, black squirrels are mutants . . . mutant gray squirrels, that is. And for those out there who collect meaningless facts, here's one: The Lansing–Detroit area is one of only five places in the United States where there is a preponderance of black squirrels, the others being Reedsburg, WI; Princeton, NJ; Galesburg, IL; and New Hartford, CT.

Michigan Dog Man

Michigan may be known for its Bigfoot sightings, but far more strange and terrifying beasts roam its deep forests. The Dog Man, as he has come to be known, has traumatized all who have encountered him in the state's northernmost logging camps and woods. With the head and fur of a wolf or dog on a manlike body, this creature is a freakish bipedal mystery. Apparently coexisting with Bigfoot in Michigan thickets and swamps, the Dog Man was known only as backwoods folklore until 1987, when Traverse City radio deejay Steve Cook (a.k.a. Bob Farley) wrote a song he called "The Legend," with lyrics pulled straight from the tales of Dog Man encounters.

Cook first played his ballad on April Fool's Day, 1987, on WTCM radio in Traverse City and was not prepared for the reaction he got. People who had had their own close encounters with the Dog Man got the shakes when they heard Cook's song. Then they picked up their phones to tell him their own stories. At right are the lyrics to Steve Cook's original "The Legend" (reprinted by permission of Steve Cook).

"The Legend"

*A cool summer mornin' in early June is when the
    legend began,
At a nameless logging camp in Wexford County
    where the Manistee River ran.
Eleven lumberjacks near the Garland Swamp found
    an animal they thought was a dog.
In a playful mood they chased it around 'til it ran
    inside a hollow log.
A logger named Johnson grabbed him a stick and
    poked around inside.
Then the thing let out an unearthly scream and came
    out . . . and stood upright.
None of those men ever said very much about
    whatever happened then.
They just packed up their belongings and left that
    night and were never heard from again.
It was ten years later in '97 when a farmer near
    Buckley was found,
Slumped over his plow, his heart had stopped.
There were dog tracks all around.
Seven years past the turn of the century they say a
    crazy old widow had a dream of dogs that
    circled her house at night.
They walked like men and screamed.
In 1917 a sheriff who was out a walkin'
Found a driverless wagon and tracks in the dust like
    wolves had been a stalkin'.
Near the roadside a four-horse team lay dead with
    their eyes open wide.
When the vet finished up his examination he said it
    looked like they died of fright.
In '37 a schooner captain said several crew members
    had reported a pack of wild dogs roaming
    Bowers Harbor.*

His story was never recorded.
In '57 a man of the cloth found claw marks on
an old church door.
The newspaper said they were made by a dog.
He'd a had to stood seven foot four.
In '67 a van load of hippies told a park ranger
named Quinlan they'd been awakened in the
night by a scratch at the winda . . .
There was a dog-man looking' in and grinnin'.
In '77 there were screams in the night near the
village of Bellaire.
Could have been a bobcat, could have been the
wind. Nobody looked up there.
Then in the summer of '87, near Luther it
happened again.
At a cabin in the woods it looked like maybe
someone had tried to break in.
There were cuts in the door that could only have
been made by very sharp teeth and claws
He didn't wear shoes cause he didn't have feet;
he walked on just two paws.
So far this spring no stories have appeared.
Have the dogmen gone away? Have they
disappeared?
Soon enough I guess we'll know 'cause summer
is almost here.
And in this decade called the 80s, the 7th year is
here.
And somewhere in the northwoods darkness a
creature walks upright
And the best advice you may ever get . . .
Is don't go out at night. (Eerie wolf howl)

Fuel was added to the campfire when a Grand Rapids deejay named Ron Bailey staged a simulated werewolf hunt in February 1992. Bailey talked the Grand Rapids Radio Players into helping him concoct a script, then broadcast the actors pretending to encounter various werewolves from a park near the city. The players crunched snow, snapped branches, screamed over alleged mauled animal carcasses, and generally pretended to be in a real-life crisis mode, à la Orson Welles's 1937 *War of the Worlds* broadcast. Many listeners called in to complain they thought they were hearing a true, live broadcast, exactly as things happened with Welles's famous radio-induced panic.

In 2002, the station issued a CD of their annual broadcast of spooky Halloween stories called *The Haunting of Northwest Michigan*. This, their fifteenth-anniversary edition, contained five stories. The first was an expanded version of "The Legend," and the other four were well-told ghost tales that were revealed as fiction at the end of the CD. However, the cut containing "The Legend" was declared to be entirely true.

Taffy, the World's Fastest Cow

No less than *Guinness World Records* has certified that a cow named Taffy, owned by Michigan State University in East Lansing, was the fastest cow in the world. Like humans, some cows are just born athletes. Taffy happened to be part of an agriculture experiment that put cows on treadmills to see if exercise affected their calving abilities. She proved to be such a nimble trotter that she caught the eye of M.S.U. associate professor and horse expert Brian Nielsen. Nielsen had heard about a sporting event for cows in Ithaca to be held June 21, 2000, called the Udder Race, and he was looking for a bovine to ride. He purchased Taffy and, like any good owner of a race animal, began to train in earnest. They rode a mile every day for almost six weeks, with Neilsen perched in an English racing saddle on the Holstein's back.

When the big day came, Taffy's winning speed was a half mile in eight minutes and 55.4 seconds. She bested five other bossies, including the runner-up, Big Bodacious Bertha. Nielsen, fully outfitted in a jockey suit, swigged a victory cocktail of milk as Taffy was crowned with the winner's wreath. Part of the reason for Taffy's big win, figured Nielsen and other M.S.U. experts, was that she was less than well endowed in the udder department, which decreased her weight and drag.

The Udder Race was the brainchild of retired dairy farmers Pete Ondrus and Barb Lambert of Gratiot County. Following their motto, "Don't milk them, race them," the pair founded the World Wide Cow Racing Association. In following years, they added events like corn silage throwing and a cow costume party.

As for Taffy, she was put out to pasture after her great victory, but she died quietly a few years later of a chronic infection. Her record has since been bested several times, but no one denies that the Michigan cow, in her time, was the fastest milkshake on four legs.

Brian Nielsen and Taffy

Waheela

In Canada, there is a magnificent river valley called the Nahanni, but natives of the area know it as Headless Valley. According to legend and to records of the mounted police, many campers and prospectors who have had the temerity to camp there have been found in their sleeping bags or even inside camping shacks with their heads bitten clean off their bodies. It would take a huge animal with massive jaws to perform this trick, and there has always been much speculation as to which monster might be responsible. The late researcher Ivan Sanderson, though, guessed the nasty head-snarfer might have been a legendary carnivore called the *Waheela*. And according to his research, the animal was also found in Michigan!

In an article he wrote for *Pursuit* magazine in October 1974, Sanderson credited fellow investigator Loren Coleman with finding an old article in the historical files of the University of Indiana. The article is regrettably vague as to exact time and place, but the story stated that three trappers were camping next to a lake somewhere in northern Michigan in colonial times, probably the late 1700s. Their tragic saga was related not by the trappers themselves, but by those who found what was left of them—horribly ravaged bodies surrounded by some type of big "wolf" tracks. The article declared flatly that the men had met up with a *Waheela*.

The *Waheela* is more often spotted around Alaska and the Northwest Territories these days. Bigger and more muscular than modern wolves, the *Waheela* has been linked to the supposedly extinct *Amphicyonid*, a "bear-wolf" combination from the Miocene and Oligocene periods. It sports snow-white fur and has a wider head and larger feet than the timber wolf. According to Native American legends, the *Waheela* is an evil spirit, with special powers for beheading human beings.

Whatzits of the Water

Michigan is unique in that it is made up of two major peninsulas, both surrounded on three sides by the Great Lakes. The state's interior spaces are also well supplied with rivers and smaller bodies of water. With such a generous watery habitat, it's small wonder that the state has earned a longtime rep for harboring lake monsters.

The Ojibwa who lived on the peninsulas long before French trappers arrived were wary of a marine creature they called *Mishipeshu*, the great horned water lynx. This strange being cruised Lake Superior, stealthily roiling the waves and smashing unwary travelers from their canoes with its whiplike tail. *Mishipeshu* was a manifestation of the evil spirit, *Matchi Manitou*, who could also appear as a merman or water serpent. The fearful name *Mishipeshu* was never uttered by the Ojibwa except in winter when ice covered every lake and stream and the people felt safer from the beast's depredations.

Ancient pictographs of both the horned lynx and the water snake are carved into rocks around the shores of Lake Superior. Their original purpose isn't clear, but some think they may mark the spots where these creatures were seen, to serve as a warning.

People who travel the lakes and rivers around Michigan might do well to remember those forms and keep an eye out . . . just in case *Mishipeshu* and the sea serpent still lurk. After all, in 1922, a six-humped water monster was spotted by two women on the Paint River, near Crystal Falls in the Upper Peninsula. And according to modern accounts, it has a few cousins around the state. Some say the strange water creatures are nothing more than giant sturgeons or oversized catfish seen through overly imaginative eyes. Others remember the legends and keep one hand on the motorboat engine's throttle while cruising the waters of the state.

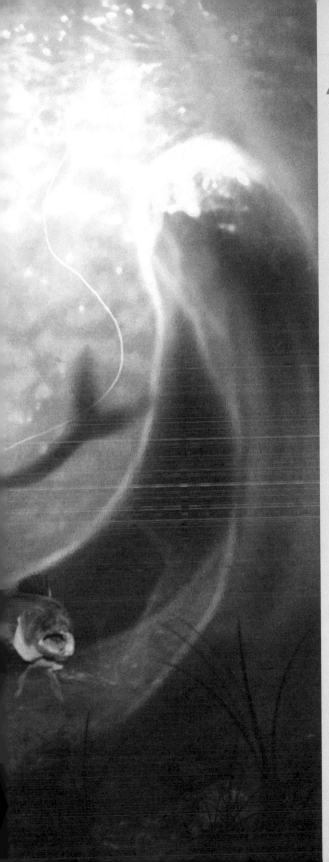

"Pressie"—Michigan's Lake Monster

Since Michigan is the Great Lakes State, it should come as no surprise that it has its own lake monster legend.

The frigid waters of Lake Superior, the largest of the Great Lakes, is said to be the home of a beast that goes by the name of Pressie, due to many sightings of the creature near the Presque Isle River in Michigan's Upper Peninsula. If witnesses are to be believed, this serpentlike monster is quite a sight to behold. It's been described as being dark in color, anywhere between thirty and seventy-five feet long, with a horselike head, a whale's tail, and whiskers similar to those of a catfish. Definitely not something you'd want to see while doing the dog paddle offshore!

Like all good lake monster legends in the United States, the mystery of Pressie begins with the country's earliest inhabitants—Native Americans. The beast it is tied to is the legend of *Mishipeshu*, the spirit guardian of the lake. Indian petroglyphs often feature serpent-like beasts surrounding *Mishipeshu* in the waters. And anything the Native Americans enjoyed, the whites were sure to pick up and make their own. Alleged reports, between 1894 and the 1930s, of an unidentified creature resembling a serpent spotted by observers from the decks of steamers and yachts have been retold on a few Internet sites devoted to this particular legend.

While there are few modern sightings of Pressie, one in 1977 produced an alleged picture of the creature. Much like the many famous pictures of lake monsters before it—Loch Ness, Lake Champlain, and so forth—the so-called Pressie Photograph shows something that could either be a monster or a rock shining in the hot summer sun.

With little to nothing to go on, some might conclude that Pressie is just another lake monster hoax. This wouldn't be surprising, considering the beast has all the hallmarks of modern lake monster culture:

Ties to ancient legends.

Alleged sightings from antiquity to the modern day.

A dubious photograph taken of the beast.

A cute name that rhymes with Nessie.

But who knows? Perhaps Pressie really is out there, watching and waiting for someone lucky, or unlucky, enough to discover it. . . .

—*John Ribner*

Lake Leelanau Monster

The story of an early-twentieth-century sea monster sighting was sent to The Shadowlands Web site by a reader whose great-grandfather was the witness. The boy was fishing for perch one day in 1910 in the shallows of Lake Leelanau in Leelanau County. The lake had been dammed in the late 1800s to provide waterpower for the local mill and to enable logging. The dam flooded much of the surrounding area, turning it into swamps and bogs punctuated by dead, standing trees.

On that particular day, the boy, William Gauthier, rowed out to a new fishing spot near the town of Lake Leelanau. Looking for good perch habitat, he paddled up close to a tree that he estimated to stand about five feet above the water, with a six-inch trunk. Gauthier was in about seven feet of water at this point and decided this would be a good place to cast a line. He stopped and began tying the boat to the tree.

That's when young William discovered the tree had eyes. They were staring him dead in the face at about four feet above water level. The boy and serpent exchanged a long gaze; then the creature went "bloop" into the water. Gauthier said later that the creature's head passed one end of the boat while the tail was still at the other end, though it was undulating very quickly through the water. The writer noted that Gauthier always admitted to having been thoroughly frightened by his encounter and that the event caused him to stay off that lake for many years.

The young Gauthier came from a prominent area family and was very well educated. After the incident, he said that he knew others who would admit privately but not publicly that they too had seen the creature. No sightings have been reported in recent times, but who knows how many people have believed they were passing by a rotting old cedar when in fact they had just grazed the Lake Leelanau monster?

Sea Monster of the Straits

The authorities tried hard to convince the public that what they saw were only giant catfish. But even the oldest, orneriest cats would be hard-pressed to attain a length of forty-five feet! The owner of a resort along the Cheboygan lakefront reported something of just that size, two of them in fact, frolicking in the Mackinac Straits on Lake Huron in front of his property, according to an article in the June 25, 1976, *Grand Rapids Press*. The day after the resort owner called authorities about it, Cheboygan County sheriff Stanley McKervey stopped by to have a look for himself. To his surprise he also was able to observe one of the creatures. "I went down to the beach, and sure enough, I'm looking at something 20, maybe 30 feet long, swimming just below the surface," he said in the article. "I was amazed. I didn't know what it was, but it sure wasn't a publicity stunt."

The sheriff continued watching the creature through binoculars. It rose only about an inch above water level, he said, but any disturbance on shore would cause it to dive deeper again. And that's exactly what happened when the sheriff ordered a couple of deputies to survey the thing in a canoe. It was gone long before the pair got there. Unfortunately, rough water conditions set in the next few days and no one could go out for another look. It wasn't observed again, and other experts theorized that perhaps it was a giant eel or carp. But neither of those sound like what the sheriff and the resort owner saw!

Werewolves of Detroit

The French settlers of Detroit not only gave their city a name from their own language (meaning the "narrows" of the river), but they also injected a healthy dose of their lore and legend into the place. One of the dominant themes in their stories was the werewolf, or *loup-garou*. In the Old World, France was considered an absolute hotbed of werewolfery, with trials, hunts, and torturous executions almost part of the daily routine in medieval times. It was only natural then, that a few *loup-garous* should slip aboard the ships sailing for America and make the landing along with their future intended victims. Perhaps a few escaped into the woods to become the Michigan Dog Man, or maybe they died out with their French ancestors. But ask any native Detroiter; the creatures were here.

The legend goes that one early Detroit man, Jacques Morand, had fallen head over heels in love with a woman named Genevieve Parent. Fair Genevieve's only passion was for God, however, and she spurned Morand's love to become a servant of the church. Morand sank into deep despair until he finally had an epiphany and ran to find one of the many witches said to inhabit the Detroit area in its early days (they were said to be children of the Snake Goddess of Belle Isle). Desperate to retrieve his adored one from the clutches of the black-habited nuns, he offered the witch his soul if she could find a way to retrieve his love.

The witch's neat solution was to turn him into a werewolf so that he would be powerful enough to snatch Genevieve from her cloister. Morand, in his fevered state, thought that sounded like a workable plan and agreed. He soon found himself able to pop back and forth as man or beast, and began spying on Genevieve from near her convent.

One day, the holy object of his affections made a pilgrimage to Grosse Pointe to worship at a shrine for the Virgin Mary. Morand saw his chance. He skulked behind her as she prayed in front of the statue, waiting for the best opportunity to grab her and run away. Suddenly, just as Morand made his leap toward her, she dropped to her knees in a fit of adoration, so that the man-beast found himself staring straight into the face of the statue. It turned him instantly to stone, taking one more *loup-garou* off the streets of Detroit.

There were more werewolves to take his place, however, and they seemed inclined to stalk and seize young women whenever they had the chance. One was bold enough to grab a young lady at her own wedding dance. He dragged Archange Simonet off to the wilds to have his way with her while her abandoned bridegroom hunted for Archange until he went quite mad. One fellow hunter got close enough to chop the creature's tail off, though, and the local Native Americans are said to still have it among their treasured possessions.

The best the groom ever managed to do was finally chase the werewolf to the shore and watch it jump into the lake. Still crazy as a loon, he swore he saw the huge furry creature jump into the maw of a giant catfish, and that was the end of his frenzied hunt.

One other mention of a Detroit werewolf has it as a helper of wood witches. It assisted them one night in thrashing a French trader who cheated the local tribespeople out of a bunch of beaver furs. As the witches pounded him in fury, the werewolf jumped on the Frenchman's back until he finally gave up his ill-gotten gains to them. He managed to flail the witches away from him, but when his rosary fell from his neck during the fray, the werewolf was forced to disappear into the earth. Later, a sulfur spring was said to have sprung up where the werewolf made his plunge; the spot was known after that time as Belle Fontaine.

Panther from the Forest of Doom

It can devour a three-hundred-pound deer, down to the head and antlers, in three hours. It once lived, evidently, in the Gogomain Swamp, a thick, marshy woods twenty-five miles south of Sault Ste. Marie, where the forest is so dense that in winter the temperature is often thirty degrees warmer inside the Gogomain than outside. (Some Michiganders call the place the Forest of Doom.) It, the thing that once resided in this perpetually dark and dank no-man's-land but finally ventured out to wander the state, is known as Michigan's Mystery Cat.

The "cat" was first spotted around 1954 in nearby Munuscong Bay and was then whispered about intermittently for decades. In 1972, deer hunter Walter Wegner was awakened one late November morning by sounds of a struggle near his tent. What roused the hunter from his sleep were snorts, a groan, and the breaking of brush and twigs. Not being the curious type apparently, Wegner waited about three hours before walking back into the area to see what was going on. Something bright red was draped over a stump, and thinking some hunter had left his jacket, Wegner walked closer. Then he realized it was the head and antlers of a ten-point buck. The experienced hunter estimated the buck would have "dressed out" at about two hundred and fifty pounds, and couldn't imagine what might have eaten the carcass so quickly.

In May 1984, a black panther made headlines when spotted creeping around houses and lawns in Manchester, only fifteen miles southwest of Ann Arbor. But a huge panther flap occurred two years later around the little town of Milford, between Ann Arbor and Flint. This time there was a casualty—a $3,000 palomino quarter horse found in its pasture, only one hundred yards from its owner's house, its throat ripped out in a deep wound that measured four by seven inches.

This was news, and area papers released a flurry of articles. The *Detroit News* edition of July 12, 1986, featured a prominent story titled ANOTHER WILD CAT ON THE PROWL; DID ELUSIVE PANTHER KILL PRIZED HORSE IN MILFORD? Milford police sergeant Ray F. Clinard said, "I think it's feline and I think it's big."

The paper stated that two years earlier, during the 1984 flap, "officers from the US Fish and Wildlife Service confirmed that a panther was on the loose."

A massive, organized cat hunt ensued. Police searched the area around the nearby General Motors Corporation Proving Grounds, and rural residents began toting guns and keeping kiddies and pets indoors. Police did see the animal twice but missed their shot both times. The *Detroit Free Press* reported that a federal wildlife official said this was not the same cat that haunted Manchester, but that it was a second black panther and both were probably brought illegally into the state. Because of that, the case was given to federal authorities, who took over the hunt. With little progress though, the Feds soon tired of the chase and left.

Things settled down over the winter, but as the weather warmed, the panther sightings bloomed again. In April, the *Detroit News* wrote, GREEN EYES GLOW IN DARK: COULD IT BE THE PANTHER? A man named Jim Trick in Oakland County said it was no treat when he saw a large animal with "glowing green eyes" on Loon Lake, not far from Milford. Trick said he encountered the panther after his dog alerted him by barking about ten forty-five p.m. He went out to investigate and was stopped short by the glowing green eyes. Man and panther stared at each other for a few seconds, he said, and then the eyes began coming toward him. Trick walked backward to his house, and the animal disappeared into the night.

Soon more loose "black leopards" were being

reported around the county. A man told Wixom police he had spotted a large black "cat" near I-96. Others reported small livestock missing; paw prints were found and cast in plaster. Some of the prints were smaller, fueling speculation that there was now a black panther family breeding in the area. Months later the man who owned the horse attacked back in 1986 came upon a black panther in the very same field and shot at it three times with a .357 handgun. He found some blood spots the next evening but no body.

The sightings continued. Two were near Muskegon in early October of 1990, one of them made by seven children who spotted the panther watching them play from under a picnic table. THE CELEBRATED BLACK PANTHER SURFACES AGAIN read a headline in the *Saginaw News* in February of that year after another family captured the animal on video from about two hundred yards as it prowled around their Camden property. The family saw the cat for two consecutive days before it hightailed it for someplace else.

As of this writing, Michigan's mysterious panther—or panthers—is still on the loose. No one has ever satisfactorily explained the sightings. The Mystery Cat is left, then, to pad around the old newspaper clippings stored in small-town library files, never quite proved and yet never erased from the memories of those who saw it with their own, startled eyes.

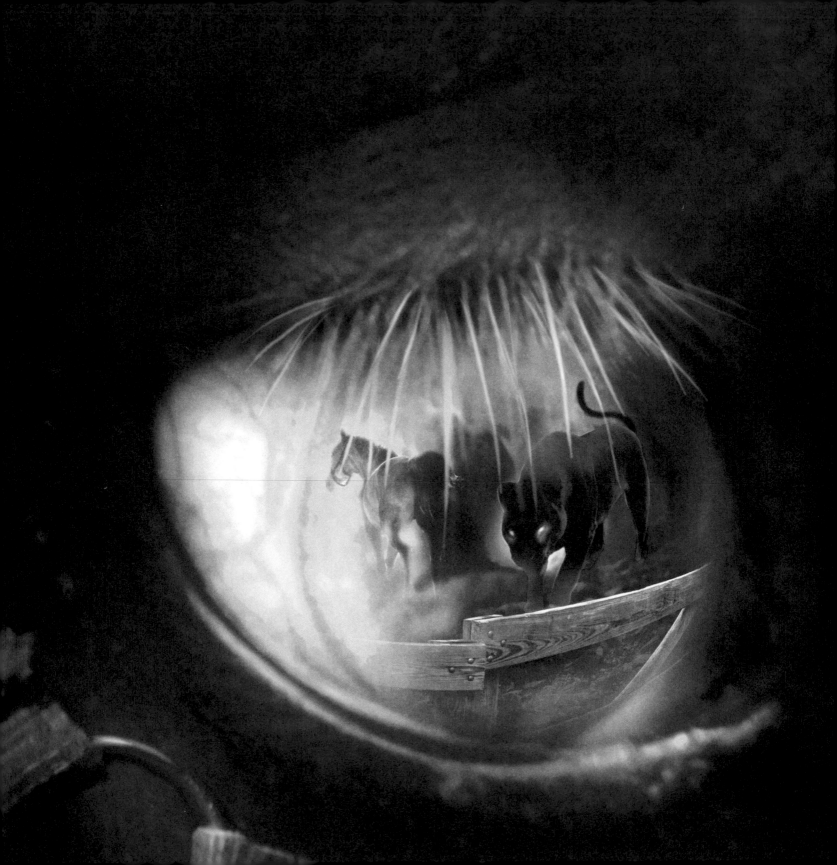

Taymouth's Tawny Cougar

Not to be outdone by its ebony relative, a tawny cougar started showing up in 1995 around Taymouth Township. One man told the *Saginaw News* he found four-inch tracks near "the mangled body of a woodchuck." A woman saw it slinking away in a field near her home. Four other people reported seeing the animal in early April. By August, residents around Flushing were calling police about mountain lions in their yards and fields. The beast evidently still lurked in the general vicinity in 1999, when an Edmore family discovered an uninvited guest at an outdoor birthday party in October. A full-grown cougar edged around the family's yard but kept its distance from the group of flabbergasted humans. The Edmore chief of police told the *Mt. Pleasant Morning Sun* he'd had two other reported sightings.

After all this activity, it was no surprise when an article in the *Saginaw News* in March of 2001 noted that a wildlife preservation group was positive that at least a "handful" of cougars were prowling the woods and fields of Michigan. The group had made a two-and-a-half-year study of the phenomenon, but their claim was still contested by state wildlife officials. Cougars are considered extinct in most of North America. If they are indeed roaming our state, they were brought here by some as yet unknown forces.

The wildlife group cited paw prints and droppings that had been subjected to DNA tests, establishing the presence of cougars at a total of six sites. They estimated that Michigan might host as many as forty-five of the animals.

Officials who pooh-poohed the cougar doo results were stumped, though, when the animals subsequently showed up near Kalkaska and attacked an 1,800-pound Percheron horse. The Kalkaska High senior who owned the horse said he saw two cats, one bigger and one smaller, up close twice. His horse was wounded on the throat and back, and scores of smaller livestock went missing in the area. And in July 2004, the Michigan Wildlife Conservancy released a video that showed two mountain lions prowling a Monroe County field.

One expert hoping to prove the existence of Midwest cougars is Clayton K. Nielsen, a university wildlife ecologist and director of scientific research for the Cougar Network. He tried to assure Midwesterners they needn't be afraid for their lives. "The likelihood of a human getting attacked by a cougar . . . is lower than death by vending machine," he said in a February 20, 2005, issue of the *Coles County Leader.*

That should be a comfort . . . but tell that to the Percheron.

Detroit Airport Kangaroo

Kangaroo sightings (outside of Australia and zoos) have become almost a regular modern-day phenomenon. Wisconsin had its famous Waukesha flap in 1978 and another in the fall of 2004, one of the rare times when the "phantom" roo was actually captured (it now resides in Vilas Zoo, in Madison, WI). But of all the sites for a displaced kangaroo to show up in Michigan, who would have thought it would choose the most densely populated area of the state, Detroit. In September 1984, an eyewitness told Detroit police that she had spotted a full-grown kangaroo leaping across the interstate highway at the airport. A sheriff's deputy also spied it the next day, but it was never caught. Did it escape from the cargo area of a plane at the airport? Hop over the fence of a local petting zoo? Enter a space-time vortex in Australia and suddenly find itself on the other side of the world? Curious Detroiters may never know.

Saginaw Water Man

The year was 1937, the place, a riverbank near Saginaw. A man sat on the bank, fishing, when he was astonished to see a man-like monster or water creature climb up on the shore. It leaned against a tree for a moment, as if catching its breath, then dove back into the river. The fisherman was so distraught by this sudden appearance, reports Loren Coleman in his book *Mysterious Encounters,* that he later "suffered a nervous breakdown." This mysterious encounter was never explained.

Witchie Wolves of Omer Plains

I grew up on the eastern shore of Lake Huron, twelve miles north of Bay City. With the limited nightlife available to teenagers in the rural area, the vast majority of teens during the mid-seventies would drive around the piney woods and wetlands looking for parties or privacy. Since at least the early sixties, it was a teenage rite for male students from Pinconning High School to pile into a car and drive twenty miles north to the wilderness known as the Omer Plains. Located a few miles west of the little town of Omer in Arenac County, this strange, uninhabited place of scrubby pines and swampland is home to the phenomenon known as the Witchie Wolves.

According to local Chippewa legend, Witchie Wolves are invisible spirit dogs that guard the graves of ancient warriors, attacking anyone foolish enough to venture out at night on foot. Although I went to the Omer Plains twice, nobody in our vehicle was brave enough to get out of the car. We could all hear the hideous, high-pitched laughing bark that came from all directions out of the near total darkness. Several times a year, a skeptical youth, usually an athlete or an outdoorsman type, would take the dare and get out of the car, only to be violently knocked to the ground by what always seemed to be an invisible wolf or dog snarling and snapping at the victim's head. Screaming and scrambling back into the car, nobody ever stuck around long enough to see what else would happen. I have seen tough guys cry while telling of their experience. I have heard claims of torn clothes and I have seen scratches and dents on roofs of cars which the owner, straight-faced and sober, would claim weren't there before the Witchie Wolf attack.

It seemed like everyone knew and accepted the Witchie Wolves. They were and probably still are given a wide berth.–*David A. Kulczyk (Originally published in* Strange Magazine 15, *reprinted by permission of David A. Kulczyk.)*

Local Notables

Every town's got at least one, but Michigan has them up the wazoo. They're the topic of every coffee shop gossip circle, the strange ones who are whispered about or shouted at—outrageous folks who may or may not be known outside the city boundaries but who stand out in their hometowns like moose in a Detroit dance club.

Some of them are dead, but they lived life so hard that they're still squeezing glory out of their earthly deeds. Others walk among us yet, spewing their own peculiar brands of eccentricity. Some of them the world could definitely do without. But others lightened the days of those around them, delightful oddballs in a neighborhood of squares. To help give them their due, we document here some of the most outstanding, the unforgettable, and the unforgivable.

Captain Jackson: One City's Superhero

He's caped, and he's a crusader. And technically, says Captain Jackson, Champion of All that Is Civil and True in the city he's named himself after, he "fits the definition of a superhero." In his purple cape, his Batman-minus-the-ears helmet mask, custom trunks, and Spandex leggings, Captain Jackson looks like a superhero. Sure, he's wearing running shoes instead of boots, and no, he can't fly or melt steel with a blast from his eyeballs. But when darkness falls in downtown Jackson, the captain prowls its back alleys and bars to let the criminal-minded know they had better think twice.

Weird Michigan couldn't resist the chance to talk to a real-life superhero, so we called and asked him if he started out by reading action comics and dressing up like Superman on Halloween. "No!" yelled the Man of Purple. "I think superhero comics are dumb! I never read comic books or dressed up as Superman!"

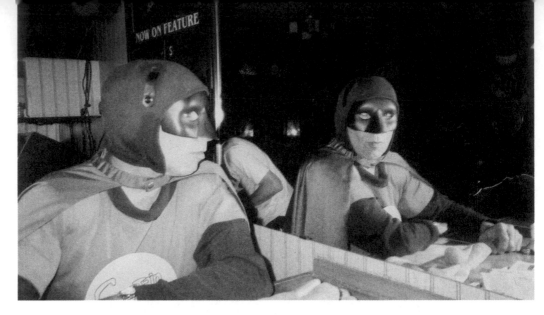

His beginnings as a masked crime fighter are much simpler, actually. Captain Jackson was born six years ago, when his alter ego (whose name we have pledged to keep confidential) moved to Jackson from Detroit and decided the local police were not visible enough in the community to keep the downtown area free of crime. "One day I called into a local talk show," said the captain, "and introduced myself as Captain Jackson. I said I just got here from Detroit, and I'm here to save this city. I had the idea of being a bridge between the police and the people."

The captain admits his first uniform (don't ever call it a costume, or you'll incur the wrath of a superhero!) was a bit on the lame side, with a homemade felt cape. The captain's original sidekick, daughter Crimefighter Girl, started at the age of nine in a flowered bathing suit with a towel pinned around her shoulders. Today the Debonair Duo (Crimefighter Girl is now fifteen) sport uniforms with custom components, including plastic logos that attach with Velcro. "A lot of the uniform is handmade," said the captain. "I mean, it's not like you can walk into Wal-Mart and ask for the superhero clothing department."

They've also added a third member to the Crime-fighter Corps, the lovely blond Queen of Hearts who, besides displaying a considerable talent for martial arts, specializes in working against domestic violence. "She just showed up on the street one night in her own uniform," said the captain. "I was like, oh, Baby! She was hot, and I was newly single." A superhero romance was born.

Captain Jackson doesn't make arrests, but he calls the police if it seems there is anything unusual going on. The police and fire departments both apparently appreciate his presence, having made him an honorary deputy fire chief and appearing with him at numerous civic events. So far, he hasn't had to fight anyone, but said he did get sucker-punched in a downtown bar one night. Within seconds, four patrons were holding the offender down, he said, so he wasn't forced to unleash his full powers upon the attacker.

The captain has loftier goals than mere safety patrols, however. His ultimate hope is to find backers for a foundation dedicated to educating people about how to take back their neighborhoods and to provide scholarships for future law-enforcement officers. At present, he pays all his expenses out of his own pocket.

Of course, every hero has his kryptonite, the inevitable Achilles' heel. The captain admits he doesn't like heights, which is one reason (besides not having spider powers) that you won't see him dangling from any rooftop parapets.

There is, by the way, one thing Captain Jackson truly wishes he could change about Jackson, but it's unlikely to happen in this age of advancing technology. "There's no phone booths!" he exclaimed. "Where's a superhero supposed to change these days?"

Bill Jarrett, Guru of Toilet Paper

Does the proper Michigander hang his or her toilet paper with the free end dangling over or under? It's the timeless bathroom question that even advice columnist Ann Landers could never manage to completely wipe out. But one stalwart Grand Rapids man, Bill Jarrett, decided to take up where Landers left off and conduct a massive nationwide poll to settle the question once and for all.

Jarrett says other polls have been conducted and that most of them came out in favor of "over." "But they weren't democratic votes with a lot of people in them," he says. "I want to find this out once and for all and decree a national toilet paper hanging way. Then the toilet paper police will have to come out to enforce it."

Jarrett estimates that he has been into toilet paper for at least twenty of his eighty years. "Toilet paper is a fine thing," he said. "It needs no instructions or batteries, and one size fits all. You can even play ball with it." Jarrett has invented a toilet paper ball game for just that purpose, using a toilet lid and a net to create a target similar to a basketball hoop. He keeps one in his TP-crammed office along with his voluminous files of toilet paper correspondence, newspaper clippings, and other toilet-related items.

Admittedly, votes are not coming in as fast as Jarrett would like. One probable reason he's fallen short of his million-vote goal is that it costs $5 to vote. People have to order and pay for the voting form, and then mail it back in. But they do get more than the form for their money. In addition, they receive a patented refrigerator magnet that includes a miniature working roll of toilet paper that people may arrange over or under, according to preference. (To get a voting kit, see www.thegreatamericantoiletpaperdebate.com.)

The Scottville Clown Band

They dress like Fred Flintstone, unshaven drag queens, and hula dancers, among other outlandish characters. But they play like a proper orchestra, whether marching in floppy clown shoes and high heels or seated in their hometown band shell. The Scottville Clown Band, in existence in various forms for over ninety years, is in high demand all over western Michigan for both its wacko appearance and fine music. With over two hundred and fifty total members, between twenty and forty musical clowns will show up for any given performance. The term "clown" is used loosely, since almost anything goes, costume-wise. This guarantees that the band is always one of the strangest-looking human assemblages to be seen on planet Earth.

Weird Michigan caught up with them at the band shell in Scottville's park one warm August evening. Playing to their usual packed house, they had just broken into a rousing version of "Margaritaville." The players, many of them anything but wasting away, appeared to range in age from about twelve to the upper seventies and beyond. One robust fellow wearing a hat that resembled a chicken led the audience in the chicken dance, accompanied by another dancer in a wig fashioned from a string mop.

Most fascinating, however, is the way the band seems to bring out the latent cross-dresser in many of its members. Men in lingerie were abundant, including one billed as "Sophie Krakowski, who put the crack back in Krakow." Sophie vamped "her" way through a simulated striptease as the band played "The Stripper."

The group was first organized in 1903, when a bunch

of locals in ordinary clothing formed to provide music for fairs and local parades. By 1930, it had somehow evolved into what they called a "ladies band," which meant men dressed as women—which explains the lingering lingerie tradition. The local newspaper archives contain numerous humorous photos of Scottville townsmen in wigs, overstuffed brassieres, and glamorous tiaras.

After a brief respite during World War II, the band reorganized and gave itself its current name. It wasn't long before it began receiving statewide recognition, and members were added in other cities so that everyone wouldn't have to travel to every event. The group still travels around ten thousand miles a year and uses the revenue it receives from selling its book, *The Big Noise from Scottville,* T-shirts, CDs, and videos to support young music students around the state. Odds are good that the Scottville Clown Band will continue to receive Michigan gigs as long as it can continue to persuade elderly male musicians to don black lace negligees and dance the hoochy-koochy.

The Real Real McCoy

Countless people have uttered the old cliché, "I want the real McCoy," without giving a thought as to what, or who, the real McCoy might be. Truth is, the real McCoy was born in 1843, the brilliant son of two African American slaves who escaped to Canada via the

Underground Railroad. The family moved to Detroit after the Civil War, and Elijah was sent to Scotland as a teenager to study mechanical engineering.

After his return to the States, McCoy took a job with the Michigan Central Railroad in Ypsilanti. Although his employee status was officially fireman, the person responsible for shoving wood into the train's firebox, he showed true genius by inventing and patenting a self-oiling lubricator for locomotive bearings. Railroad companies across the country rushed to buy the new McCoy lubricating cup because it saved expensive maintenance stops. And to make sure they weren't being sold some inferior brand, they began to ask for "the real McCoy." The phrase stuck and trickled into common usage.

McCoy was issued many more patents over the years and even had his own manufacturing company for a while. His final years were less than pleasant, however. He lost his business and spent a year in the Eloise Asylum in Westland before succumbing to various illnesses of old age in 1929. He had no children to carry on his name, but his marvelous lubricating invention did that job for him.

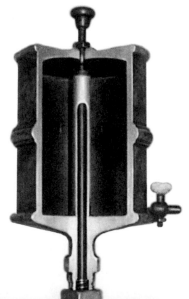

Streakers of Detroit

There's something about Motown that seems to make people want to run around in the buff. Whatever the quirky catalyst might be, it's been there for centuries. In the 1820s, according to *The Detroit Almanac,* one downtown business owner named Robert McNiff was so enslaved by demon rum that he would trade whatever clothing he had on at any given moment for a bottle, then hoof it back home in his birthday suit. At least he had the bottle to use as occasional strategic cover.

In 1974, about one hundred and fifty years after McNiff's shocking runs, some baseball fans took advantage of opening day at Tiger Stadium to shuck their apparel and dance around the arena's upper deck au naturel. Before being apprehended, several dozen of them managed to simultaneously entertain and dismay the crowd by running through the bleacher aisles and dangling themselves from the scoreboard. The temperature that day? A mere thirty-eight degrees. Newspaper accounts do not say whether the young men needed treatment for frostbite of any body parts.

One other near streaker of note was known as the Belle Isle Skulker in 1970. The man seemed to have a strange compulsion to strip down to his undies, dive off the Belle Isle Bridge, then swim through dangerous currents and river flotsam to the other side. When police were finally able to catch up with him, they saw to it that he received professional help for his hazardous obsession.

Shakey Jake of Ann Arbor

Shakey Jake Woods claims he's a hundred and three years old. But then, he's been claiming that for at least twenty years. And even though he doesn't get around as well as he used to, he's still as much a part of downtown Ann Arbor as the streetlights or the refurbished brick storefronts. Woods makes a living by passing the hat after street corner serenades and selling bumper stickers that read BRAKE FOR JAKE. For a while, one downtown bagel store also sold stickers that said WE BAKE FOR JAKE. He's even been featured in *Rolling Stone* Magazine, although Carol Lopez, owner of The Peaceable Kingdom store, says the *RS* writer got him all wrong.

"They said he was really an eccentric millionaire who rides around town in a Cadillac," Lopez says. "But they were mixing him up with another of our town characters, Cadillac Joe, who has several vintage Cadillacs that he drives very slowly with the windows all down, playing music very loudly."

Jake's two favorite spots are on the corner of Main and Liberty, or down in the campus area. He has a reputation as something of a kidder. When anyone says hello to him, says Lopez, whether he knows the person or not, he's likely to respond, "Where you been? I ain't seen you in a long time!"

One of Jake's crowning moments came some years ago when the downtown hosted an ethnic festival with a stage set up on his street corner. When a Greek dancing group didn't show up in time, someone shouted, "Put Jake up there!" Lopez said, "He got up and sang, 'Swing low, sweet chair-io', for fifteen minutes. When he was done, the crowd made a huge noise and began throwing money up on the stage. It took a long time to pick up all that money."

Born in Little Rock, Arkansas, just ten miles from Bill Clinton's boyhood home, Jake says he grew up with

fourteen brothers and sisters, and that his mother died at the age of a hundred and six. He claims he earned his blues chops in the 1940s on Bourbon Street in New Orleans, playing with B. B. King and James Brown (he also says he used to play softball with boxer Joe Louis) until a group of Ann Arbor students coaxed him into coming north for a visit. Once he arrived, he never left. He still shows up downtown every day, even playing in the winter when the temperature allows. And when that sweet chair-io finally does swing low, here's hoping it finds Shakey Jake with one full hat.

"Wolverine Guy" Jeffrey Ford

Move over, Wolverine of the superhero comics fame. There's a new Wolverine Guy in town. He may not grow giant claws when rankled, but that's what people are calling Deckerville high school science teacher Jeffrey Ford of Ubly.

Ford has pulled off an achievement near to the hearts of every loyal Michigander . . . actually sighting a live specimen of Michigan's state animal, the wolverine. Despite its official status, the feisty brown-haired mammal has been officially absent from Michigan for at least two hundred years—which has been a tad embarrassing for state athletic teams and others using it for their mascot. All of this has made the hunt for a genuine *Gulo gulo*

become Michigan's version of the quest for the Holy Grail: endless and unrewarding.

Ford has changed all that, however. He started on the wolverine trail after hearing back in February 2004 that some local coyote hunters had flushed a *Gulo* from the woods near Ubly. He found his first evidence of the animal Native Americans called carcajou, or "mountain devil," not long after that. Later he was able to capture video footage using cameras set to detect heat and motion near a site he and fellow woodsmen Jason Rosser and Steve Noble baited with chicken and venison.

Although many have claimed to have seen wolverines, Ford's film was the first official documented sighting of the animal in the state of Michigan. Besides the film, Ford cast footprints for evidence of the sighting and found hair samples to submit for DNA analysis to establish the gender, although its size indicates this is probably a guy *Gulo.* Full-grown wolverines weigh around thirty-five to forty pounds.

Ford's most thrilling moment, however, was actually encountering the creature at his bait site in April 2005 and watching incredulously as the beast ferociously charged him from the underbrush. "I kept thinking, I'm gonna die, I'm gonna die," Ford told the *Bay City Times* in December 2005. After all, wolverines have been known to best eight-hundred-pound grizzly bears. Luckily, when the animal came within about five yards of Ford, it seemed to realize he was not its usual prey and turned and hightailed it out of there. Ford emphasizes that the wolverine is not dangerous to humans, a fact that has become his mantra as he continually assures neighbors that it will not be eating their children.

Since becoming Wolverine Guy, Ford has invested at least $3,000 of his own money and, he estimates, at least a thousand hours in his furry obsession. He operates a Web site, wolverineguy.com, where people can buy a twenty-minute video titled *Gulo Madness,* resin replicas of the paw print, or a glossy eight-by-ten pinup photo.

The Lubrimental Journey of Prophet Jones

In the year 2000, all humanity was to receive the gift of immortality as heaven descended to earth to wipe out sickness and death forever. This now obviously failed prophecy was often repeated during the mid-twentieth century by Detroit's most audacious man of the cloth, the Reverend James F. Prophet Jones. The catch was that when heaven descended, those who had previously failed to obey the Prophet's fifty-some rules for living would somehow not be around to enjoy the new paradise. To become heaven-worthy, among other things, men and women were instructed to wear girdles to keep their bellies and rear ends from protruding. Female followers spent much of their time and money on manicures, redoing their nails twice a day to follow the Prophet's demand that they wear clear polish in the daytime and red at night.

The amazing thing was that people—lots of them—complied with these rules. Enough so that in the 1940s and '50s, as many as twenty-five hundred followers packed the old Oriole Theater (later named the Shrine of Lady Catherine after Jones's mother) five times a week for marathon services that began at ten p.m. and lasted until seven or eight in the morning; they were broadcast live on local TV every Sunday night.

Services at Jones's Church of the Universal Triumph, the Dominion of God, began with great pomp as Prophet Jones strode to his elaborate, thronelike chair in a long, red velvet coat that covered a sequined ruby robe. He owned four hundred expensive suits for everyday use and a white mink coat given to him by parishioners. His sermons could be puzzling. Jones often employed an unknown tongue called glossolalia. And when he did preach in English, his sermons were peppered with original, unexplained phrases. He once solemnly told fellow preacher Father Divine, of Philadelphia, "I know the chassis of your mind has been carried up into a divine cosmic lubritorium." Whatever that meant, this strange idea seemed to be a key point of his theology, since he often shouted praises for the "lubritorium of lubrimentality" during his sermons. The Reverend's power to mesmerize an audience was said to be spectacular, however, and he never failed to whip his congregation to an emotional, fevered pitch.

Born in 1907 in Birmingham, Alabama, Jones was a religious child prodigy. He made his first prophecy at the age of two, telling his mother one morning that when his daddy, a railroad worker, came home that night, he would have blood on him. Sure enough, that day his father tried to pull a hitchhiker off the train and received a blow to the head with a sharp hunk of coal, drawing blood. The Prophet began preaching at the ripe old age of six and became a full-time minister when he was only eleven. His Alabama church sent him to Detroit at the age of twenty-one, charging him to

and furniture fit for royalty. The house was referred to as his castle, and everyone close to him received a title of Prince, Princess, Lord, or Lady.

Unfortunately for Jones's flamboyant kingdom, the Dominion eventually lost its steam. In 1956 the Prophet was charged with gross indecency, and although he was acquitted, his popularity began to wane.

He did continue to make prophecies, though they proved less than accurate—such as his 1966 prediction that the United States would decisively win the war in Vietnam. In 1971, he died of a heart attack in a private home on Detroit's LaSalle Boulevard. Jones was buried in Elmwood Cemetery, dressed to the nines in an embroidered robe, ready for his journey to that cosmic lubritorium in the sky.

begin a new mission church, a task he accomplished in short order.

Jones broke away and formed his own, separate group in 1938. People flocked to his grandiose worship style, and the Prophet became known nationwide with profiles in *Time, LIFE,* and the *Saturday Evening Post,* which called him the Messiah in Mink. He lived in a French chateau-style mansion with fifty-four rooms at 75 Arden Park and decorated it with gold ceilings

The Unabomber, Killer Math Whiz

That's Una, for the university scholars many attacks were aimed at, and bomber, for airplane bomber. Put them together, as did detectives on the trail of this elusive killer (their original codeword was Unabom), and you get the wild-haired, Chicago-born Ted Kaczynski. Although he killed three innocent people and wounded almost two dozen others with mail bombs before he was finally apprehended in 1996, he was once the leading math genius of the University of Michigan in Ann Arbor.

Kaczynski earned both a master's degree and a Ph.D. in math at U-Mich and impressed his professors with feats such as solving a math problem neither the professors nor other mathematicians had been able to figure out. He taught for three years in Ann Arbor while publishing brilliant papers in professional journals. Even though he was a complete social outcast, distancing himself from peers by such habits as wearing a sport coat and tie to Michigan classes in the era of bell-bottomed jeans and tie-dyed T-shirts, his future in academia looked dazzling.

Something inside Kaczynski just couldn't hang onto that success, however. Criminologists who've studied his life say it was during his five years in Michigan that he not only seemed to crystallize his core philosophy of

personal anarchy and hatred of modern technology, but showed clear signs that he was teetering on a dangerous psychotic edge. Psychologists have tried to explain the strange twist his life took by pointing out that as a baby he became ill and was restricted to a hospital room for weeks, while his normally loving parents were prevented from even touching him. According to his mother, little Ted never recovered emotionally from that experience.

Kaczynski was offered an assistant professorship at the University of California, Berkeley, in 1967, and spent two years teaching there before he resigned in 1969. He took the job mainly to earn enough money to afford a remote hideout where he could carry out his plans for killing people. When he was arrested, he was living in a ten- by twelve-foot shack in a Montana forest.

The Unabomber started his career with an explosive device sent to an engineering professor at Evanston, Illinois' Northwestern University in 1978. He managed to elude authorities and continue his diabolical obsession for the better part of two decades. It ended only when several national newspapers published Kaczynski's thirty-five-thousand-word manifesto which outlined his philosophy, in return for the killer's pledge to stop the mail bombs. The rambling document made Kaczynski's own brother, David, realize that his sibling, Ted, was probably behind all the madness. David sorrowfully tipped off authorities.

Ted Kaczynski was sentenced in 1998 to life in prison without possibility of parole and is still incarcerated in a Federal Supermax in Florence, Colorado. Ironically, Michigan ended up with what might be the most lasting reminder of the havoc his strange mind devised. In June 2005, Kaczynski fought to donate his autobiography, many letters, bomb tools, books, and other papers to the University of Michigan's famed Labadie Collection, a research archive of social protest materials. Kaczynski's massive and murderous paper trail now takes up five linear feet of shelving in the library of the serial killer's alma mater.

Andrew Kehoe, Too Cruel for School

It was the explosion that rocked and shocked a state. On the morning of May 18, 1927, the treasurer of the school board in the small community of Bath ran suddenly amok. No one in Bath had any idea that Andrew Philip Kehoe was about to snap, but all the signs were there. He had been secretly stealing from school funds because his farm was failing. He had a sick wife and couldn't afford her medicine, and the bank was threatening to foreclose on his home. Moreover, he was incensed that local property taxes had been raised to build a new, consolidated school for the area's students.

According to one longtime Bath researcher, Kehoe had suffered a fall earlier in life while studying to be an electric lineman and went into a coma. Although he eventually recovered, this event was said to have permanently affected his personality. When he was forty, he was also suspected of abetting the burning death of his stepmother (widely misreported as happening when he was fourteen).

With all this strange history, the diabolical plot Kehoe hatched to amend his Bath woes is slightly more understandable. It's hard to say exactly when he decided on his course of action, but he had started accumulating explosives and hiding them in the ceiling of the new school basement months before the event. Kehoe had several chilling objectives. One was to completely remove any value from his farm so that the bank would have nothing but the land when it foreclosed. Another was to take revenge on the man

he blamed most for the new school building, Emory Huyck.

His major goal, of course, was the elimination of the building he hated so much. The day before his planned disaster, he started out by killing his wife, crushing her head with a blunt instrument. That left her free from any retribution and him free to spend the rest of the day finalizing his murderous plan.

The next morning Kehoe was up bright and early and began his tasks with manic zest. He sawed through his grove of maple and fruit trees, killing them one by one. He had already wired his house and all the outbuildings with an abundance of explosives. Just before nine a.m., he got into his pickup truck, drove it to a safe distance, then watched as the accumulated material possessions of his life, along with his dead spouse, exploded like a volcano, spewing debris as far away as the next farm. He warned the neighbors who came running that they had better

go to the school instead, then sped off toward town.

At the school, only the younger children were present because the older high school students were in the church next door, practicing for the upcoming commencement exercises. Kehoe had previously set the school explosives with a battery and a clock. People had barely recovered from hearing the giant blast at his farm when the homemade firebomb detonated in the Bath school's basement. It was like Armageddon to shocked villagers, the northwest side of the building completely gone, the rest of the school in flames and rubble. Thankfully, though, Kehoe had set several separate charges and the first blast somehow disabled the others.

Still, the carnage was unthinkable. Kehoe's bomb had killed thirty-eight children, mostly in the lower elementary grades, and several teachers. At least fifty more were wounded to various degrees.

Within half an hour of the explosion, the insane

mastermind drove up in his truck to survey his handiwork. The back of his pickup was crammed not only with explosives, but also with an assortment of metal farm trash designed to turn the truck into a shrapnel-filled terrorist bomb on wheels. As he looked over the scene, Kehoe spotted his hated opponent, Superintendent Huyck, and motioned for him to come closer. As soon as Huyck was within range, Kehoe coolly turned and squeezed off one well-placed rifle shot into the truck's deadly cargo. Huyck, the town postmaster,

SCHOOL BLDG. BATH MICH
DESTROYED BY DYNAMITE MAY 18-27
PHOTO BY LEAVENWORTH—LANSING.

PICTURE SHOWS FOUR TRAGEDY VICTIMS RECOVERING

Four of the child victims of the tragedy at Bath, Mich. where a crazed farmer dynamited the consolidated school, are at hospital in Lansing in the accompanying pictures taken by Norman Mauger of the Blade camera staff. From left to right, Dorothy Fulton, 11, Ruth Barnes, 13 and Marion Beckbruch, 11, with her nurse, Mrs. Green. At the bottom left is shown At the right workmen are shown digging graves for some of the 44 children and adults who were killed in the explosion.

CRIMINALS ARE MADE, NOT BORN.

and a young boy who had managed to escape the school blast were all killed.

The bloody remains of Andrew Kehoe landed in a nearby flower garden. Authorities removed 504 pounds of additional, unexploded dynamite from the remainder of the school. The new building had to be scrapped, as Kehoe had planned, but another one was built in its place by townspeople determined not to let the crazed farmer have the final say on their educational program. That school was eventually torn down, and today a small park occupies the former site of destruction, with various memorials and the original school's red-topped cupola serving as centerpiece.

As for Kehoe, his chief memorial will always be the brief message on the handmade wooden sign he left in a safe place on his farm for everyone to read after he was gone. It read, CRIMINALS ARE MADE. NOT BORN.

Personalized Properties

In a world of cookie-cutter houses and big box store land-scaping, those who dare to veer from the norm in their places of abode are usually looked upon with a mix of puzzlement, disdain, and sometimes outright hostility. Why would a person embellish his backyard with broken doll parts rearranged into enigmatic dioramas? Who would want to fill his entire property with a massive block of intricately linked, brightly painted, giant whirligigs? Luckily, the folks who concoct these wacky visual delights carry on despite anyone's approval or disapproval. They think, therefore they art.

The intelligentsia of the world call this type of work "outsider" or "visionary" art, but most of these artists refuse to pigeonhole themselves with labels. A few don't even consider themselves artists at all—just people who like to make stuff. Ignoring traditional media like oil paints or bronze, their chosen materials are often whatever happens to be closest at hand: concrete, old bottles, even worn stuffed animals. Their messages are much much more than their media.

The world may sniff at these audacious people, but *Weird Michigan* embraces them as guardians of the independent spirit of humanity. We can all use a good shaking-up now and then, and they are just the people to do it.

Stonehenge of Nunica

Why should Great Britain have all the good Druidic ruins? That's what one Michigan couple asked themselves. And the answer was . . . Michigan deserves an ancient—or at least ancient-looking—ceremonial center too! Accordingly, Fred and Pam Levin, of rural Nunica, have turned the front yard of their seven-acre horse farm into the site of a Styrofoam-and-stucco sculpture replicating England's famed Stonehenge.

The Levins went online to find the original site's actual measurements, then tinkered a bit to bring them into proportion with their yard. The foam megaliths in the Levin yard stand thirteen feet tall, almost the same height as Stonehenge on the Salisbury Plain, but the New World arrangement's diameter is only about half that of the original. And although the British Stonehenge took about one thousand years to complete, the Levins' contractor did the work in six weeks, using a variety of photographs as a placement guide and working from the family's horse barn. Each foam block is anchored by a metal beam set into the ground below. And the replica is not finished yet. "It's an ongoing project," Pam Levin told *Weird Michigan.*

The couple is interested in sacred spaces from a variety of belief systems worldwide and has also created a Cretan labyrinth-style meditation path and an American Indian medicine wheel garden. "I think they symbolize spirituality and the mystery of life," said Pam. "That's kind of what the theme is." Fred, an orthopedic surgeon, has also enlarged a natural spring on his property to add ponds and streams. "We're just really into gardening," adds Pam, in a classic understatement.

While England's Stonehenge is a favorite spot for modern-day Druids and other New Agers to congregate, the Levins are thankful that local would-be worshippers appear to understand that their site is part of a family home and, so far, have not tried to perform mystical rites in the yard. Or perhaps area neo-Druids simply realize that Styrofoam blocks don't have quite the same geomagnetic properties as the solid rock originals. Building a replica is one thing; duplicating serious ancient mojo is another.

The Nunica Stonehenge sculpture is on private property—no trespassing allowed—but it can be seen from the street just south of town on Leonard Road.

The Pickle Barrel House of Grand Marais

Forget the old woman who lived in a shoe, Jack Sprat (who moved his wife into a pumpkin shell), and others who have laid dubious claim to living in strange objects. Grand Marais had a real-life author who lived in a pickle barrel, and the authentic barrel turned house still stands seventy-five years later as a monument to the sheer audacity of it all.

The Pickle Barrel House started with the unlikely premise of a newspaper comic called the "Teenie Weenies," originally created in 1914 for the *Chicago Tribune.* To the delight of early-twentieth-century Americans, writer and illustrator William Donahey dreamed up the Lilliputian beings who stood about two inches tall and inhabited an enchanted rosebush. Donahey and his mini-minions entranced readers nationwide for more than fifty years.

Like many popular figures today, the tiny people attracted commercial sponsors who saw them as natural sales boosters, and the comic pixies were soon shilling for Monarch Foods. Donahey drew individual "Teenie Weenie" stories for each ad, one of which depicted a charming newlywed hideaway fashioned from a barrel modeled after the wooden kegs in which Teenie Weenie Sweet Pickles were sold. The cartoon home was so fetching that Donahey commissioned a house-size replica from the Pioneer Cooperage Company and had it shipped to Sable Lake near Grand Marais to use as a summer cottage.

Actually, the house is made of two pickle barrels, with a smaller one attached to the rear to form a kitchen. It has two stories, with a bedroom up and a living room down. Donahey and his wife, Mary Dickerson Donahey (an author in her own right), found the lakeside barrel home an inspiring location from which to create their stories. Donahey penned a number of Teenie Weenie books in the structure, along with many comic strips and pickle ads.

However, as the house's fame spread, throngs of sightseers began disturbing the tranquil hideaway. After about ten years of putting up with Sunday gawkers, Donahey decided to deed the little place to a local entrepreneur, who dragged it into Grand Marais. It became an ice-cream shop in its second life, as well as a tourist info center and a souvenir stand. But over the years, the giant pickle barrel lost some of its luster as the wood weathered and the hoops began to rust.

In April 1970, the once shining pride of Grand Marais was eclipsed in media attention by a huge throng of deer that overran the village and ate everything within reach, including underwear on clotheslines. The Pickle House managed to survive both the whitetail hordes and other ravages of time, however, and was finally opened as a museum by the Grand Marais Historical Society in July of 2005. The group furnished the house to reflect its original inhabitants, and tourists 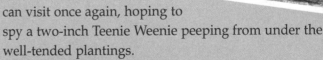 can visit once again, hoping to spy a two-inch Teenie Weenie peeping from under the well-tended plantings.

The pickle barrel was not the only object Donahey turned into a house for wee folk. A home created from a man's hat was featured in his first comic strip. Aficionados of object houses can only hope the rest of Donahey's creations will be replicated someday, to create a human-size Teenie Weenie City.

Milligan's Giant Cairnscape, Sault Ste. Marie

All over the world, ancient civilizations erected giant cairns, a fancy word for rock piles, to mark sacred places, trails, or other spots with special significance. Today's archaeologists study the old cairns, analyze their structures and alignments, and try to figure out who built them and why.

Kevin Milligan, a forty-eight-year-old contractor and landscaper from Sault Ste. Marie, has left one heck of a rock puzzle for future archaeologists to ponder. Milligan has put together what looks like a landscape from another world by carefully placing massive cairns around his Seymour Street property on the edge of town. The huge boulders are accented with implanted upside-down trees, whose sky-thrust roots curl against the clouds like wooden tentacles. Milligan's surreal arrangements create a setting worthy of the weirdest science fiction story, a perfect backdrop for improbable creatures or interdimensional windows to pop out against.

Milligan had nothing so large-scale in mind when he started back in 1983, however. It all happened quite by accident. The road in front of his house was being repaired, he told *Weird Michigan,* and the workers dug out a large boulder and rolled it onto his yard. "When I came home from work, they asked me if I wanted it," said Milligan. "I said yes, I'll take it."

Unsure what to do with the lone boulder at first,

Milligan left it near his house until he found a second rock while working in a nearby wooded area. He began to think about putting several rocks together and started checking gravel pits for unwanted boulders. When he found one, he hauled it home on a trailer, and he gradually began stacking and arranged the boulders to his liking.

The upended trees were also an accidental discovery, said Milligan. "I used to work in the woods a lot," he explained, "and one day I had to push some trees over and I realized they were nice, straight oak trees and I liked the way the roots looked, so I thought I'd take them home and add them to the rocks." Milligan hopes that birds will nest in them eventually to add living biological components to his works.

Milligan, forty-eight, has had no formal training in art, and yet his cairns have a sense of balance and composition worthy of any modern earth sculptor or Zen rock gardener. Although his cairn field feels like a sacred area, Milligan says it has no such meaning; he just likes moving rocks around. The piles include a variety of colors and shapes. Some rocks carry deep grooves worn by local rivers; others are striped with white or red to reveal strata compressed eons ago. One 110-ton behemoth, hoisted with a crane from a sandpit near Mackinac Trail, stands out in a somber shade of black.

The cairnscape is not complete, said Milligan. Over

the past summer, he discovered a wooded area that contained a number of boulders near the surface, and he has been busy hauling them in. "I know where there's a fifty-ton rock I'm thinking of getting," he added. Whatever the eventual size of the project, Milligan's cairns may already be called a monumental success in every sense of the word. And some day in the distant future, they are bound to drive some curious archaeologist wacko.

Don Crossman's Sculpture Garden, Beulah

It's Don Crossman's vision of a perfect world. Bucolic farm animals—cows, pigs, and chickens—peacefully coexist with elephants and giraffes. Cartoon characters burst to life, Uncle Sam is on hand to keep us patriotic, and Jesus is in plain sight to remind everyone "that there is a Jesus. "You put it all together, it sounds about like what I'd want in the world," the seventy-one-year-old retired welder says.

Crossman used to run a small farm with a few animals, and when he retired five years ago, he decided it would be nice to have some cows around, but he didn't want to bother with milking them. He had always tinkered with small art projects in his spare time and discovered he liked to weld objects together to create small sculptures. Now he went for the big time. He started by turning a big tank into a giant cow, and it received a lot of attention from the neighbors and family. People started dropping off other old tanks, and Crossman began scouring local junkyards for appropriate materials. "Then my grandkids started saying, why don't you make this and why don't you make that," he says.

Most of the figures took about a week to create, says Crossman. "The painting's what took the time. As far as slapping them together, I could do that in two or three days. I made them out of my head."

The Jesus figure, arms outstretched in welcome, was Crossman's last creation, and he won't be making any more, he says. People are always asking to buy them, but the sculptures aren't for sale. "Then I wouldn't have them," he explained, "and they're all one of a kind. I hope you enjoy them—it's one of the reasons I done it, so people enjoy it."

Don's Sculpture Garden can be seen at 8775 U.S. Highway 31 between Honor and Beulah in Benzie County.

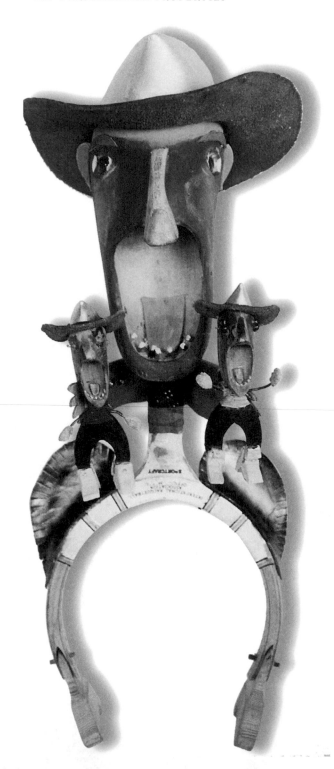

From Doctoring to Dutch Cowboys

Beulah's Dewey Blocksma may be self-taught as an artist, but he is certainly not uneducated. He began making toylike artworks as his own self-prescribed antidote to the trauma he experienced in his day job as an emergency-room doctor. Spending his working hours trying to prevent people from gushing blood, picking bullets out of gunshot victims, and witnessing a never-ending parade of human misery made him turn for relief to the "comprehensive universal language" he found in the world of toys and art. "The more gun wounds and stabbings he saw," a reporter for the Michigan magazine *Traverse,* noted, "the more he made art, and the sleeping giant inside him awoke." Blocksma told *Weird Michigan,* "Those difficult experiences in the emergency room gave me a unique perspective on what it means to be alive, and I took down my doctor's shingle to become a full-time artist." He was thirty-six years old at the time.

Blocksma didn't have a big savings stash to fall back on, but he had other, more important resources. When he was a child, his military surgeon father took his family to live in Lahore, Pakistan, far from the American cornucopia of manufactured, store-bought toys. There, out of necessity, Blocksma learned to create his own playthings. He and his Pakistani friends made their own kites, coating the strings with ground glass and then battling one another in the sky. He learned to scrounge for scrap metal and other discarded items to use as toy parts. This experience proved invaluable when he began making sculptures for a living.

Blocksma was also inspired by a number of folk artists, including Howard Finster of Summerville, Georgia, a prolific painter who said he got a message from God on his thumbnail telling him to make art. Finster obeyed and created close to fifty thousand primitive works on plywood cutouts. Blocksma owns a Finster self-portrait called *Finster in a Shoe,* complete with a hand-lettered warning: "Don't be faike."

Blocksma evidently took those words to heart. He began to construct his own unique working, moving sculptures out of items such as old Jell-O mold cups, bicycle wheels, turbines, and

Dutch wooden shoes. People liked them, so Blocksma began selling his artwork at galleries and art fairs throughout Michigan and the rest of the United States.

He wasn't always confident about his work, however. He credits a friend with rescuing an early piece he had dejectedly thrown in the trash. The friend sent it to a gallery, which immediately accepted it and asked for more, to Blocksma's delight and surprise. Since then, he's been included in a major book on outsider art called *American Folk Art of the Twentieth Century,* as well as many magazine and newspaper articles.

"I don't fit any particular mold," Blocksma says now. "I needed to define my own little universe and explore that. I work with found objects. I like to use wooden shoes because I'm Dutch and I also lived in Holland, Michigan. I use them as heads, like Edvard Munch's *The Scream,* and combine them with the country images like cowboys because I was born in Texas on an air force base."

Blocksma continues to fill his yard near Beulah in Benzie County with standing wind machines and other multimedia sculptures. They can be seen on Warren Road between Crystal Lake and Platte Lake and are for sale at the Tamarack Gallery in Omena. He also created a major work called *River Guardian,* which stands on the riverbank in Traverse City. The sculpture consists of an "earth mother" figure made from a canoe, accompanied by a wind machine representing a variety of animals. Although it was extremely controversial when unveiled in 1999, residents have come to accept it for the original, playful statement it makes. Blocksma remains undaunted. "I'm making art from my own experience, which started in the emergency room," he said. And the cowboys scream on.

Kaleva's Bottle House

It's a triumph of folk art, recycling, and innovative architecture all squared up into one unique abode. No one who sees the compact house John J. Makinen built from glass bottles can fail to admire the use of sixty thousand former soda containers all stacked bottoms out to create four sturdy walls. Makinen once owned a bottling company, so he had access to all the

glass bottles he needed, but only someone with the heart of an outsider artist would have thought of using them as a building material.

Makinen was born in Finland in 1871 but moved to Kaleva in Manistee County around 1903. He didn't start building the bottle house on Wuoski Avenue, one block north of the center of town, until later in his life. He finished it in 1941, the year he turned seventy. But in a sad twist, Makinen died before he was able to move into the glassy dwelling. His family, though, enjoyed the place for many years before the Kaleva Historical Society bought it in 1980. The society opens it for tours on summer Saturday afternoons and features exhibits inside on local lumbering history.

Makinen built diamond patterns and other designs into the walls using different colors of bottles, so there is a lot of rich detail to look at. *Weird Michigan* travel tip: Be warned that staring at the bottle house for too long can incite deep thirst, which may necessitate an immediate trip to a place of liquid refreshment. We also learned the hard way that no, you can't see inside the house by putting your eye up to the bottoms of the bottles and attempting to peer in.

Tower of Bottles

The tiny hilly town of Matherton, about twenty-five miles northwest of Lansing, doesn't have many tourist attractions. And the one it does boast is little known, although it deserves some measure of fame. After all, you don't find a twenty-odd-foot-tall tower of glass bottles standing around just any old place.

The bottle tower rises jauntily on the lawn of the Evans family home, off School Road, which is really just a gravel driveway. It was built by the late Michael Evans between 1973 and 1983, after he was disabled in an auto accident. "He needed something to do," Carole Evans, Michael's widow, told *Weird Michigan.* "People brought him bottles, and he also picked 'em up."

Evans got the idea, she said, from a bottle fence someone else had built near Farwell. The fence is now long gone, but it started Evans on an obsessive quest to make his own bottle creation. "He just thought it would be really neat," she said, "and he and the kids would go out along the road collecting bottles."

Stacking the bottles was not physically easy for Evans, who endured seven operations on his back and also had heart problems. Once the tower was up, though, it did begin to attract attention. Evans and his creation were featured on several television shows and in newspaper articles. The location is so out of the way, however, that interest in it eventually lagged. Evans died in 1987 at the age of forty-eight.

His tower, shaped something like a big bottle itself, with windows, a door, and designs built into the sides, has seen better days. It was vandalized once and needs a few broken bottles replaced. Still, it's Matherton's treasure as well as a victory of the spirit of the former factory worker who created it.

Whirligig World Gone Wild

"I do not believe it myself," Dmytro Syzlak says as he gazes in awe at the magnificent, thirty-foot-high amalgamation of wooden and metal sculptures, signs, and whirligigs packed into his little backyard in Hamtramck. It is a little hard to believe, but there it is, the fruit of over a decade of painstaking labor, fabricated in Syzlak's tiny garage studio after he retired from General Motors. The studio is packed with unused found objects he's either collected or been given, along with neatly arranged hand and power tools. The house is at 12087 Klinger Street, but the front entrance of the artwork is off the little alley between Klinger and Sobieski.

Too much for the eye to take in at once, Syzlak's life-work demands a slow pace with frequent pauses to absorb the variety of interconnected, brightly painted forms. A sign that fronts the display in the yard reads WELCOME TO ART SHOW DISNEYLAND, but that's a bit misleading. This is no pale imitation of Disney characters. Syzlak invents his own images of American icons: Cowboys and Indians cavort with mermaids and airplanes while whirligigs and recycled electric fans move in the wind as the atmosphere wills them. The display is bedecked with every color in the spectrum, although patriotic red, white, and blue predominate, with a proud Uncle Sam overseeing the spectacle. Discarded store mannequins and ceramic doodads, even American flags and dime store paintings add a punchy touch of the bizarre.

Syzlak is an aviation fan, and it shows in his original take on the Concorde supersonic jet (complete with tiny passengers and an interior light). There's a rocket ship too and a helicopter bringing Santa Claus.

A few of the artworks are wired to move electrically, and some light up, as well— especially the topmost sculptures—turning the whole thing into a frenzied, kinetic light show after dark. Syzlak can also play recorded tunes through an old car speaker when he feels like adding sound to the jumbled mix.

The assemblage is meant to last. Syzlak

Eventually, the small patch of grass around his home filled completely up, and Syzlak's daily chores turned to maintenance rather than building. The figures constantly need dabs of fresh paint, the windmills require oiling and tweaking to keep turning smoothly, and nails and bolts need to be rehammered and tightened. Syzlak is in his eighties now, and it's not easy for him to reach some of his high-altitude pieces, but that doesn't stop him from trying. People come from all over the world to see his work, which has been featured in *Raw Vision* Magazine and Randy Mason and Mike Murphy's book *Rare Visions & Roadside Revelations*. Some may ask what keeps him going, but Syzlak has said many times that he made it all for the public, as his gift to the world. *Weird Michigan* hopes the world remembers to send him a thank-you note.

proudly told us that it survived the tornado of 1997. No surprise, since he had the heritage of a craftsman to draw upon when he began the project. Born in the Ukrainian village of Lwiw in 1920, Syzlak made wooden barrels in a small German village before emigrating to the United States in 1949. Here, he toiled on the General Motors assembly line in Detroit for thirty-two years. He and his wife, Katherine, raised three daughters in their modest home in this neighborhood known for its concentration of Polish and Eastern European immigrants. But Syzlak, used to working hard, was not the type to sit out his retirement in a rocking chair. He threw himself into creating his fantasy world with the same energy he had once applied to assembling automobiles.

God, Mother, and Country in Cement

When Silvio Barile was a child in Italy during World War II, his family was sent to live in a Nazi relocation camp. He had no toys, so to amuse himself he learned to make small objects out of clay he scraped from the ground. After the war, the family came to the United States, and for the past thirty-five years, Barile has continued making things to amuse himself. Working out of a building at 26417 Plymouth Road in Redford, where he once ran a pizzeria, Barile creates large cement sculptures embellished with rocks, marbles, and other found objects.

But there are larger ideas beyond the fantastic facsimiles of men, women, and children that inhabit his private universe. "I do it for the sake of art, family, and religion," the outspoken Barile says. "You can make anything, but to me it's the message that's most important. It's the significato, as we say in Italian."

Although the health department recently forced Barile to stop making pizza on the premises, he still keeps his place open to sell wine, sausage, and packaged goods. But the rooms and back courtyard are packed with sixty or seventy sculptures on topics significato to Barile. He recently finished a work he calls *Mother of Peace.*

"It's my mother, actually," he told us. "And America needs a mother that stays with the father and children. There's too many divorces."

Barile is divorced himself and has five children. But the ideal principles of life are what he tries to express in his artwork. "The first

thing they teach you when you go to school in Italy is morals," he said, "and that's what drives me."

Not everyone agrees with Barile's message, of course. He says some women have called him a "chauvinist pig." But though some may argue with his exuberantly moralistic ideas, it's impossible to doubt his passion. He's eager to explain the exact vision he's built into every piece of his work.

For instance, there's the recent project he calls *The American Venus,* based partly on a painting by Botticelli. "She's very very beautiful," he said. "She's breast-feeding as she emerges from the sea."

Another, called *Columbus Dream,* depicts Christopher Columbus with the words TERRA, for discovering new land, and BENEFACTOR OF HUMANITY, for the gifts Barile says he brought to the Americas, written on his arms. All the parts of this sculpture symbolize something specific: There are fish and squid for the Atlantic Ocean, Native Americans to represent the New World, and even three small figures he says are King Ferdinand, Queen Isabella, and the Pope, who together paid for the voyage.

Making art is not his only talent; Barile is also known for his habit of breaking into song on the least provocation. "I got a golden voice," he says, and promptly sings a few verses of an Italian song, "Vento" (meaning, "wind"), in a very agreeable baritone. "I was brought up where Caruso came from," he explains.

Barile, sixty-six, isn't sure exactly

how long he will keep making sculptures. Pieces are accumulating, and he has sold a few in the past, but doesn't want to part with any more. Noted Detroit-area professional sculptor Sergio DeGiusti has been photographing and documenting the works for years, and thinks Barile is one of the best and yet least appreciated outsider artists in the country. "I think of Silvio as the Gaudí of Redford," he told *Weird Michigan*, chuckling. He hopes that the Barile collection will stay together and eventually receive the attention he feels is its due.

Barile, meanwhile, continues to go for the gusto in his art, song, and extravagant statements about the world and how it should be. "I'm still full of life," he declares. "I do these things for the love of people."

Doll Garden of Frights

Is it art or a Barbie nightmare? *Toy Story* gone bonkers? An apocalyptic version of a Disney ride through yapping dolls of every land? Madison Heights artist Michael Anthony Dion, who signs his work "M80" (it's an acronym for his initials), has filled his backyard with his own macabre vision of what happens when good dolls go bad. Visible through a chain-link fence from the sidewalk on Campbell (between 12 Mile and 13 Mile roads) is a great variety of dismembered and tattered dolls in bleak metal and wooden assemblages. There's a black-haired doll head wearing a white cowboy hat, for instance. It's anchored to an old wagon wheel, which is attached to a wooden

chair frame, with a small arm waving from the seat. A one-legged Barbie stands sentinel next to a wooden box that contains a pleading child doll next to a few crumbling flowerpots. A plastic chicken wears a cracked baby doll head instead of its own beaked noggin.

This is not your mother's dollhouse. Dion refers to the yard tableau he's been working on since 1991 as an "installation." "I move things within the installation," he told *Weird Michigan.* "It pulses in and of itself as I add and subtract things." Despite the dark, prickly street ambience of the exhibits, he has said that there exists something "sweet and tender" within his work that he thinks comes from rescuing discarded dolls and giving them a second life. Perhaps it's this tension between strange and sweet that makes the doll garden so mesmerizing.

Dion has a day job that blends perfectly with his passion. "I sell old stuff and collectibles that I find as I'm out there looking for components for my art," he explains. A self-taught artist, he first began making assemblages with found objects when he had a brainstorm for making unusual bolo ties. "I thought, Why do they have to look western? So I made them from TV knobs, old Legos, and they got a good reaction." From the bolos, Dion eventually graduated to larger objects. He often exhibits in galleries, but his backyard serves as his main ongoing venue. And the work does provoke reactions from people.

"They get creeped out by the dolls," says Dion. "But I use them just as I find them in the trash. People come to me with a whole meaning that the work has for them, and I think it's important that everyone works that out for themselves. I'm not the type to say what or how to think." And when Dion tries to explain the true intent behind his work, he insists it's rather like Jerry Seinfeld's "show about nothing."

"And yet," he goes on, "obviously it has some meaning to people, so there's a conflict they can see. I feel it's important to get the viewers to process the conflict for themselves."

Whatever emotions the forlorn recycled dolls evoke in visitors, Dion's backyard remains an ironic turnabout on the typical green, empty lawns of American suburbia. Populated with the unpretty, literal outcasts of society, the doll garden beckons to the traffic rushing by on busy Campbell Street. It pleads with the drivers to stop and observe the dolls in their quietude. Hopes the visitors wave back before they leave. Believes that if visitors look long enough, they really will find something in nothing.

The Heidelberg Project

Tyree Guyton had a vision for his art that was larger than himself. A college-educated artist, Guyton turned his personal passion for the free-spirited forms associated with outsider art into a mission. He looked at the blighted neighborhood surrounding Heidelberg Street in the mid-1980s and wondered what art could do for the people who lived there, if only they had the chance to experience it. Then he got out his paintbrush and started transforming his house, his street, and the neighborhood into an open-air art gallery and environment.

Founded in 1986 with Guyton's former wife, Karen, and his grandfather Sam Mackey, the project kicked off by transforming the first house on Heidelberg Street with refuse collected from cleaning up vacant lots. Guyton called it Funhouse. His next project was Baby Doll House, with broken dolls nailed from the ground to the roof. Guyton covered one structure with multicolored polka dots— it was dubbed the Dotty Wotty House—and splashed bright primitive faces on the hoods of old cars parked permanently on the streets. Guyton's vision didn't limit itself to paint; he used collected objects such as rows of discarded shoes to symbolize old-time lynchings or people standing in unemployment lines. He covered trees with hubcaps, bicycles, cars, clocks, and even old purses to make various social comments on the plight of Detroit. People slowly became aware that something major was happening here.

Within two years, the Heidelberg Project was the subject of major articles in *Newsweek* and *People* magazines. It now attracts over 275,000 visitors a year and has been ranked in the top three most visited places in Detroit. But not everyone saw the eclectic conglomeration as art. Unbelievably, in 1991 the city of Detroit bulldozed four of the decorated houses, declaring them "trash" and "eyesores." The city's brutish act earned Guyton worldwide sympathy. The Heidelberg Project sued the city and later won the right to adorn its houses with art as it saw fit.

Today there are new places to look at, such as the house covered with stuffed animals and the *House that Makes Sense* project, which aims to side an entire house with pennies—800,000

House and artwork of artist Tim Burke, who also lives on Heidelberg Street

of them. Many of the pennies are donated by school-children, and student crews have done much of the work—preparing surfaces and mounting the pennies on cement board. A wire mesh will cover them to quash anyone tempted to pick up a little quick change. The penny-covered structure was formerly known as the OJ House, which stood both for O. J. Simpson and Obstruction of Justice. It was covered with many signs and symbols referring to the Simpson murder trial, which have since been removed.

Guyton has always created his own solo work and concepts, but the Heidelberg Project has evolved into an entire chorus of contributors involving numerous projects with schools and other community groups. The day *Weird Michigan* visited, its founder was out in front of one of the houses, wielding his usual tools: paintbrush, saw, and hammer. Neighborhood children pedaled bicycles around the art zone, whizzing past discarded TVs turned into installation art and picnic tables used as workstations for summer camp art projects. Several young tourists pulled up to have a look at the colorful environment. "The Heidelberg Project has had its setbacks, but it's never been completely torn down," Executive Director Jenenne Whitfield told us. "Our goal is to completely transform each building on a street so it becomes functional. But every artwork has a particular thought and idea behind it. The whole concept is to create a type of artist colony, and transcend racial, social, and economic boundaries."

The project maintains a Web site at www.heidelberg.org.

Marvin's Marvelous Mechanical Museum

Weird Michigan Travel Tip: Empty the piggy-bank, fill your pockets with change, steal Junior's lunch money—but do not come dimeless to Marvin's Marvelous Mechanical Museum in Farmington Hills. Marvin's is the stupendous result of one man's lifetime pursuit of coin-operated amusement machines of every type, from the oldest gypsy fortune-telling machines to a hand-carved farm scene made by a murderer, the Butcher of Alcatraz. Marvin Yagoda spent over five decades gathering the darkest, corniest, wackiest machines ever created to part a fool from his money, and then opened his 5,500-square-foot combination museum and modern video game arcade in the early 1990s to house them all.

According to Yagoda, the most popular machines have to do with either love or torture. A top favorite is the cheerful Spanish Inquisitor, which urges the user to "witness abominable tortures" such as the flogging of a miniature character. Torture of a different kind follows from dropping a coin into an ominous-looking machine that promises the Disgusting Spectacle. The player gets to watch in suspense as a man slowly raises his hand . . . to stick his finger in his nose.

Weird Michigan enjoyed a vintage machine titled Career Pilot. It asked, "Will you be a school-teacher, nudist, psychiatrist or stooge?" If the machine was right, *Weird Michigan* will eventually

have to begin seeking out clothing-optional beaches.

But there are so many more buttons to push. Experience the Drunkard's Nightmare, where demons pop from the cupboards and the booze jug is inhabited by a snake. Or see the two-headed baby if you're feeling freakish. Test how long your nerves can hold out in the presence of a snarling rabid dog. The possibilities for the terminally curious never end. And if one does get bored, all a person need do is stare at the ceiling to watch circling airplanes, talking and smoking deer and buffalo heads, and flashing neon in all colors and shapes. There's even a mini-carousel making endless circles. It's a sensory overload far past the maximum threshold that human neural systems were built to endure.

Yagoda, a pharmacist by trade, started his massive collection with one $500 nickelodeon he found in a store in Ann Arbor. A natural adventurer, he began amassing other old machines and oddities of all kinds, personally bagging thirty-two large game animals on a number of African safaris over the years. Yagoda became well known not only for his craze for antique machines, but for his inspired wardrobe items such as spring-bottomed shoes, stars-and-stripes suspenders, and "tattoos" on his teeth.

His son, Jeremy, now runs the museum. Jeremy, who unlike his flamboyant dad appears outwardly normal, told *Weird Michigan* that since he grew up with the collection,

IN THIS CHAIR OVER 30 PEOPLE WERE ELECTROCUTED AT SING SING PRISON, IN NEW YORK STATE 1921-1950's

MARVIN'S MARVELOUS MECHANICAL MUSEUM

BIG MARVIN'S USED FURNITURE

none of it ever seemed weird to him. "I was an only child," he said, "so I always got all the fun things." He was excited on the day we were there because a load of working automatons from England's Cabaret Mechanical Theater had just arrived. "The exhibit always keeps changing," he said. "We can't keep it the same."

Marvin's is located in a strip mall on 31085 Orchard Lake Road at 14 Mile Road. And one other thing . . . whatever happens, do NOT, repeat, NOT lift Burt Reynolds's fig leaf!

Roadside Oddities

Like overdressed actors in a surreal dream play, large and strange objects loiter on the roadsides of Michigan highways, begging passersby to acknowledge them as Lords of the Scenery. *Weird Michigan* can't forget the time we came sailing down a hill near Onaway in the *Weird*mobile, only to be confronted with a giant steel head of George Washington gleaming incongruously in the middle of a field. The spectacle of the enormous cutout Santa in the town called Christmas will ho-ho in our minds forever. And we suffer recurring nightmares of being mowed down on the slopes by the oversized fiberglass ski-boy of the Upper Peninsula.

Michigan does boast incredible natural beauty along its roadways, of course, especially with so many miles of Great Lakes shoreline. But even sky-blue waters and acres of leafy forest can eventually be taken for granted by the road-fatigued. So, while adding some man-made wackiness to nature's handiwork may seem like gilding the lily, we'd argue that occasional absurd attractions enhance our viewing pleasure simply by making us look.

This chapter is an attempt to document some of our favorites before they disappear either from the landscape or from our fickle minds. Consider the stories and photos presented here your personal Michigan road gallery. Better still, see how many road trip pix you can click of yourself standing under giant bear paws or next to ridiculous Santa moon-faces, and create your own album of the weird.

Okay, everybody. Say cheese!

Dead Dog in a Sleigh

Crane's Pie Pantry & Restaurant in Fennville may have built its reputation on the freshness of its pies and other baked goods, but its on-site canine mascot is ironically un-fresh, having been dead for about sixty years now. Dashing through the porch, in a no-horse open sleigh sits Dead Betty the Dog, a decades-old mounted mutt who presides over the funky country establishment. It's a local tradition to wave to Betty when entering the building. Woe to those who forget and pass her by!

Betty, who lived in Chicago from 1930 to 1937, according to an attached sign, was inherited by the aunt of one of the store's bakers. Exactly why she ended up preserved here for eternity is uncertain, but she wound up as guardian of the unheated porch of the old farm, her main companion a mannequin dressed in traditional farmer's overalls.

Around the corner from Betty hangs a section of chicken coop occupied by a stuffed Buff Orpington and a Plymouth Rock hen, but thankfully the taxidermy mania ends there. The interior of the restaurant is crammed with fun antique memorabilia and collections, with old wartime paratrooper toys hanging from the ceilings and mannequins posed and costumed in every nook and cranny. Betty can be visited on weekends only, two miles west of Fennville on M-89. Hours can be sporadic. Betty can be unresponsive.

Teeing Off

This Giant Golfer stands in front of the Riverbend Driving Range in Chesterfield. The driving range is next door to the World's Finest Frozen Custard which has a mini golf with another giant man and several other fiberglass figures. I don't know if the two businesses are related or were at one time.—*Debra Jane Seltzer*

World's Tallest Indian

Dwarfing the Ironwood residential neighborhood around him, the World's Tallest Indian looms fifty-two feet over the abandoned iron mines that once lay at his gargantuan feet. Nicknamed Hiawatha, the 18,000-pound fiberglass statue was placed here in 1964, in what local papers called his Erection Ceremony. Although the statue was popular enough to inspire the sales of hundreds of replica banks sold through Ironwood's chamber of commerce (not to mention T-shirts, buttons, magnets, ornaments, and other bric-a-brac), critics have rightly pointed out that this Hiawatha is dressed as a Plains Indian, not as one of the forest tribes, such as the Ojibwa, who would have populated the Ironwood area before Europeans took over.

Easily the tallest object on the horizon, Hiawatha is not hard to find. He was located at the old mine area in hopes of developing interest in the historic caves there. Statue seekers can simply follow the main drag to the end of Burma Street to get a view. While there, they may contemplate the fact that this massive *objet d'art* was somehow spirited away from its seventy-foot trailer the night before the big erection ceremony. It was found within twenty-four hours, probably when the culprits realized they couldn't fit it inside any door in Ironwood.

The thieves were never identified, and the ceremony was held the next day, with the mayor sporting a feather headdress and a riding group called the Saddleites leading the statue procession. Today it not only draws tourists from around the world but serves as centerpiece for the annual Hiawatha Days Festival. Best of all, Hiawatha is available for viewing 24-7, whatever the weather.

Giant Bear

Created by John Radlovitz, a Chicago sculptor, this concrete and steel bruin stands seventeen feet tall and measures twenty-eight feet from nose to tail. Why did Radlovitz craft a massive bear to stand along Highway 2 near Vulcan? Probably because he could. A sign next to the sculpture says the bear was made in 2000 and that Radlovitz may make more. So far the bear stands alone on his corner lot, next to a small, unoccupied shop with a FOR RENT sign in its window.

World's Largest Bear Trap

If the huge cement bear in Vulcan ever shakes loose its moorings and needs trapping, an Upper Peninsula man in Chassell will be ready with the properly sized trap. Actually, Ed Sauvola calls the massive replica that takes up a good portion of his front lawn the Tourist Trap, implying that it's intended to catch more than bears. To make his point, he sometimes hoists an old snowmobile into the trap's steel jaws.

The trap stands a little over nine feet tall and is thirty-two feet wide, exactly twelve times bigger than the real trap the expert welder used as a model. Sauvola is hoping businesses or individuals will commission him to build giant-scale models of other objects. But he has expansive plans of his own too. "I want a ninety-foot one big enough to hold an RV," Sauvola said as we stood surveying his deadly creation. "Or," he added, "I'd make one that functions if someone wants to crush their car."

Sauvola glanced meaningfully at the *Weird*mobile. We gulped a little, said our thanks, and peeled out.

That's One Gigundo Stove

Before Detroit had the automobile, before Detroit had Motown, Detroit had . . . major stove manufacturing! Hence, the World's Largest Stove is located in that city. The stove sits out at the Michigan County fairgrounds, actually, and is a bit hard to see off-season, when the grounds are closed, but it's one gigundo cooking apparatus. Of course, if anyone actually lit this twenty-five-foot-high replica of a Garland wood-burning stove, they would find it to be exactly that: wood, burning. The "stove" is actually made out of oak and was created in 1893 to be exhibited at the Columbian Exposition in Chicago. Drive through the intersection of Woodward Avenue and Eight-mile Road and cast a glance at the southeast corner to see the stove rising up from the fairgrounds like something from the land of Mother Goose.

Another outsized Detroit artifact is the famed Giant Tire. Tall as an eight-story building, the tire was made for New York's 1964 World's Fair as the center of a Ferris wheel. The twenty-four gondolas have long since been removed, but the attraction continues to earn its pay as the main decor at the Uniroyal-Goodrich Tire Company. It has undergone several renovations, including a new hubcap, but can still be spotted on I-94 East, in Allen Park.

World's Largest Lugnut

When Lansing acquired a minor league baseball team in 1995, there was much ado about what to name it, especially when the team announced that it would be calling itself the Lansing Lugnuts. The people of Lansing went into a furor, but the team refused to budge. It had successfully pleaded with the Hasbro toy company to give up the Lugnut trademark it had reserved for a future toy design, and the team was sticking with the name it had won. Eventually the furor turned into equally heartfelt support. "Let's Go Nuts!" is the town's favorite cheer. Besides, ya gotta love a mascot named the Big Lug (along with his sidekick, Ratchet).

Although the team inexplicably chose to display a large bolt as its insignia, a factory about a block south of Oldsmobile Park Stadium erected the World's Largest Lugnut on its smokestack so that fans could have a clear image of what their team is really all about. Its silver gleam can be seen from the stadium, with the best close-up viewing at the corner of Larch and Michigan.

World's Largest Cherry Pie Tin

It only stands to reason, if you want to bake the world's largest cherry pie, you need the world's largest cherry pie tin. Will-Flow Corporation built one in 1976 so that the giant cherry pie could be baked on the grounds of the Medusa Concrete Company in Charlevoix Township. The pie was over fourteen feet in diameter and contained around five thousand pounds of red, tart cherries. The concrete company constructed a special oven for the occasion, and the pie held its title until 1987. Today the tilted tin, looking like some kind of '50s flying saucer display, contains one forlorn and faded slice of faux cherry pie. It can be seen in front of the Charlevoix Fire Department station on U.S. 31, between Charlevoix and Traverse City.

Giant Chair, Mio

A chair is a symbol of hearth and home, exactly the places Debby Bellow aims to help people beautify through her store, Genevieve's Flowers and Gifts, on Caldwell Road outside Mio. It made perfect sense to her, then, to commission wood artist James Jennings to craft a giant chair to stand outside her shop. "Years ago I saw a show on Michigan artists," Bellow explained when we visited her lush little place, "and one guy made big grapevine chairs, but I knew they would deteriorate. My chair is hand-carved cedar."

The giant sitz place stands twenty-five feet tall and was erected outside the store in November 2004. People constantly ask Bellow if they can climb into it, but she has to say no for safety and insurance reasons.

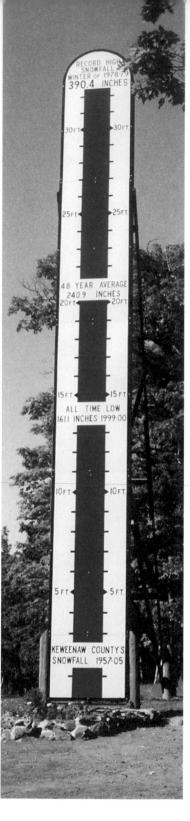

Giant Snow Gauge

It may look like a joke to tourists, but the thirty-two-foot-high Snow Thermometer on U.S. 41 between Mohawk and Phoenix is no laughing matter to the locals who slog through almost that many feet of white stuff every winter. Standing in a roadside park so motorists can pull over and read the amazing snow totals up close, the monument reveals that this Keweenaw Peninsula location receives a staggering average of 250 inches of snow annually. That's a cumulative total, of course: Because snow melts and recedes between falls, the snow bed seldom grows higher than half a dozen feet at a time. Still, that's high enough to bury a fairly tall man, and snow removal is a major industry on the Keweenaw. Many people here plant their own twelve- or fourteen-foot snow sticks in their front yards so they can tell exactly how snowed-in they are after a storm. But the giant stick on 41 is the grandpap of them all.

World's ALMOST Largest Hairball

This is not exactly a roadside oddity, since you have to get off the highway and trudge past the ivy-covered buildings of Michigan State University to the school's museum to see it. But East Lansing's giant hairball, extracted from the stomach of an ill-fated cow, is worth the detour.

Anyone with a cat knows that mammals can gag up disgusting masses of hair that have congealed in their stomachs. But who knew that a bovine could collect one the size of a basketball? The bogged-down bossy who produced this record-setter, however, did not regurgitate the nine-inch-wide ball. It was discovered only after her death. According to the museum signage, hairballs are caused by mineral deficiencies that result in "depraved appetites" that make animals lick their own fur.

University officials are quick to note they can't claim this is the world's largest anymore, however, since there are at least two that beat it: a fifty-five-pounder in Garden City, Kansas, that was found in a slaughterhouse, and another in Alexandria, Indiana, originally pulled from a city sewer and now existing only in replica. Alexandria, by the way, also boasts the World's Largest Ball of Paint and (we are not making this up) sells T-shirts with their town slogan, WE'VE GOT BIG BALLS!

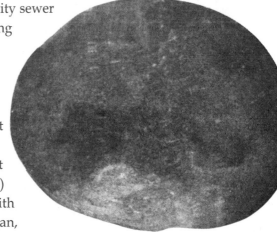

Big Powderhorn Ski Boy

The ski industry is one of northern Michigan's biggest tourist pulls, hence the giant fiberglass Ski Boy you'll see bracing for his downhill slalom at the gates to Big Powderhorn Mountain along Highway 2 between Ironwood and Bessemer.

You'll admire his jutting Superman chin. But with his permanently tinted shades and classic "knitted ski-cap," Ski Boy may look a bit out of place from April through October, when he's surrounded by green slopes. The rest of the year he looks right at home.

Sand and Gravel "Crash Site"

Travelers driving on State Road M-37 west of Hastings are greeted with an unusual sight: a small airplane buried tail up in a bank of sand. This is Airport Sand & Gravel's sign, which has become a local landmark and conversation piece. Owner Bruce Firlik originally bought the plane, a 1940s-era Luskin Taildragger, twelve years ago, with the intention of advertising his business on its wings. Apparently, the craft was damaged in a North Carolina hurricane several years ago, severing its tail and rendering it more or less junk. After Firlik patched the tail back on and applied some lettering, a very unique business card was born!–*Marc A. Sebright, Contributor*

Trash Bag Eagle, Iron River

It's amazing how the humblest material can be used to portray the loftiest of ideals. Who needs bronze or marble when you've got cinch sacks? A giant and majestic eagle made from plastic trash bags beckons travelers from its perch alongside U.S. 2, just outside the Into the Woods Gift Shop. The traffic-stopping sculpture was created in 2003 by members of the West Iron County Fire Department for area parades. The big bird stands nine feet tall, and each wing is ten feet long, for a total wingspan of twenty-five feet. "When we used it for parades, it was almost too wide to go down some streets," one fire department member told us.

The firemen chose to sculpt an eagle both for patriotic reasons and because it is their department emblem. They covered a wood and chicken-wire frame with 3,600 bags stuffed in pom-pom style after deciding the plastic would be more weatherproof than traditional tissue-paper puffs. Red reflector eyes add a predatory glare to the eagle's head. The nameless bird is put into storage every winter but resumes his eagle-eyed watch over U.S. 2 once the snow melts in the spring.

Weird Christmas

Maybe it's because Michigan is one of the northernmost states, or perhaps it's the great volume of snow the Great Lakes dump over the land every winter. Could be it's just a statewide infatuation with old men in red suits, a psychic impression left over from the days when everyone wore crimson long johns to get through the frosty winters. Whatever the reason, Michigan seems to have more than its fair share of odd Christmas connections. For starters, it has a town called Christmas, with a post office that gets busy every December out of all proportion to the size of the community. Midland boasts the Oldest Santa School in the World, a 1987 transplant from Albion, New York. Then there is Frankenmuth, known as the Christmas Capital of the World. Each of these places has its own unique jingle bell persona, and each, of course, supplies giant Santas for a year-round Yuletide ambience. Sniffing weird potential, off we flew, like the down on a thistle, to investigate the state's holly jolly side.

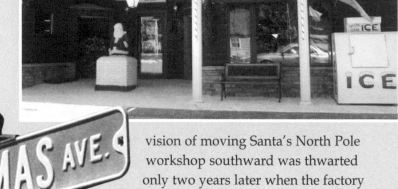

The Village of Christmas

It's not easy being red . . . and super-tall. But although he's proclaimed the World's Largest Santa Claus, the seventy-five-foot plywood Santa in the unincorporated village of Christmas doesn't have to stand alone in his notoriety. Santa spoons with a fifty-foot Missus Claus, although she isn't billed as the World's Largest Santa Spouse. The place got its name in 1938 when a Munising man named Julius Thorson built a factory here to make Christmas gifts. His vision of moving Santa's North Pole workshop southward was thwarted only two years later when the factory burned to the ground. Reportedly, all the elves escaped. But although the holiday gift factory was never rebuilt, the name Christmas stuck.

Actual Christmas attractions beyond the Santa and Mrs. Claus statues are pretty sparse, however. The highlight is a gift shop called the Christmas Mall, which hosts a U.S. postal station where people can have their mail postmarked CHRISTMAS, MICHIGAN. People can mail their stamped envelopes to Christmas and ask to have them cancelled there by sending to Christmas Post Office, #7989 W. M-28, Christmas, MI 49862. A few other plywood cutouts, related to nursery rhymes, fill out the area next to the Christmas Mall parking lot. We particularly enjoyed posing in the Peter Pumpkin Eater window, although we couldn't really say why.

Santa may eventually be edged out as the jolliest attraction in Christmas, however. The busy Kewadin Christmas Casino lurks only a block away, with slot machines lit up like a Christmas tree all year long and eager customers hoping Santa's sleigh will be loaded with rolls of quarters.

Giant Neon Kielbasa

It's just a neon sign, really, but who can resist a giant kielbasa sausage that glows? The Kowalski Sausage Company erected its landmark sign in Hamtramck, a once Polish suburb of Detroit, in the early '50s, and it has served as a festive backdrop to the annual Labor Day Sausage Fest ever since. The big red sign proudly honors the tasty mix of unmentionable animal parts that go into a kielbasa sausage at 2270 Holbrook Street, Kowalski headquarters.

Two-Story Outhouse

Visitors to the little town of Cedar Lake on M-46 have long believed that its famous two-story outhouse used to belong to a hotel at a railroad depot. According to town legend, the top one was for ladies and the lower one for gents. In a way, that last part is true. The outhouse belonged to the home of a man who employed loggers, and he didn't want his half-dozen daughters mingling with the hired men. So he constructed the bottom half for the gents, while his family walked over an elevated bridge to access the privy's top floor, according to a former Cedar Lake resident.

The house-to-outhouse bridge is long gone, but the dilapidated john still stands, its lower siding mostly missing, behind a two-story white house. The outhouse can be seen from the road; the white house is on Academy Road, just past Pine Street and behind the town's thrift shop.

Cherry Bowl Drive-in

Like a scene from some crazy Dadaist painting, the yard outside the Cherry Bowl Drive-In Theater teems with the absurd. A giant white chicken, the rear end of a groovy turquoise cruisemobile seemingly slammed into a fence, a pink VW bug topped by a grinning clown, and a giant hot dog poised high above the grass make the vintage 1953 outdoor theater a treasure trove of weirdness. Near Honor, eighteen miles southwest of Traverse City on U.S. 31 South, the theater is also unusual in that it has operated continuously since its grand opening, when it played Cecil B. DeMille's *The Greatest Show on Earth*. The Cherry Bowl prides itself on always offering a double feature, plus vintage cartoons and newsreels. And what visitors hear through the old post speakers comes from the original vacuum tube Motiograph amps. The speaker posts light up and glow red during the movies so that no one accidentally runs into them on the way to the refreshment stand, which is crammed with old movie memorabilia. They really don't make 'em like this anymore.

Paul Bunyan, Oscoda's Homeboy

That titan of a logger, Paul Bunyan, belongs to every Midwest state where logging camps once ruled the north woods. But the tiny northwest town of Oscoda claims to be the true birthplace of the legend of Paul Bunyan and has gone so far as to introduce a resolution to that effect to the Michigan House of Representatives. It is now resolved that "Oscoda, Michigan, is recognized as the true birthplace of the legend of Paul Bunyan as first set in ink by James MacGillivray based on the life of logger Fabian Fournier," says the official document.

True, a big statue of Paul Bunyan has stood in Oscoda's Furtaw Park, at the corner of State and Evergreen, for years, serving as the spark for the town's annual Paul Bunyan Festival. Statues, however, are not proof. The final word comes thanks to the sleuthing of a determined town historian, the late Mary Jane Hennigar, and a passel of international researchers.

According to an article in the *Oscoda Press* on November 8, 2005, MacGillivray was editor and publisher of the *Press* in the early 1900s. Before he became a newspaperman, though, MacGillivray toiled as a logger and absorbed the logging lore told by old-timers around the campfire. He had plenty of background to draw from, therefore, when he wrote "Round River," a story of the grandiose exploits of an imaginary lumberjack whom MacGillivray dubbed Paul Bunyan. The *Oscoda Press* can point proudly to its August 10, 1906, edition as proof of the "Round River" story debut.

MacGillivray, however, drifted on to another paper, *The Detroit News Tribune,* and in 1910 his story was printed there. With a larger circulation, the Detroit paper transformed Paul Bunyan and his blue ox, Babe, into instant folklore celebrities.

Other statues of Paul Bunyan can be found in Ossineke, Manistique, Alpena (thirty feet tall and made of car parts), beneath the Castle Rock Lookout in St. Ignace, and at Stagecoach Stop USA, Irish Hills (south of Detroit), on U.S. 12.

Lunker's Fish Kitsch

A lunker, for the uninitiated in fishing lingo, is an overly large fish. Lunker's, a sporting-goods store and restaurant in Edwardsburg, is full of them. There's a massive rotating bass on the sign outside the store, and indoors the enormous front end of an even bigger bass appears to burst through the bricks of one of the walls. There are smaller fish too—live ones. The entire restaurant area is surrounded by the Lunk-quarium, a wall of fishtanks that are decorated according to different themes, such as the patriotic tank, the butterfly tank, and the Sponge Bob Squarepants tank. Warning: Fishophiles will be hooked and may need to be lured from the place.

The Underwater Crucifix

At the opposite end of the spectrum from those who believe that giant crucifixes should be placed near highways for maximum visibility are those who think giant crucifixes should be placed completely out of the view of almost everyone—say, about twenty-five feet underwater in a Great Lakes harbor. The Underwater Crucifix Shrine in Petoskey, in Little Traverse Bay, off of Lake Michigan, represents the latter opinion. But there is method to Petoskey's madness. Every winter around Valentine's Day a private diving crew clears the snow off the ice over the shrine, sets lights underwater, and allows people to walk out and view the eleven-foot statue of Jesus on the cross. The rest of the year viewing is restricted to scuba divers and people in boats on very clear, calm days.

Turns out this statue has a story behind it. Veteran diver and policeman Denny Jessick, who has devoted much of his life to caring for the shrine, told *Weird Michigan* about the strange journey the statue took to reach this place.

The white, Italian marble sculpture is dedicated to divers who passed away in the line of duty, searching for lost victims of boating mishaps. Given its history, it is oddly appropriate as a memorial to terrible accidents. The sculpture was originally ordered from Italy, intended as a land monument for a young man named Jerald Schipinski from Rapson, who was killed four days after his fifteenth birthday in a tragic gun accident. Schipinski had gone out to a field on his family farm to retrieve an implement for his father and took his new shotgun along to shoot the crows that liked to gobble the family's seed corn. The gun accidentally discharged, fatally wounding him.

The boy's grieving parents awaited the statue's arrival from Italy, but found it had been damaged in the sea crossing, with fractures under both arms. They ordered a second statue, but that one was struck by lightning and reportedly now resides in a cemetery at Mio. A third statue finally made it to the Rapson Cemetery unscathed.

In the meantime, a diving club bought the original statue for $50 and planted it in the harbor in 1962 in honor of fellow diver Charles Raymond, who had been lost in Torch Lake. They dedicated the shrine to other divers as well. Many plaques representing lost divers also lie on the lakebed near the shrine. The divers give the statue a thorough cleaning every year and lately find themselves also having to remove thousands of zebra mussels from its surface.

The hidden crucifix is so popular that the Petoskey chamber of commerce has had to remove most of the information on it from their Web site because they were overwhelmed with requests to view the monument. They would love to offer greater access, they say, but at present there is no way for the public to see it most of the time other than in photos at the small information center next to Petoskey Harbor. For eleven months of the year, most people will have to content themselves with the comfort of knowing the statue is down there, keeping company with the spirits of those who gave their lives to help the lost of Michigan's waterways.

One Man's "Insanity" Lures a Town

While makers of modern musical instruments might protest, a Cadillac high school band teacher has been busy proving that sounds made by items from nature can be as beautiful as anything coming out of a brass trumpet or French horn. He's also shown that, however rustic, proto-instruments can look as good as they sound.

Located on busy Chestnut Street in the downtown area, the Cadillac Sound Garden whistles, groans, and otherwise sings to beckon people out of their cars and into the garden. There they can spend a few moments banging wooden branches together, pounding on drums, and whacking improvised giant wind chimes to hear the tones of ancient forests come back to life.

The attraction's creator, Frank Youngman, made his first sound garden in his own backyard after noticing the sounds different firewood logs made as he unloaded them from his pickup truck one day. The log instruments he subsequently created might have stayed on his lawn forever, though, if highway authorities had not decided to run a bypass around Cadillac. That sent the city scurrying for a suitable project to draw people back into town. Someone heard of Youngman's Sound Garden, and after a little coaxing the city council was persuaded to build a replica on Chestnut Street, across from the Clam River bridge.

Construction became a community affair, with Cadillac residents thronging to peel bark and hoist massive logs. Service clubs and organizations donated grants of money, and woodcarvers, blacksmiths, landscapers, and construction companies jumped aboard. When it was finished, the project earned a first place national award for creative innovation among municipalities.

And it became wildly popular with the locals, succeeding beyond the city council's wildest dreams at luring freeway traffic. Youngman formed a group of local high school percussionists, called the Log-Rhythmics, to demonstrate and perform on the giant sound stage, but all kinds of people, from senior citizens to preschoolers, seem to have no problem banging away on their own. Teacher Youngman still seems amazed at how far his original inspiration has come. He said in an article posted on cadillacmichigan.com, "It is pretty scary to go public with your insanity."

Fighter Jets and Voodoo Avenue

It's a long drive to the middle of nowhere to get to the former K. I. Sawyer Air Force Base in Marquette County. Now a civilian community, it's probably the only town in Michigan that has fighter jets scattered around its streets. K. I. Sawyer was named after the county highway supervisor in charge when the field was first envisioned in the early 1940s. The base was closed in 1993, but the military ambience remains, with hangars in the center of town and jets hanging around various places. In addition, the streets are named for fighter planes, with monikers like Voodoo Avenue in honor of the F-101 Voodoo jet.

Giant Head of Washington and More

Chugging down M-68 on our way to Onaway, a small town on the northern tip of the Lower Peninsula, *Weird Michigan* was expecting anything but what suddenly popped into view: a twelve-foot-high steel head of George Washington, complete with curly wig, sitting by itself in the middle of a large field. Gleaming in the sun as if elves had just given him a good polish, George appeared to stare thoughtfully toward the highway. We noticed that the field was adjacent to the Moran Iron Works and surmised there might be a connection; turns out we were right.

Tom Moran, owner of Moran Iron Works, is the self-taught artist responsible not only for George, but for a number of other super-sized steel sculptures that now grace Michigan byways.

Moran didn't set out to be a sculptor. "I grew up poor. My father was a lumberjack," he says. "My best class in high school was shop, and I soon became the school repairman. By the time I graduated, I already had a clientele." Moran worked for his dad as a logger for several years, continuing to repair and weld things in his spare time, and after a few years had more work than he could handle.

The first sculptures came about as attractions for the local Fourth of July parade. Moran usually begins working on each year's project around

Christmas, then spends the next six months welding on nights and weekends. One year he made a giant fishtank with a four-foot sturgeon in it, since Onaway calls itself the Sturgeon Capital of the World. Another year, as a special fund raiser, he fabricated a giant pig roaster, which actually cooked a porker as it rolled along the parade route behind the high school marching band.

"One year I did a fifty-six-foot-long muzzle-loader rifle," he says. "At first we planned to shoot it at a car or something, but it was so violent we ended up stuffing it with confetti and splattering it all over the crowd. It was very popular."

Moran has some big dreams for future projects, but doesn't like to reveal what the next parade item will be for fear it won't turn out. And although many have suggested he fill the field next to Moran Iron Works with more sculptures, that isn't going to happen. "I'm afraid of having it look like a junkyard," he admits. "I only tolerate George because he looks right there. There's something solitary about that look and that spot."

And when George occasionally goes missing—

usually to ride in someone's parade—the locals get upset, Moran says. "They'll call to make sure I didn't scrap him."

It would be a lot of scrap. The statue, which took eight hundred man-hours to create, weighs 6,000 pounds and used 4,000 pounds of eight-inch steel and 2,000 pounds of "hair strands." Creating the sculptures provides a welcome break from Moran's usual work, which he describes as serious industrial stuff. He has a hard time putting into words exactly what inspires him to make his art though. "It's hard to explain inspiration. It's just something inside you."

When Buildings Look Good Enough to Eat

Customers looking for a summer ice-cream treat don't need to worry; there is no hemlock (the drink Aristotle did himself in with) in the soft-serve cones at the Hemlock Whippy Dip. It gets its name from the town west of Saginaw on M-46. The fanciful building, designed to resemble a giant soft-serve cone, was the brainchild of owners Alfred and Kathy Smith. "I had seen a similar building in Perry, and it caught my eye," Kathy told *Weird Michigan.* "I thought, What better way to sell ice-cream? Every kid that sees it is going to want to stop."

The cone was designed by a company in Missouri and shipped in three parts to its site, where it was attached to a preexisting building. Inside, it looks like the interior of an igloo, although the Smiths did install a ceiling to cut down on energy costs. The stand also sells coney dogs, hot dogs, and nachos, April through September. (Note: the Perry ice-cream shop that inspired Kathy has a cherry on top and can be seen on M-52.)

World's Largest Weather Vane

There is a bit of dispute over the title, but what is usually referred to as the World's Largest Weather Vane stands forty-eight feet tall in a little park in downtown Montague on Dowling and Water streets. Its wind arrow is twenty-six feet long, and it's decorated with a fourteen-foot replica of a doomed schooner called the *Ella Ellenwood.* The ship's nameplate was all that was left after the vessel was scuttled during a storm near Milwaukee in 1901. Miraculously, the *Ellenwood*'s nameplate somehow floated back to White Lake, where it was rescued from the drink, ensconced in the Montague City Hall, and memorialized by the Whitehall Products Company, which specializes in weather vanes.

The giant apparatus is made of hand-forged aluminum and weighs 4,300 pounds, making it safe from even the most dizzying exhalations of Mother Nature.

Up in the Yukon Territory of Canada, however, at Whitehorse International Airport, spins another weather vane, which the Canucks claim is the world's largest. Actually a refurbished DC-3 airplane set on a pole so that it spins with the wind, it has a wingspan of ninety-five feet and is about sixty-five feet long. *Weird Michigan* did the math and must agree, the DC-3 beats Montague's wind instrument in sheer footage. But all is not in "vane": Montague can still claim to have the largest intentionally designed weather vane in the world.

Why put big, goofy animals along roadsides? For one thing, animals sell; every advertising mogul knows that. Whether related to the product or not, animals always get a second glance and usually a gush of emotion as well. And sometimes they outlast their original commission and live on as landmarks too beloved to kill. Who could blast apart a concrete, polka-dotted dinosaur and still look himself in the mirror the next day? Building an animal can be just plain fun. Why make a boring faux human when you can make a big grasshopper instead?

Giant Grasshopper: Real Art, Fake Lore

Tucked into Centennial Park in Kaleva is a giant grasshopper poised for flight. You can find the big bug by following Wuoski Street to Walta. Hang a left and then look in the park to the right, and there it is. The metal hopper was created in 2000 by students from Lutheran Brethren High School with the help of a local welder, as part of a long-term plan they conceived to renovate their aging city and commemorate the town's Finnish heritage.

Kaleva was originally named after the "land of heroes," a place in Finnish mythology. The legend supposedly behind the grasshopper, however, is fake. The holiday known as St. Urho's Day, named for a saint who allegedly drove the grasshoppers from Finland, is a joke invented by two Minnesotan Finns riffing on the legend of Saint Patrick's banishing snakes from Ireland. Humor-loving Finns soon adopted the day as their own, and the Kalevan students figured the grasshopper would be the perfect subject for their centerpiece sculpture. They also created a totem pole based on Finnish myth, among other beautification and weirdification projects.

Bear Statue: Make Love, Not War?

Touted as the World's Largest Bronze Wildlife Sculpture, the two bears in a permanent tussle in front of mega–sporting-goods store Cabela's in Dundee have been the source of some controversy since the Titanic-scale artwork was installed. Are the bruins fighting or preparing for amour? Some claim it looks more like they are smooching than wrestling. Although the sculpture probably wasn't intended to convey a double impression, we think it's nice to have an artwork that can satisfy both hawks and doves at the same time.

Oswald's Bear Ranch

If Michiganders hadn't chosen the wolverine as their state animal, logic might have dictated the black bear for their mascot. Bruins do roam freely throughout much of the northern half of the state and the Upper Peninsula. But at Oswald's Bear Ranch on M-123 four miles north of Newberry, people can experience a much closer encounter with the animals than they might prefer if they were in the wild. Still, these bears are not Yogi and Booboo, and are treated like the wild animals they remain. The entrance is hard to miss, with a large bear sculpture marking the driveway. The park has an old-fashioned, mom-and-pop ambience, with bears cavorting in three outdoor habitats, bear sculptures, and a gift shop filled with all things ursine. Although the exhibits are open only from Memorial Day through September, the statue is worth a drive-by anytime.

The Moose in Big Boy Pants

It's always pleasant when big corporations can adapt themselves to the local culture. Our collective heart was gladdened, then, when we passed the Big Boy Restaurant on Highway 2 in St. Ignace and saw this proud animal of the north decked out in red-and-white-checkered pants. It seemed to have somehow kept its dignity as king of the northern forest, even duded up as it was. And so far as we know, the place was not serving mooseburgers.

Key to Dinosaur Longevity

Ever watched the movie *Pee-wee's Big Adventure* and wished you too could climb a ladder up into a hollow dinosaur's belly to watch the sun rise? Then hitch the next ride to Ossineke, on Michigan's northwest shore, and visit the Dinosaur Gardens. The kitschy artistic vision of self-taught sculptor Paul N. Domke, these Jurassic critters were created almost six decades ago but show nary a crack or fissure in their carefully textured hides. Domke concocted his sculpture material using a formula of his own invention, Gardens manager Jean Cousineau reports. "He said he had a secret ingredient in his cement that would make it last forever," she said while keeping an eye on tourists milling around the well-stocked gift shop. "The mix included horse hair or deer hair and we don't know what else."

The walk-in brontosaurus (now renamed an apatosaurus) weighs 60,000 pounds, with an equal mass of concrete below ground to support the structure. Climb the stairs, and in the belly of the beast, you will find a religious icon, an oil painting of Jesus Christ set into the blood-red heart. That tableau and a statue of Jesus holding the world in one hand in front of the museum symbolize Domke's devout belief that evolution and dinosaurs are compatible with the Bible. A pious German Lutheran, Domke treated his faith and his prehistoric kingdom with equal veneration and zeal.

Domke, who traveled the world as a navy medic, was disappointed that most people could visit only the skeletons of dinosaurs. He wanted everyone to be able to see the creatures fleshed out in living color. That vision soon became an over-powering dream.

When Domke returned to his native Presque Isle after his Navy tour was over, it occurred to him that the cedar swamps around Ossineke must look much the same as they did at the time of the dinosaurs. So he purchased a tract of land and began to create his dream park. By day, he ran an Ossineke gas station, but worked nights, weekends, and early mornings on his obsession, assisted occasionally by several nephews who mixed the mysterious cement and dug holes for the supports. Domke worked on various projects almost to the day of his death at age ninety-four in 1981, and it's hard telling how many dinosaurs would have eventually inhabited his gardens. By the time he stopped, he had created over two dozen life-size figures, spread out over forty acres of dense woodland. All the creatures boast educational signage.

The dinosaurs are far better detailed and proportioned than the humans (Domke's cavemanlike conceptions of prehistoric man) in the park. It's easy to see where his interests lie. "Mr. Domke would be the first to tell you that he wasn't good with people," says Cousineau. "When he was making the statue of Christ, he blew the hands off four times," she said. "It shattered all the windows in his house and the one next door, just because he didn't like the way they turned out."

Most who knew him agree that the misanthropy applied to both his art and his interpersonal skills. "I don't neighbor," he gruffly told the folks next door before they could get too friendly, according to an undated *Metropolitan Detroit* article pinned to the gift shop wall. And Domke didn't care whether anyone came to tour his creation or not, eschewing advertising almost completely. Strangely, he also had plans for a Utopian village on the grounds, but it was never begun.

Weird Michigan toured the Dinosaur Gardens the day after a rainstorm, as a lingering mist raised steam from the stands of fern and fomented swarms of period-correct but all-too-live mosquitoes. We saw that, despite his religious piety, Domke wasn't one to shy away from bloody confrontations or anatomical correctness in his displays. A young mastodon bogged in a tar pit bleeds red paint as it's torn to shreds by ravening wolves, while nearby a carnivorous dino chews a gory hunk out of the green back of a corythosaurus. In another vignette, dark-haired cave people, the ladies shamelessly topless, throw spears and rocks to finish off a trapped mastodon while another member of their clan succumbs to the contractions of a huge snake.

Cousineau is devoted to the preservation of this remarkable trove of folk art and aims to preserve the acreage for posterity in all its gaudy and fantastic splendor. "I love it here," she says, "or I wouldn't have been here for twenty-three years."

Roads Less Traveled

Roads *have always been* the favored haunt of fairies, goblins, the devil, and all sorts of apparitions. There's something about those long ribbons leading off into the distance, sometimes to hazards the state highway department never warns us about.

Americans are particularly susceptible to road myths, spending as much time in our cars as we do. The streets we traverse become more than just an empty space between our starting point and our destination; they grow enmeshed in the journeys of our lives. In a very real way, we live on the streets we frequent. It's only natural that we should observe them closely and find significance in the darting shadow or the furtive wisp of white we glimpse in the rearview window.

The teenagers among us probably understand this best. They have made road legend an art form. Stories originate, mutate, are aided and abetted by hoaxers, and become excuses for steaming up the Chevy windows for legions of young people. Spook roads are their heritage, old bridges and shoe trees their shrines.

Ride along as *Weird Michigan* explores a few of these twists and turns on tire-worn gravel and rutted asphalt. Please fasten your seat belts, keep arms and legs within the vehicle, and when the screaming begins, NEVER roll down your window!

Blue Lady of Denton Road Bridge

Denton Road is a perfectly normal-looking thoroughfare with a historic old bridge. It runs north and south just west of Detroit, from Denton to Canton in Wayne County. But what happens there after dark sounds like anything but normal.

Supposedly, a cheating wife and her son were both killed under the Denton Road Bridge sometime in the early Victorian era. The woman was said to have lived in a nearby farmhouse. Her farmer husband slew her lover with an axe, then took off after his wife and caught her under the bridge, where she had hidden with a lantern and their baby. Stories vary as to whether he killed the baby as well as the woman, but that's when the ghost troubles began. The road and bridge are said to be plagued by spook lights — bright orbs that represent the murder victims' spirits — even though the old one-lane, graffiti-covered bridge was replaced by a newer, two-lane structure in 2001.

Some people have reported hearing the cries of a baby coming from beneath the bridge, and others have been run off the road by phantom headlights before they could even cross the haunted structure. Car windows unaccountably fog up, and baby footprints appear on the glass. At least one carload of bridge-crossers claimed that the lights actually touched their car and left burn marks. Sometimes an apparition of the farmwife, called the Blue Lady, is seen.

Even the *Detroit Free Press* has reported the strange phenomena on the Denton Bridge. On Halloween 1999, an article appeared titled "Sprawl May Scare Away the Legendary Denton Road Ghost." It described how the burgeoning population of Canton Township was forcing the paving of old Denton Road as well as bridge improvements. But according to the writer, Ron Dzwonkowski, as many teens were responsible for the legends as were scared by them. Some kids would hide under the bridge, he said, and imitate crying babies. He also noted that a favorite prank played by nearby college students was to strand new fraternity members in a Denton Road cornfield and supply them with a lantern on a pole to help them find their way out. It's not hard to imagine how spooky the swaying light must have looked from the road and bridge.

Still, the *Free Press* writer found at least one person who testified that her teenage daughter and friends drove onto the bridge one night and felt their car suddenly accelerate on its own, causing the teens to accelerate even faster to get past the scary place. Ironically, the story notes that the bridge is near a Halloween funhouse called Krazy Hilda's Trail of Terrors.

If our correspondence is any indication, teens are still flocking to the Denton Bridge, watching for tiny footprints on their windows. Perhaps the Blue Lady will stay no matter how many people move into Canton Township. It appears she would be missed if she left.

Brothers Bond on Denton Bridge

My younger brother is ten years younger than me, so growing up, we didn't have the usual experiences siblings closer in age share together. We were never in the same school at the same time, and by the time he had graduated high school, I had children of my own. We finally found something to truly connect on when we converged on my parents' house this Thanksgiving and realized that we both held an affinity for the haunted Denton Bridge.

My brother was surprised to hear that I spent a few years going down that road nearly every weekend, and that I knew it before it was all fixed up, when it was truly scary. I told him about the first time I saw the ghostly light that lives near the bridge and how it changed me to my core.

I saw the light once and only once. I had driven down the road dozens of times, and had spent many tense minutes

sitting in silence listening for the cries of babies underneath the bridge. Nothing scary had happened. This night was different, though. I had been driving around with a friend of mine, aimlessly. We didn't even mean to make our way down the road. A friend of ours had recently died in a car crash and it was the first time the two of us had really spoken about it. We drove for hours, and without even consciously choosing to, headed towards the Denton Bridge.

We stopped the car, since it was so desolate around there back then and it seemed private. We talked for about twenty more minutes when before I even knew what was going on, I realized that the area around the car was getting faintly brighter than before. My friend and I froze. We both turned and looked behind us and saw a blue orb, about the size of a basketball, floating a few feet above the ground and slowly moving down the road. It went past us, and about fifty feet further down the road it dissipated and eventually disappeared. That night changed everything about how I felt about the supernatural, about the afterlife, and about driving aimlessly around.

Years later, it also changed how my kid brother felt about me. —*Sam Skinnis*

Grabbed in the Graveyard

I couldn't make out his eyes or any facial features. In fact, I couldn't help but notice I could make out the tree behind him . . . not just BEHIND him, but almost THROUGH him.

In Belleville, where I grew up, there's an abandoned road not too far from town known as Old Denton Rd. Down this road was an old cemetery everyone in town called the Soop. It was named after the first man buried there, "Something" Soop. Growing up as kids, my elders would always warn my friends and I to stay away from this road, because it was haunted (or possessed massive demonic activity, depending on who you talked to).

As we got older, this same group of friends and I had a hard time finding things to do in our boring little town. Soon visiting "The Soop" turned into a pastime of ours. But not for very long. The very first adventure we had there turned out to be an experience that we seldom talk about unless we are all at a safe distance from this wicked place.

Five of us drove up to the Soop and parked our car down the dirt road away from the entrance, and then proceeded to venture in. Carefully making sure not to step on any of the gravestones, we all seemed to look up at the same time and noticed a figure of what appeared to be a black male, standing underneath a tree some 20 feet away. The figure didn't move. I decided to be the daredevil of the bunch and proceeded towards the man. As I drew closer however, I noticed something wasn't right. Though I was only about 10 feet from him, I couldn't make out his eyes or any facial features. In fact, I couldn't help but notice I could make out the tree behind him . . . not just BEHIND him, but almost THROUGH him.

Stopping dead in my tracks, I turned and motioned for the others to come up to where I was, but when I turned back to the man, to my surprise and horror, he was no longer there. As I looked around rapidly I noticed a figure walking through the dark cemetery.

I turned back to look at my friends, who were now standing right behind me, and by the looks on their faces I could tell they had seen this too.

As we neared the back of the cemetery, my best friend kept saying there was some sort of animal back there, because she could see the red eyes glowing. I could definitely feel something in this place, something indescribable. Still I pressed onward staying in the middle of the pack. Out of nowhere a blood curdling scream pierced the darkness; everyone had heard it. We turned to run all at the same time, in the process I grabbed on to one of the arms of a friend.

I felt something cool latch onto my leg from the side my friend WASN'T on. I tried to kick free from it, fearful of turning around to see what it was, and instead fell face first into the dirt. Seconds later my friend hit the dirt as well, screaming. I proceeded to shout out the Lord's Prayer. I couldn't move; I couldn't speak. I lay in the middle of the cemetery daring to not so much as open my eyes to turn and see what had my friend. Another friend came running back towards us, grabbing both mine and the other's hand and pulled us free from some invisible force holding us. Whatever it was broke free and we were able to get up and run. After peeling away down the road, we all dared to turn and look back, seeing two figures in the back of the cemetery that seemed to be watching the car.

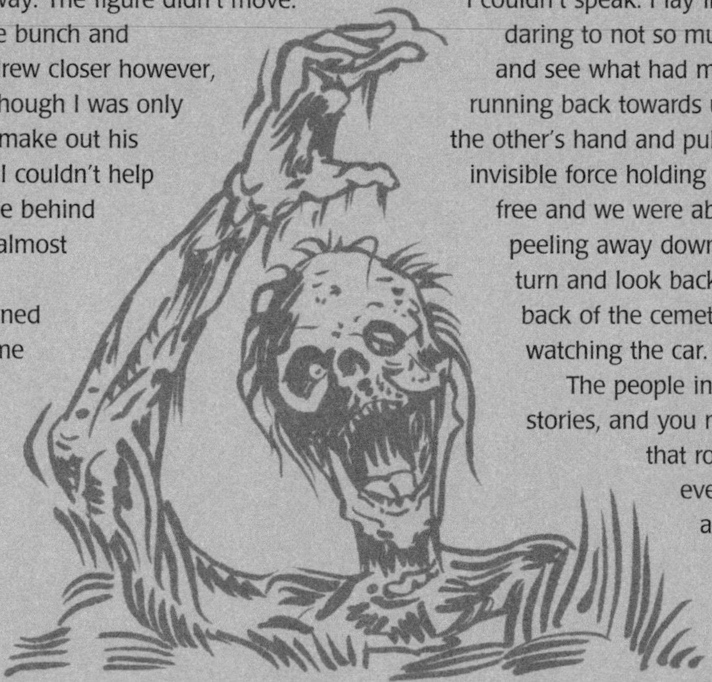

The people in Belleville all know the stories, and you never see many people near that road, day or night, and rarely ever do you hear any stories of anyone else venturing in the cemetery. Even the cops in the town warn teenagers of weird things happening in there.– *Kristy Bird*

Hell's Bridge

"The devil screams at midnight." That promise was enough to lure *Weird Michigan* to the famed steel footbridge in Algoma Township. We pulled up to the small circular turnaround and parking lot off Friske Road and easily found the path next to a sign that read FOOT TRAFFIC ONLY. It wasn't midnight, just late afternoon, and a red SUV was already parked there. The underbrush looked dense, but we plunged in without so much as a shot of bug spray.

The narrow footpath wound for about a quarter mile through a thick woods lined with poison oak vines here and there. Our directions said to veer to the right when we came to the fork in the path, and we did, passing someone's abandoned picnic blanket still neatly spread on the grass. We wondered where the picnickers had vanished to. Suddenly the cursed bridge loomed in front of us, spanning the river in a short, handrail-less walk.

According to legend, Elias Friske, for whom the road was named back when the area was known as Laphamville, killed an unknown number of children and dumped their bodies into the Rogue River, right beneath where the bridge is now. He claimed at the time that the devil made him do it. Word is that you can still hear the children crying or laughing there, that there are odd splashing sounds as if their bodies are still hitting the water, and that, at midnight, the devil will scream in victory. Occasionally a lone, misty figure is also spotted standing near the bridge.

In the afternoon sunlight, the place with its overhanging trees and softly gurgling water seemed spooky enough. The bridge felt solid, but without handrails it wasn't a place you'd want to tap dance or jump around. We took our photos, wondered again where the picnickers were, and finally made our way back down the muddy path, slapping at mosquitoes and making mental notes to bring plenty of flashlights if we ever came back at night. Others have done just that—here are some of their tales:

Hell's Bridge a Freaky Experience

So far, we've been there six times and each time we come away with something different. But in most of the photos we've taken (and we've taken a lot) there is always an orb directly over the middle of the bridge or really close by. If someone is standing on the bridge when the pic is taken, the orb always seems to be right next to their shoulder or directly above their head. I am certain that this is not dust or anything like that. Our meters all indicate paranormal activity at this place.

You take the path on the right-hand side as you cross the bridge and follow it a ways into the woods. You will find that EMF meters go crazy and there are quite a few "cold spots" as well. Several of our group members have also had the sensation of feeling "pushed" while sitting or standing on the bridge at midnight. I have never heard the "Devil" scream at midnight, although we did hear some very odd noises coming from just beyond the bridge. Something was thrown at us and landed in the river. We're pretty sure we were the only ones there at the time.

We have still been unable to obtain any EVPs there. The crickets are very very loud and that interferes with any recording we try to do. I get a different feeling every time I go out there.— *Dave, Grand Rapids Area Paranormal Enthusiasts, www.geocities.com/ghosthunterpara*

The Baby Screams at Hell's Bridge

Recently, my sister and her friends went camping near Hell's Bridge near the Upper Peninsula. At midnight they videotaped the bridge. When they watched the tape, they heard the screams of an infant and stopped the tape. As soon as they stopped the tape, the scream stopped just as fast. The wails were coming from the tape. I asked her if she heard the baby screaming during the visit, and she said no. Also, there were two orbs that went by on the tape that no one saw in person. I finally looked it up on the Internet and it said that Hell's Bridge is where the Devil kills infants and children and throws them into the river below.— *Riley Alexandra Vruggink*

The Little Ghost of Knock-Knock Road

It's a sweltering summer day in Detroit, but the little girl wheels joyfully down the sidewalk on her new bicycle, unmindful of the heat. Suddenly, as small children sometimes do, she accidentally veers down a driveway and into the busy traffic on Strasburg Road, just south of Seven Mile. Tires screech; an awful thud resounds as the car's front end clashes with the bike and little rider. In moments, the child lies dead on the scorching pavement.

However, according to legend, although her body is carefully removed and laid to rest, the little girl's spirit never leaves the scene. She spends her endless nights approaching cars on Strasburg and knocking on their doors to see if they might conceal the driver who ended her short life.

Nicknamed Knock-Knock Road, Strasburg has been a favored cruising spot for decades for Detroit's thrill-seeking teens, all hoping to hear something come a-rapping on the sides of their vehicles. Other streets eventually claimed the same legend, but according to an article in Wayne State University's student newspaper, *South End*, no one has ever managed to find a record attesting to such a death at any of these locations.

Still, droves of thrill seekers have claimed they heard the knocks on Strasburg. Some of the sounds were undoubtedly made by companions dangling their arms out an open window to give a few raps when no one was looking. Others may have come from bumps or potholes in the road itself. Whichever, enough people have claimed to have heard the mysterious sounds to keep the story alive from generation to generation. Interestingly, a new paving job on Strasburg that smoothed the street considerably did not stop the stories. The knocking, insists the Strasburg sojourners, continues just as it did before. The source of the enigmatic noises, if there is one, remains unknown to this day.

Another Crash on Knock-Knock

I heard that a bunch of kids in a car were driving down Knock-Knock Road and were going too fast and hit a pole head-on. They crashed and all burned alive. While they were burning, they were pounding on the windows trying to get out. Now, whenever you drive down that street you can hear and feel them knocking and pounding on your doors yelling and screaming for help!—*Valerie S.*

Ghost Is Clocking Your Speed

I have heard that Knock-Knock Road works most of the time, but is most reliable when you are going the exact speed those kids were going when they veered off the road—76 miles per hour. I have tried it many times, and the closer you get to that speed, the more likely it is to happen. I can vouch for it personally, as I have heard it on four different occasions now.– *Ali Marko*

Rolling Bass-Ackward Up Gravity Hill

It's a confounding experience, watching the scenery go by the wrong way as you roll backward up a hill with your car in neutral and foot off the gas pedal. But that's exactly what *Weird Michigan* experienced at the Putney Corners gravity hill, one of several places in the country where gravity seems to take a vacation. We've experienced a few of these and usually bring our trusty bubble level to prove that, contrary to what our eyes are telling us, we are actually rolling downhill, not up. We'd forgotten it that day, but no matter, all of these hills are optical illusions. Really.

The Putney Corners slope is especially effective, however. The perspective, the landscape, everything works together to make you swear your car is being pushed by invisible forces. And speedily! By the time we got to the driveway of the church at the top of the "hill," we had to brake to keep from going through the intersection.

Local legends say, in fact, that the Blaine Christian Church drags sinners upward toward its doors. If that's the case, the *Weird Michigan*-mobile was bound for glory! We tried it three times.

Putney Road is in Benzie County. Take M-31 north to Joyfield Road. Go left on Joyfield to Putney. The church marks Putney Corners. Turn left (south) and go slowly to the bottom of the first hill until the STOP AHEAD sign shows up in your rearview mirror. Shift into neutral and feel the irresistible church doors drawing you up the hill toward them.

Sinners Saved in Putney Corners

Putney Road, in Putney Corners, is a well-traveled street—backwards and forwards. A portion of the road has strange powers that pull your car uphill backwards. Legend says that the Blaine Christian Church, sitting at the top of the hill, pulls anyone who is a sinner towards its doors. To experience the phenomenon, make sure you are on the south side of Putney Road, and that you can see the STOP AHEAD sign in your rear view mirror. – *Anonymous*

Feeling Gravity's Pull

In July of 2003, my husband took me on a birthday tour of the northeastern portion of Michigan's Lower Peninsula. While we were traveling the back roads of Benzie County, he suddenly remembered a place he'd known about—a road where cars seem to defy gravity! I thought he was pulling my leg, until he told me to get out of the car and watch what happened when he put it into neutral.

Sure enough, though the car seemed to be slanting uphill, it actually rolled in the uphill direction! I was duly amazed, and when we returned to our home, I couldn't wait to research the Internet. The Benzie County mystery spot information can be found here: www.coheadquarters.com/PennLibr/BenzieCounty/PutneyWonder1.htm.

I'm hoping to visit some more of these places because, even though some web sites have somewhat dispelled the mystery of them, I still find the idea fascinating. –*Mrs. Terry Gordon*

Alien Footprints at Rose City Gravity Hill

My husband and I went to check out the Gravity Hill in Rose City. When we were almost there we hit a snowstorm and did not realize we had a flat tire. Once in Rose City we pulled into a gas station to get directions and fix the flat. The clerk there directed us to the road but said he'd never checked it out himself. By the time we got there, there was a fresh blanket of snow on the ground so the only tracks made were from our car. The stories were right. Our car appeared to be coasting up the hill in neutral.

My husband Bob decided to get out of the car to watch how this works. Once out, he yelled for me to get out too and look at what he was seeing. I did and there appeared to be hundreds of little footprints all around our car and also coming out of the woods. We stayed for a while and headed back toward the gas station. We told the clerk that the hill does indeed work and also explained the footprints. A customer in line said, "probably the aliens!" Not thinking much about his comment we headed home to Grand Rapids. The next day I decided to call Rose City Chamber of Commerce to explain about the footprints. The man on the other end of the phone said, "probably the aliens!" Now I questioned this one. He said folklore has it a craft crashed there years ago. I'm not sure about that one but I am sure about the footprints–*T.*

Tunnel of Trees and Devil's Elbow

If ever there was a place that looks suited for ancient legend, it would be Michigan's Tunnel of Trees, a winding stretch of M-119 covered with a bower of interlocking tree branches so dense in places that car headlights turn on automatically even on bright days. The road twines around the shore of Lake Michigan from Harbor Springs to Cross Village, and in places, the spiritual pulse is almost palpable.

The Ottawa (Odawa) who lived here first knew that. The Thorne Swift Nature Preserve is traditionally believed to be occupied by a capricious water spirit. The cedar swamp allows it to come and go as it wishes, and it can play tricks as innocent as blowing boaters around the lake in directions they do not wish to go or as tragic as plucking away an unguarded child. The trees in this place are over one hundred years old, adding to its sacred aura.

The area is full of historic significance. On Lower Shore Drive, an old Jesuit church marks the site of a tribal cemetery, and two miles south of Cross Village is a ravine where the British and some Native American tribes signed a treaty joining them as allies against the fledgling United States. But the ravine has an older meaning for Native Americans. According to their lore, this is where a huge battle between the Thunderbirds, or sky spirits, and water panther spirits was fought. The Thunderbirds used massive lightning strikes to drive the water panthers deeper into their aqueous home, carving out the massive ravine in the process.

Devil's Elbow is the slightly misnamed hairpin turn marked by a wooden sign explaining the Ottawa legend behind it. The sign reads MOTCHIMANITOU, DEVIL'S ELBOW: A FLOWING SPRING IN THIS RAVINE WAS BELIEVED BY AREA ODAWA INDIAN BANDS TO BE THE HOME OF SPIRITS WHO MADE THEIR PRESENCE KNOWN IN THIS LOCATION DURING THE HOURS OF DARKNESS.

Strange lights and unexplained occurrences here have caused the place to be regarded with caution not only by indigenous people, but everyone who has come since. The Ottawa name actually means "where the spirits live," but like many similar Indian place-names, it fell victim to the white man's almost universal substitution of "devil" for "spirit" in translation. Nevertheless, the Tunnel of Trees is a mystical area, and people of all cultures feel it.

A Night Alone in the Tunnel of Trees

I would highly recommend against driving alone down the Tunnel of Trees. It is quite a spooky place. I know from firsthand experience that it turns out better when you have someone there to share the experience with. Once, when I was just past the Devil's Elbow, my car went completely haywire. At the same exact time, my engine cut out and all the electrical systems turned on. Believe me, there's nothing more disorienting than realizing your car isn't moving and at the same time trying to understand why you're suddenly being barraged with old Journey songs on the radio you didn't turn on. I had to sit out there and wait for a tow truck for over forty minutes. And on that road, there's nothing to do but sit around and think about which evil spirit jumped inside your engine and turned it into mush. So at the very least, bring a friend, so you have someone to talk to when you're out there thinking way too hard about ghouls and phantoms. —*Rick Pico*

Legend of the Halfway Station

The Halfway Station, a gas station and store on Hawks County Road 451, halfway between Hawks and Millersburg, has a reputation that precedes it. The story goes that two teens went on a murder spree there, killing several people and then committing suicide. It is said that if you visit the Halfway Station—especially after midnight—and you circle the building three times, the ghosts of these two evil teens will chase you off the property or even follow the car down the road.

A Western Michigan Ghost Hunters Society investigation into the story uncovered these facts:

The two men were Darrel Jarvis, twenty-one, and James Siebert, twenty, both from Pontiac. In November of 1976, they engaged in a two-day escapade (along with Jarvis's sixteen-year-old female cousin) that began with the abduction of David Pfaff, thirty, and the theft of Mr. Pfaff's 1976 Monte Carlo.

The two men and the cousin drove the stolen car with the victim in the back seat to Presque Isle County. Jarvis drove the car to a gravel pit that is located behind the Qcqueoc Township Cemetery, ordered Pfaff out of the back seat, and at gun point and carrying a shovel, led him to the gravel pit where the victim was ordered to dig his own grave. The cousin testified that she stayed at the car, but could see the event. Siebert then made Pfaff lie facedown in the grave and shot him in the back of the head. Siebert ended up returning to the car to reload the shotgun, saying, "the S.O.B. isn't dead yet."

The shotgun was reloaded, and Siebert shot Pfaff once again. Jarvis and Siebert then finished the burial. After getting about two miles away, they realized that they forgot to steal Pfaff's wallet, so they returned to the murder site, where all three dug the body back up, took the wallet, buried the victim once again, took money out

of the wallet, and then tossed the wallet into the Rainy River.

The following day, Jarvis and Siebert traveled, still in the stolen Monte Carlo, to a store called the Halfway Station. It was a family-run store where the wife/mother was working at the time. Jarvis and Siebert were in the middle of savagely beating and stabbing the mother when her ten-year-old son came home from school. The boy walked in on the assault, and was in turn also horribly beaten and repeatedly stabbed. They robbed the store and left, and the father/husband found the victims two hours later. Both mother and child survived the attack. . . .

Jarvis and Siebert are now serving, between the two of them, fourteen life sentences and both are incarcerated at Oaks Correctional Facility. Since the sentencing, Jarvis has had two more sentences added—both stemming from attempted prison escapes. The sixteen-year-old female cousin was given immunity in exchange for testimony.

Since neither murderer committed suicide, it is impossible for their ghosts to be chasing people off the property. Also, no deaths occurred at the Halfway Station, as the legend also states.— *Nicole Bray, Contributor*

The Helpful Spook

Back in the late 1800s, when automobiles and ambulances were as yet unknown, a country physician named Dr. Lucas was hurrying along Romeo Plank Road one foggy night in Clinton Township. The good doctor was on his way to see a patient, when his horse and carriage somehow went awry and doctor, horse, and buggy all tumbled over the Clinton River Bridge. Doc Lucas never made it to another bedside.

Some say a light still appears there on Romeo Plank Road when travelers are in danger and that the light is the doctor waving his house-call lantern as he continues his mission of helping humanity. Sometimes, an ancient black buggy is seen racing along with the light, pulled by an unseen horse. Others ascribe the bouncing luminescence to a railroad worker killed about the same time in the same vicinity who swings his rail lantern to light the way. Either way, it's nice to know there are some ghosts who have our best interests at heart.

Beware of Luke the Spook!

If you are a nonbeliever in Luke the Spook you should not be. I am sixty years old now, but when I was 15 or 16 we used to park on that flat bridge many nights. On two occasions we saw that light winding along the stream and we were scared. On one occasion we had trouble starting the car. We were always told about the doctor and his carriage. I know that something or someone is there. So disbelievers beware. I saw this and will never forget it and the fear I felt.— *Carol*

Witches on Blood Road?

Rumor has it that many witches and devil worshippers migrated to this state during the witch trials taking place back east in the 1600s, mainly because of all the woods and hiding places here. In 1990 my friend and I began reading about devil worship and began hearing rumors about a road just outside of Metamora called Blood Road. They were frightening stories of how kids would drive down the road at night and witness trees following them, and of being chased by a truck with bright lights.

The first time we went down the road, it was just after midnight. We had the windows rolled down to see and hear better. About halfway down the road we began to notice that the road was wet, although it had not rained in days. The road began to wind, the trees thickened, then it seemed as if the road was sinking. The water on the road was increasing as we watched!

As the road slowly disappeared, we noticed that it was a strange water, thick. We both opened the doors and saw that it was red in color. My buddy turned on his brights, and the whole road was covered in this blood-like substance. He turned the truck around and we began to leave, then we saw off in the distance a fire, with people in white robes standing around it chanting. As we kept driving we saw a few of them even run across the road. We got the hell out of there.— *Rypple*

Don't Mess with the Blood Road Gang!

I've heard that Blood Road is a huge hangout for a gang of Satanists. A friend was once down there, and he and his boys had parked their car on the side of the road. They got out when they saw a few people kneeling around a tree. They watched from about fifty yards away. They were surprised when a young blond lady, dressed all in black, snuck up behind them and asked them what they were doing there. They were totally freaked out and way too scared to answer. She pointed back to their car and told them to go.

She said, "You'd better leave before any of them realize you're here and don't come back. We don't give second chances."

Needless to say they left. My friends are tough, tough guys. They wouldn't back down from anything except a real challenge. Please let anyone who reads this know—Blood Road is absolutely not to be trifled with.— *James P. Cobb*

Testimonies of Murder or Funky Road Art?

Searching for a shoe tree can be a bit like following a will-o'-the-wisp. We're not talking about those old metal things that people once put in their shoes to keep the leather shapely. We mean your average maple or elm that has somehow become festooned from trunk to tip with castoff shoes. It may be there when you arrive at the purported address, or it may have disappeared, gone the way of some landowner's fit of pique at having his forest desecrated with strands of oxfords, pumps, and bedraggled old Nikes.

Several different trees, or groups of trees (the con-

dition appears to be infectious) have been reported in various stages of dress around Michigan, from Kalkaska to Atlanta. *Weird Michigan* homed in on the magnificent specimen on Highway M-33 outside Comins in Oscoda County, where two doughty hardwoods stood blooming with every imaginable kind and size of shoe. Some of the footgear had fallen, so that the ground too had become part of the exhibition. We kicked at an expensive black wing tip, sans shoelaces, moldering in the dewy weeds. A child's red flip-flop lay flung onto a nearby stump. A squawking blackbird claimed a pile of dirty sneakers.

So why do people travel miles of Michigan highway just to fling their shoes into the sky? Some say it's only a desire to be part of a group phenomenon—a reprise of the "happenings" of the late '60s. Others are hooked in by the legends that surround some places, such as the tree that allegedly contains a section of tiny antique shoes—purportedly torn from the feet of dead children ravaged by a demented killer who memorialized his dirty deeds by creating the first shoe tree. Another legend involves a boy who died in a swamp after bullies teased him by hanging his sneakers high on a branch. Of course the boy still haunts the place, letting loose an unearthly wail when people scream at the tree.

People have also reported seeing mysterious shadows emerge from the woods near shoe trees or experiencing electrical difficulties with their cars while parked nearby. Most shoe tree pilgrims, though, just want to admire the incongruity of the whole thing. (Other Michigan shoe trees are or have been reported at Novi, Sheldon, Kalkaska, Atlanta, St. Helen, and along I-96 in Livingston County near Howell.)

Flatfoots Watch for Unlawful Soles

On Highway 131, north of Kalkaska, is the famous Shoe Tree. Hundreds of pairs of shoes have been tossed into the tree over the years. They first appeared early in 2001 and have multiplied in growth greatly since then. State police are keeping their eyes peeled for the perpetrator, although admittedly, it's not too high on their list of priorities. *—Anonymous*

Those Shoes Are Murder!

I just wanted to tell you a story about the Shoe Tree. Legend has it that a recluse lured a number of young children to his isolated shack, where he murdered them. Before disposing of their bodies, he removed their shoes as mementos, hanging them on a nearby tree. The tree is still there—and so are the shoes! Visitors claim that the tree remains warm to the touch even in the dead of winter. Many report inexplicable car failure when they try to leave the site. *—Dan*

Haunted Michigan

You could say Michigan's history gave it a head (or would that be headless?) start in the ghost department. Besides the legacy of its many indigenous people, who've been here from time immemorial, Michigan's peninsula status lured European settlers—French fur traders, adventurous Jesuits—to the state almost a full century earlier than to much of the rest of the Midwest. Times were tough in those days, and more than one of these intrepid pioneers came to a violent or otherwise unhappy end. Ghosts, some people say, linger in this realm because something about the way they died left their souls unsettled. Some of these early Michiganders may haunt us now, everlastingly trying to come to terms with the circumstances of their deaths.

Other people say that ghosts are entities who don't know they're dead. So they stay on, scaring the daylights out of the rest of us. Whichever the case, Michigan is loaded to its lake monster gills with haunted woods, inns, theaters, lighthouses, you name it.

With this embarrassment of otherworldly riches to choose from, our collection is by necessity a mere sampling of some of *Weird Michigan*'s favorite ghost stories. But a few of the misty visages you will encounter here may not yet have crossed your path. We hope they never do.

Seul Choix Lighthouse

The name is French; the ghost is British. But the stories about the haunting of the lighthouse near Gulliver on Michigan's Upper Peninsula are pure American folklore.

While traveling to investigate this spirit-drenched place, *Weird Michigan* committed an innocent faux pas when we stopped at a local gas station and asked how to get to the "Sool Choy" lighthouse. We were told, a bit disdainfully, that the "Sis Schwah" complex could be found along CR 432 and then 431. Oops! Pardon our French!

The name means "only choice," and the harbor it stands upon was so dubbed by fur traders who once found the rocky point literally their only port in a raging Lake Michigan storm. The nearby tiny town of Gulliver shelters a brace of haunted old houses clustered next to an ancient Indian grave that is visited regularly by the ghost of a Native American woman. Or so says Michigan writer Frederick Stonehouse. The houses might be haunted by any number of people. Unexplained activity ranges from items returning after being thrown away to the ghostly appearance of a young girl in the windows. The skeleton of a girl was found buried in the cellar of one of the houses, and coffin remnants were uncovered just outside the place. It's unknown how many other undiscovered bodies lie in the area.

But it's the lighthouse that offers a chance to glimpse the locally famous ghost known as William. The tower's charming brick house, refurnished appropriately for its era, is now open for visitors and proudly displays portraits of its resident haunt, former sea captain Joseph William Townshend.

After arriving in the United States just before the turn of the twentieth century, William worked his way up from Mackinac dockhand to keeper of the Seul Choix lighthouse in 1902. Light keepers often lasted no more than a few years at the lonely occupation, so William did well to still be

polishing the Fresnel lens eight years later in 1910.

Unfortunately, illness struck the old captain that year, and he died a very painful death in the lighthouse bedroom to the left of the top of the stairs. However, many think he never left his last home in spirit and that he lingers, especially in that bedroom. Several people have reported looking in the room's dresser mirror, only to find themselves staring back into the dark eyes of the long-deceased William! (*Weird Michigan* tried, but the captain was apparently not in a reflective mood that day.)

One of the museum's longtime tour guides told us that several times when he showed the house in the morning, the kitchen silverware would be set American-style on the old wooden table, with the fork lying alongside the plate, but when he returned a few minutes later after touring the adjacent rooms, the forks would be lying across the plates according to the British custom. "Others have seen him in the windows," added the guide. William has also been seen skulking near the woods behind the lighthouse, eyeing visitors warily.

There is no doubt about what William looks like, since several portraits sit on a table in the front parlor. The tour guides take the old guy in stride and include him as part of their spiel. Maybe that's one reason he finds it so hard to leave.

The Ontonagon Lighthouse . . . Is It Haunted?

Do we believe in ghosts? Well, if you are going to call up images of spooks flitting about in white sheets, the answer is probably no . . . but hauntings, which can mean the presence of an entity from the past, are a different matter. Such an entity, or rather, entities, are believed by some to inhabit the old lighthouse at the mouth of the Ontonagon River in Michigan's Upper Peninsula.

In daylight, the lighthouse is not very imposing. It's a yellow brick structure surrounded now by a large industrial complex. The lighthouse was in service for ninety-seven years, from 1866 until the fall of 1963. During that time, nine lighthouse keepers and their families lived in the dwelling portion.

The first keeper was a perky little Irishman named Tom Stripe. Though Stripe was married and had children, for the most part he worked alone at the lighthouse, his family staying at their home in the nearby village of Ontonagon, across the river from the lighthouse.

Stripe had lost his left arm above the elbow in an accident but was still able to carry out his duties as light tender. However, the five-gallon oil can used to carry fuel up the winding staircase of the tower to the lantern room must have presented a special challenge. Stripe would have had to carry the heavy can up the stairs without the use of a left hand on the banister to help him keep his balance. Once in the tower, the little Irishman had to go through contortions to get the can on his shoulder in order to fill the fuel tank for the beacon, which was originally fired with whale oil and later with kerosene. The beacon burned fuel at a rate that required topping off the tank every four hours, so Tom Stripe carried that heavy oil can up those stairs literally hundreds of times between 1866 to October 18, 1883, when he was relieved as light keeper.

Late-night visitors to the lighthouse have reported hearing the clanking sound of the heavy oil can being set down on the steps of the metal stairs, as if Tom Stripe is putting it down so he can rest a moment before resuming his climb.

Once, when a lighthouse tour guide from the historical society (which operates the lighthouse as a tourist attraction) was in the tower late at night checking on a string of Christmas lights strung for the holidays, the clanking sound of the oil can was heard coming up the stairs. Upon investigation, the oil can, which only minutes earlier had been in the lower hall on display, was found on the second-floor landing!

On another occasion, a tour guide was climbing the tower stairs in broad daylight when he came up against a cold barrier—something, or someone, was actually blocking the tower stairway to the second floor. There was nothing to be seen, but some force kept the guide from going upstairs for a few moments, and then there was a clanking sound in the tower, as if the entity was again moving up the staircase. The noise ended, and the tour guide was able to go up to the lantern room, only a little shaky from the strange encounter.—*Bruce H. Johanson*

The Baffling Haunting

A brilliant white tower still lords it over Presque Isle Bay on Lake Huron, although the old lighthouse, which is now a thirty-nine-stair museum, was shut down and severed from power back in 1871. Unlike many unused towers, the Presque Isle Station was allowed to stand, and in 1972, almost exactly one hundred years from the old tower's disconnection, George and Lorraine Parris were hired as caretakers. Ten years later George died. That same year, in May, Lorraine made the strange discovery that a light was burning in the old tower, despite the fact that there was no power. "Every day the light comes on at dusk and goes off at midnight," said Lorraine in the 1999 video *True Lighthouse Hauntings*. Many people have witnessed the light, and it has actually guided at least one boat into safe harbor during a storm, but no one has been able to figure out how it occurs. Is it the ghost of former caretaker George Parris, determined to bring the historic treasure back to a working life?

Light is not the only reported haunting of the lighthouse. According to local legend, one Presque Isle light keeper regularly locked his wife in the tower while he pursued a tryst in the neighboring town. Eventually, the keeper got tired of hearing her enraged screams, so he did away with her. Little did he know that she would only scream louder and longer once she was dead. Her angry cries are still heard on very windy nights.

The Capitol Theatre

Located in downtown Flint, this used to be my (and many others') local punk rock hangout during the late '80s–early '90s. Many people who have worked the theater during these local music shows have reported ghost sightings. The three main ones are: 1. Ghost of an usher who reportedly can be seen in the theater's balcony. 2. Screams and knocking noises of someone who was allegedly sealed in a wall. 3. Ghost of a workman. All the times I've been there, I've never seen anything; however, I can say that the Capitol Theatre has a very weird "vibe" about it, for lack of a better word. It's a very creepy place that used to give me a weird feeling every time I went there.

—*Ribby*

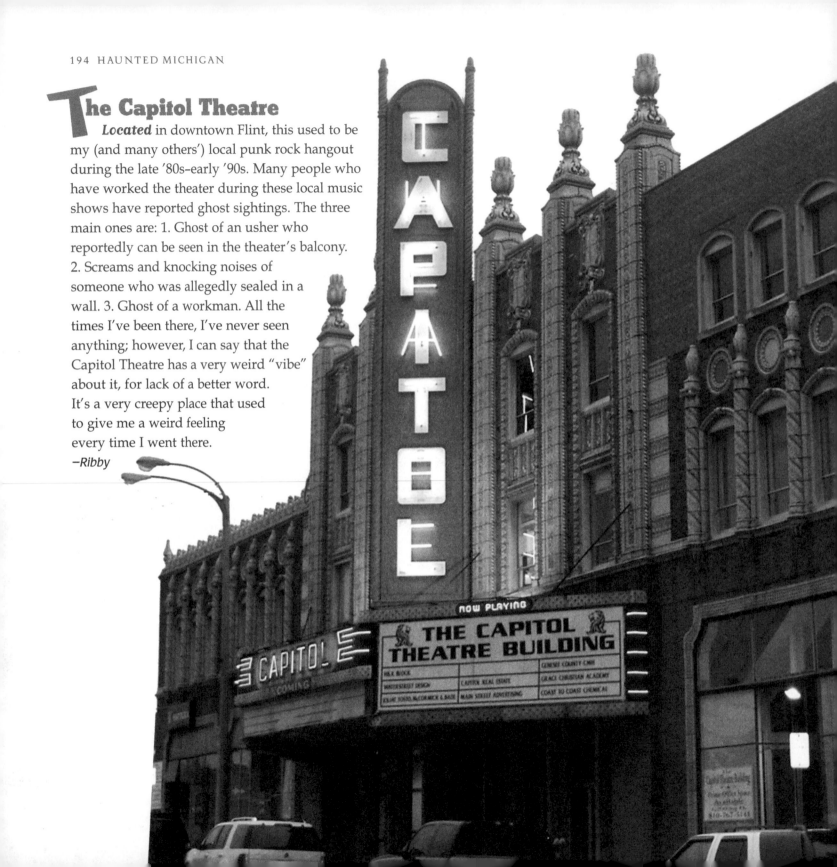

NOW PLAYING

🦁 THE CAPITOL 🦁
THEATRE BUILDING

Calumet Theater

Remember the cartoon character Casper, the Friendly Ghost? He was meant to overturn the old cliché of ghosts as menacing, frightening creatures. The Calumet Theater, an architectural gem in the Upper Peninsula city of Calumet, has its own friendly and helpful ghost, the spirit of a famous Polish actress named Helena Modjeska. It is said that she actually appeared in 1958 to actress Adysse Lane, who was stuck in the throes of stage fright, and whispered the woman's forgotten lines from Shakespeare's *Taming of the Shrew,* "Fie, fie, unknit that threatening unkind brow. . . ."

The theater was built with riches from the local copper mines, and the history marker affixed to its brick exterior says that its 1900 opening was "the greatest social event ever known in copperdom's metropolis." It even featured a fabulous electrified copper chandelier. When *Weird Michigan* visited the still ornate theater, we came face-to-face with the same imposing portrait of Modjeska that tipped off Miss Lane to the identity of the floating, whispering lady.

The portrait hangs on the back wall of the theater, where we were allowed to take a photo of it, all the while hoping Modjeska would come floating along in one of her opulent stage costumes. After all, others have spotted her all over the theater, even in the dressing rooms. People have felt an eerie presence near her portrait, and poltergeist activity increases when the portrait is taken down periodically. Employees hear loud crashes and report having the lights turned off and on by unseen hands.

No one seems to know why Modjeska chose this particular theater to haunt. A belle of the 1880s and '90s, she made her home in California and flitted from coast to coast, playing all the best venues and many of the rural houses in between. She died in 1909 at the age of sixty-nine and could have chosen to bestow her eternal presence on any number of equally magnificent theaters. Perhaps Modjeska simply remembered the beauty of the Calumet or was attracted by the staging of her favorite Shakespeare play. Maybe she just had a thing for copper. Whatever her reasons, actors here can take the stage confidently, knowing there is someone waiting in the wings to whisper their forgotten lines in a sexy Polish accent.

Haunted Howell

Howell is a town that has weathered reports of crop circles, ice circles, UFO waves, and other strange phenomena, so it's no big surprise that the place should also be rife with ghosts. Owners of the Howell theater, its big screen now dark and idle, long heard midsummer complaints from patrons subjected to unexplained icy blasts in the unair-conditioned theatre. But moviegoers hardly knew the half of it.

One of the theater's ghosts was evidently prone to locker-room humor. The building's manager, according to a 1999 *Detroit News* article, was startled to receive a stinging smack on his bare posterior after he took a shower there one night. No one else was in the building. The manager told the paper he "freaked" and that it had to be Wilma, a former school bus driver who owned the theater with her husband, Clayton McDaniels. They both died in the late 1970s, but apparently stayed on to play tricks such as making an astonished janitor's vacuum cleaner zoom up an incline by itself.

The upstairs of a pub located in what used to be Howell's Livingston Hotel is also supposed to be haunted. Patrons hear noises, and a previous owner continually caught glimpses of a white figure wandering the old guest rooms.

Also, the local newspaper related the eerie experience of the owner of a senior care home in nearby Brighton. The woman visited the Howell Library's resident historian to see if he could explain why voices haunted the halls of her place at night, upsetting residents. After some research, the historian discovered the home had been built on the grounds of a cemetery. The woman was left to wonder if all the bodies had indeed been removed or if some remained to complain about finding a building atop their place of eternal rest.

Kalamazoo's Ghost: Thelma

I used to volunteer at the Kalamazoo Civic theatre, and it is DEFINITELY haunted. They used to tell us not to tick off "Thelma" because she would mess up your show if you did. However, she's really saved the butts of some performers and crew members during shows. I personally have had three run-ins with Thelma, including one where she spoke to me. I had no idea I was talking to a ghost until she disappeared!

I was in a production of *Steel Magnolias* and had several quick costume changes, so an hour before the show I had to check and make sure all my costume pieces were set where they needed to be. I was doing this before one performance when I saw an older woman standing in one of the wings. It was way before show time, and I knew the lobby wasn't even open yet, so I asked her if she was lost. She laughed and said, "Oh, no, I think I know my way around here pretty well." Then she turned away, chuckling, and completely disappeared before my eyes.

Later, during the run of that same show, a pipe burst in my dressing room and flooded the cubbyhole where I had stowed my wig and the pregnancy suit I had to wear in the second act. I was the first to discover the flood, and I found that all my things had been carefully moved from where I'd left them the night before to a safe, dry shelf across the room. The theatre staff insisted no one had been in the dressing rooms all day long.

The legend around the theatre goes that Thelma liked theatre and donated some of her things to the Civic Players when they'd been in another auditorium. Then when she died, she haunted the props she donated, moved with them to the new building, and installed herself permanently. But no one knows for sure.–*Jen*

The Enchanted Ramsdell Theatre

Traverse Magazine says the Ramsdell Theatre, a porticoed old landmark in Manistee, is enchanted. An article by intern Jenny Gavacs tells the story of a tradesman working in the theater basement who was surprised when he noticed a young girl with long hair, dressed in white, standing in a nearby doorway surveying him. As he turned to face her, she told him, "Follow me to your fortune," then vanished.

The worker was left wondering what his fortune might have been had he been able to vanish with her. Others have seen the White Lady drifting languidly through the Victorian splendor of the theater's interior. The legend goes that her father was Thomas Jefferson Ramsdell, founder of the theater and co-haunter. He likes to appear dressed suitably for an evening at the opera, in a period tuxedo. A well-respected pillar of Manistee's early society, Ramsdell hired a professional painter and his own artist son to decorate the lobby with naked nymphs frolicking in two moon-shaped panels. Supposedly, the scandalous nudes were given the faces of a few ladies known around town for their tongue-wagging and especially for their derogatory remarks about Ramsdell.

The theater is now on the National Register of Historic Places and is used for performances by the Manistee Civic Players and other acting and music organizations. These groups know that no matter what the turnout, they will always have an audience in the shades of Ramsdell and his enigmatic daughter.

Thomas Jefferson Ramsdell, founder of the theater and co-haunter, likes to appear dressed suitably for an evening at the opera, in a period tuxedo.

Jeffers High: Too Ghoul for School

From a former Upper Peninsula teacher and union official we'll call Hal, *Weird Michigan* learned that some staff members at Jeffers High School in Painesdale have had a few experiences that put a whole new twist on the concept of higher education. They seemingly encountered something from a loftier plane in this venerable place of learning.

"It's a nice, old school," our informant said, "probably one of the first in the area to have a swimming pool. I was up there one day, getting ready to have a negotiation meeting with the board of education, the superintendent, and some of the support staff. I was standing in the hall looking at this picture of Frederick Jeffers and his wife, Cora. Jeffers was superintendent of the school from 1899 till the early 1960s! His wife was the principal, and between the two of them they had over seventy-five years in education at the time the portraits were taken."

While Hal stood looking at the picture, a member of the Houghton County Board of Commissioners came over and said, "Yes, that's Fred Jeffers, all right. He's still here, you know." Hal was startled, since he knew Jeffers was deceased, and asked for an explanation. The commissioner took Hal downstairs to meet with some custodians and one of the cooks, who proceeded to fill him in on the school's strange happenings.

The first person with a tale was the cook. She was the old-fashioned kind who didn't like to use canned or frozen food. Surplus commodities were still available in the schools then, and this cook made homemade rolls and hamburger buns. One morning the woman had gone in early to get the bread rising and walked into a little anteroom with a door that leads to the kitchen proper. The door had a window of diamond-patterned glass, so that it wasn't exactly transparent but someone moving on the other side could be seen. As the cook was taking off her coat, she saw someone moving through the glass. "Who is in my kitchen?" she yelled, then opened up the door and walked in. No one there. So she closed the door and stepped back into the anteroom. Again she saw someone moving in the kitchen. She opened the door, found no one, and again closed it. Suddenly something pink appeared on the other side of the glass. It was a face looking right back at her! Again she quickly opened the door, and again no one was there. The woman left and refused to go into the building alone after that.

The next person to talk was the commissioner himself, whose name we were given but have withheld by request. He was in the building at about five thirty one morning to run a routine boiler check when he heard a basketball being bounced on the floor. "Who the heck's in here?" he yelled, and turned on the lights. A basketball was lying in the middle of the gym floor. He figured someone had just left it there, so he turned the lights off and started to leave. Then he heard the bouncing sound once more. He ran back and turned on the lights, and there's the basketball noise again—a little closer to him. The same thing happened a third time, but this time the basketball was bouncing faster and,

when the commissioner turned on the lights, the ball was lying right at his feet!

But the oldest custodian had the strangest story of all. He had been ordered by the fire marshal to clean out all the papers in the attic above the study hall. Bit by bit the yellowing papers, old schoolbooks, and records were hauled out, including some old records and checks signed by Fred Jeffers. The custodian was reluctant to throw these mementoes away, but he'd been told to get rid of everything, so he did. Fifteen boxes of papers were removed and sent to the landfill. Job over.

Not quite. A few weeks later the superintendent called the old custodian into his office.

The superintendent was very upset. "I thought I asked you to get all those old books out of there," he said. "The fire marshal was just here, and he's going to cite us."

The old custodian protested that he had done his job and hauled out everything. But when he looked in the attic, he found all the books and papers right back where they had been. "I told him he could move them all himself. I ain't going back up there again," the man said.

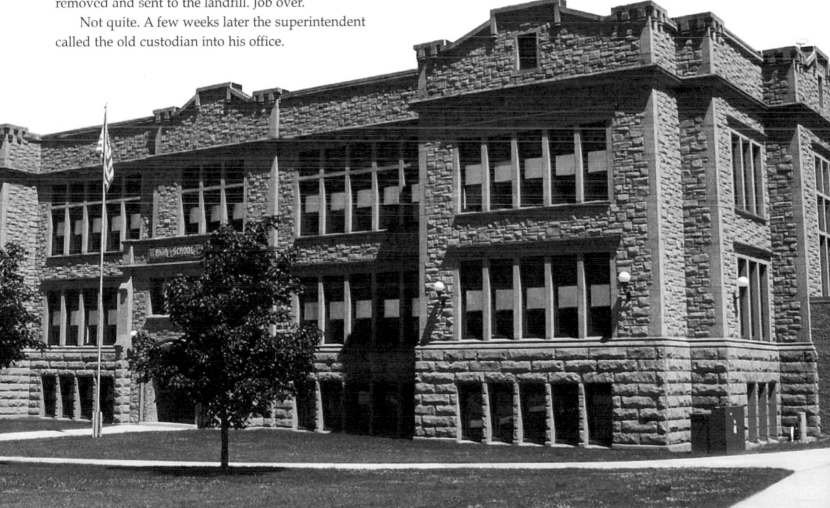

House of Ludington

Weird Michigan arrived at the swanky House of Ludington in Escanaba on a Saturday afternoon just as wedding guests—dressed to the nines—were arriving for a reception inside the stately old brick building. How many of them knew, we wondered, that they were walking straight into one of Michigan's most haunted places?

In a town made famous for deer hunting in the movie *Escanaba in da Moonlight,* the House of Ludington stands out as an elegant throwback to the past, with its antiques-filled lobby and carefully decorated guest rooms. And yet this gracious old place is filled with paranormal hot spots. Visiting investigators have reported not only feeling "presences," but also experiencing strange sightings, sounds, and smells. One ghost encountered was a man who left a swath of tobacco odor mingled with pungent B.O., and who exuded feelings of grouchiness. There is evidence that a man fitting that description lived in the hotel at one time.

However, present operators Edward and Suzell Eisenberger say the main spirit in this place is a colorful former owner—former Chicagoan Pat Hayes, who bought the building in 1939. He'd previously owned another business that went bankrupt, but somehow came up with $10,000 to buy the grand hotel. Townspeople were even more surprised when Hayes again filed bankruptcy only thirty days after buying the House of Ludington, and the judge on the case inexplicably awarded the hotel to Hayes on the ground that it was his home. It all seemed very unlikely. Whispers of probable connections with the Chicago Mafia swept the town.

Hayes was determined to make his place a success, however, and ran things his own way. One of his peculiarities was that if anyone dared to order a well-done steak, he either threw the person out or served him

fish or chicken. Hayes also installed the first glass elevator in Michigan in the House of Ludington in 1959, over the objections of a city official. Hayes told the fellow that the elevator was being built, and he would sit in the street with his shotgun and shoot anyone who tried to stop him. The elevator still works today. And sometimes it works without anyone in it!

Although Hayes died in the hotel of prostate cancer in 1969, Eisenberger believes he's still running some things—like that elevator. When Ed and Suzell first moved in and began making their own renovations in 1998, the elevator would glide up and down endlessly, completely on its own. It still does on occasion, he says.

Around the time the inn reopened, one of the

Pat Hayes, left, poses with an unidentified guest

waitresses came running to Eisenberger yelling that there was a big problem in the ladies' room. He rushed to the scene and stood astonished to see all three toilets shooting up water like porcelain fountains. Fearing the worst, he called a plumber, who conducted a thorough examination and then reported, scratching his head, that there was absolutely nothing wrong with the toilets or pipes and he couldn't explain it. The spectacle never happened again.

The strangest event, though, occurred while a busboy was serving a wedding party one night. The lad was known for being a tad on the clumsy side, and as he hoisted a giant shrimp-filled crystal bowl to carry it into the dining room, Suzell admonished him not to drop it. Ed heard her say that, but wasn't watching when the room suddenly filled with the tremendous, crashing sound of glass breaking and shattering all over the floor. He rushed over, determined to fire the busboy, and arrived just in time to see the young man setting the intact bowl down safely. Nothing was broken anywhere, yet people were streaming in from all the serving areas to see what had made the huge noise. "It sounded like a whole pantry full of dishes coming down," said Eisenberger. "Lots of people heard it." They finally pinned the ghastly practical joke on Hayes. Evidently, when that judge awarded him the hotel, it was for eternity.

The Bloody Stairway

Inside an 1852 frame farmhouse situated on a gravel road outside Fowlerville in Livingston County, family members trod lightly whenever they climbed the stairs to the second floor. The wooden stairs bore bloodstains that would not come out, no matter what cleaning methods were used.

The chilling story of the house with the bloody stairway was printed in the November 3, 1982, issue of the *Fowlerville Review.* The family who lived there had owned the home for fourteen years and said the previous occupants never bothered to clue them in that someone else was living there . . . and would probably be staying on.

It didn't take long for the new family to find that out, however. As soon as they moved in, the phenomena began. Doors would slam for no reason, lights would operate independently of switches, the vacuum cleaner would careen around the floor on its own, like a scene from an updated *Sorcerer's Apprentice.* The family heard eerie footsteps on the bloody staircase and the second floor. They would hang pictures, only to experience the frightening spectacle of their artwork detaching itself from the wall and crashing to the floor. The ghost even chased the husband out of the house the first time he stayed there alone.

A medium once told the family that the spirit was a "big man with black hair, dressed like a lumberjack." Perhaps taking issue with the description, the ghost proceeded to physically push the woman out the door. The family said that was the only time it "touched" anyone, the article noted. However, the ghost did create a melee anytime company came. Doors slammed hard, the footsteps intensified, and objects levitated until the visitors were too frightened to stay. This happened the day the couple brought home their youngest child from

the hospital too. And that baby, said the article, grew up to be able to see the ghost and talk with him—and he said the spook's name was Arnold.

Was that Arnold's blood spilled for all time on the stairway? The family never found out. It's unknown who lives in that farmhouse now or even if it is still standing. But one thing is sure. That was one highly tolerant family to have put up with such exuberant manifestations for so many years.

Buried Brandy at Bowers Harbor Inn

Ten miles out on Old Mission Peninsula, which juts north from Traverse City, the genteel Bowers Harbor Inn enjoys both a fabulous view of Lake Michigan and the presence of a well-known ghost. Her name is Genevive, and she was the discontented wife of lumber baron J. W. Stickney, who built the place during the 1880s as a summer mansion. According to an article issued by the inn, Genevive's all-absorbing passion in life was concocting her own fruit brandies. Evidently suffering from some sort of paranoia complex, she was so afraid of thieves coming after her tasty creations that she actually buried them around the shady lawns. The article describes her as an "obese and jealous woman," who had a trick mirror installed in her bedroom that gave her an illusion of slimness.

In her later years, Genevive needed both an elevator and a nurse. The nurse soon became closer to Mr. Stickney than perhaps she ought. When the lumber magnate died, he left the bulk of his fortune to his mistress and only the Bowers Harbor estate to Genevive. In despair, the betrayed widow hanged herself inside the elevator shaft, thus beginning the long tradition of hauntings. Almost immediately, lights began to misbehave, mirrors and paintings dropped from the walls, and the elevator would tootle up and down with no one inside.

The hauntings continued after the home was turned into a restaurant in 1959. In 1964, one guest had near hysterics after looking into Genevive's gilded fun-house mirror and seeing the troubled woman's reflection standing next to her own, hair pulled into the brandy-maker's trademark bun. The woman identified Genevive from photos.

One guest also reported seeing the old philanderer himself, J. W., riding in the elevator one day. The current owners of the inn, Schelde Enterprises, are accepting and almost protective of their (usually) unseen guest, and ask those who encounter Genevive's shade to "be kind, for she has surrendered to an eternity of discontent and sorrow." We guess a little kindness thrown her way couldn't hurt.

Ashtrays Fly

According to area ghost hunters, if you go into the old section of the Amway Grand Plaza Hotel in Grand Rapids, there is an area where items such as ashtrays will move around by themselves. Truthfully, when *Weird Michigan* was there, the place was quiet and stately, with all decorations seemingly nailed down, but then it was a Sunday morning and far past most witching hours. However, the place definitely has a spooky and historic atmosphere, and you have to believe that with all the soap salespeople who have stayed there, at least a few must have been tormented enough by not making their monthly quota to leave behind some poltergeist angst. Knowing Amway, they are bound to have at least one product guaranteed to wash ghosts away, however.

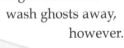

Rowdy Ghosts

The Fenton Hotel, a former inn turned gourmet restaurant in the small mid-state town of Fenton, is an establishment that prides itself on hanging on to things from its historic past. All the original tin ceilings still adorn the dining room, and the foyer looks much as it did back in stagecoach days. Hints of the second story's glory days still exist in its tile-floor ballroom, the communal men's and women's bathrooms, and the dingy corner room once reserved for Emery, the place's late, longtime custodian. But the old brick building retains something far beyond old chairs and ancient porcelain fixtures in its aging halls.

Many people say the Fenton Hotel still hosts Emery himself, along with an entire cast of ghostly hangers-on. People can hear Emery walking around in his former upstairs digs, his footsteps reverberating in the tin ceiling. Sometimes he thumps on the walls after customers leave, as if to tell the staff to get a move on. But Emery was a gentleman, say staff members at the Fenton. That's how they know it's some other ghost that sometimes gropes the arms or buttocks of unsuspecting waitresses.

And there are other spooks here, each with his or her unique "signature" activity. The restaurant hostess told *Weird Michigan* in hushed tones that the incidents are no passing fantasies. "Things are still going on," she said ominously as she seated us at one of the green linen–covered tables.

Built in 1856, the Fenton boasts its own official state historical marker, which explains why the interior is still much the same as it was in the past, although the exterior's old front porch fell victim to a team of runaway horses in 1904. The side of the building that faces the parking lot is embellished with paintings of ghostly inhabitants from another time, which only adds to the feeling of having stepped back into an earlier century.

The bar area off the foyer is probably the building's hottest ghost spot. A bartender named Brittany told us that she has heard someone call her name when no one else was in the room and felt something brush her leg. On several occasions, customers have told her they saw someone hugging her at a time when she could see or feel no one.

Besides the phantom cuddler, there is the recurring case of the mysterious man at table 32. Every now and then a man seated there will order a shot of Jack Daniels on the rocks, and the bartender will duly pour one, but upon attempting to serve it to the customer, finds nothing but thin air. Speculation is that one of the house ghosts wants a drink badly enough to show himself and order one, but lacks the throat to gulp it down. So he just skulks off.

Weird Michigan was given a guided tour of the closed upper level, which generally is not allowed, since it is used now only for storage. We didn't see anything unusual; even Emery's small, cold room was quiet, although we couldn't help but wonder if the old custodian was upset at our intrusion. But while standing in the darkened hallway, one of us heard a female voice whispering close by, a voice we could not explain. Strangest of all was the fact that after we descended the stairs, we found a small glob of melted candle wax near the viewfinder on our digital camera. There was no candle on our dining-room table, and we saw none on the second floor. The wax globule was not there earlier while we were shooting other pictures. Perhaps one of the old hotel guests was examining us at closer range than we realized, using the lighting methods available in 1856! Or maybe someone was trying to tell us not to look at the upper-story inhabitants through that viewfinder.

According to a hotel brochure, several séances have been performed on the premises, but the ghosts seem determined to stay. Perhaps for them, the Fenton Hotel is like the Eagles' hit song "Hotel California": *You can check out any time you'd like, but you can never leave.*

How May I Haunt You?

Audrey and Jason are only two of the purported spirits hanging out at the Osceola Inn in Reed City, a burg more widely known as the hometown of the Reverend George Bennard, who wrote the popular hymn "The Old Rugged Cross." (There is a cross memorial and museum just outside town.) But the block-long hotel and restaurant, closed for renovation at this writing, has attracted its own media attention after hosting teams of paranormal investigators who hoped to get to the bottom of long-told rumors about the place.

So how do we know the ghosts have names? According to a July 2005 *Cadillac News* story by reporter Mardi Suhs, paranormal investigator Michelle Hajdu was conducting an investigation at the inn when she captured a male voice on a camcorder declaring, "My name is Jason." No males were in the room at the time, and a separate story on the incident reported that the voice also registered on a second investigator's camcorder. Audrey's unseen presence had been grist for the local ghost rumor mill for decades.

Hajdu and her group of investigators were joined by clinical psychologist and ghost hunter Timothy Hunt on an overnight surveillance of the inn, using various electronic monitors including infrared thermometers and computer systems engineered to gauge a range of energy fields. Hajdu had interviewed skittish inn employees before the hotel closed, the article said, and she told Suhs that the lobby used to bear a sign instructing guests "to report any and all ghost activity to the front desk."

In Suhs's follow-up article, she revealed that the inn's general manager, Bruce Krouse, had heard a mysterious voice on the building's loudspeaker and that he had witnessed other strange phenomena such as doors being opened and closed by unseen hands. And when investigator Hunt first peered into the building's windows, he saw a white, wraithlike figure waft through a first-floor room. The group affirmed that their electronic readings also showed likely ghostly activity. No word on whether the spirits will be ready for the new clientele when the remodeling is complete.

Nashville's Haunted Library

The Putnam Library in Nashville, about ten miles south of Lake Odessa, was the site of a particularly tragic suicide in the 1930s when a doctor suffering from tuberculosis killed himself there. The red brick, white-shuttered building was used as a residence at that time. But the place has been haunted ever since, say Nashvillians in the know.

Kalamazoo Regional Psychiatric Hospital

There's nothing like a mental hospital to bring on troubled spirits. The old building on Oakland and Howard has it all: noises, lights, mysterious writing appearing on the walls by an unseen hand, and, of course, ghostly forms. Only a portion remains of the former vast hospital grounds, one building with a classic 1895 Queen Anne water tower, a 175-foot-tall landmark.

In the asylum's beginning days, a typical patient might have been someone like the unfortunate teen in the following 1875 excerpt from the *Fowlerville Review*:

> Miss Minnie Kylestorm, a young lady 17 years old, who has been living with her sister at Muskegon for two years past, has been taken to the asylum at Kalamazoo. At the time of the Peshtigo fire she saw her mother, a sister, aged 18, and two brothers, one 22 and the other 9 years old, burned to death, and only escaped the terrible death by clinging to a lumber raft and diving under the water when the heat became too intense. She has since been insane.

—From the Mardos Memorial Library of On-line Books & Maps at www.memoriallibrary.com

Spirits of Ishpeming

A little boy in blue pajamas haunts an old green house near the downtown area of this Upper Peninsula city. There are also supposed to be many leftover spirits from the Indian burial ground the town is built upon, as well as not-quite-departed miners from the days when gold was struck nearby and the town was inundated with brawling gold-rushers. These spirits are said to wreak periodic havoc on the town's electrical and phone systems, showing up in darkened streets and alleyways as faintly glowing figures bent on electromagnetic mischief.

Old Veterans Home

The beautifully wooded grounds of this old hospital on the north side of Grand Rapids are said to literally crawl with wounded ghosts of old Civil War veterans. They've been reported peeking from the woods and windows, spooking motorists who drive by at night.

The Haunted Hamilton House

It was 1986 when an intrepid small-town reporter went out canvassing the historic village of Tecumseh for some good Halloween ghost stories. Nancy Niemann wasn't disappointed. She finally coaxed area residents into telling tales about one of the town's stately old Victorians.

Known as the Hamilton House for the doctor who built it in 1840, the place had developed a reputation for people moving in and then almost as quickly posting a FOR SALE sign. Niemann interviewed the owners at the time, Chuck and Margaret Gross, who had good-humoredly nicknamed their resident ghost Dr. Hamilton. Although the Grosses didn't know of any traumatic event that had transpired there other than a chimney fire, they've experienced all the typical signs of a haunting: lights that go on and off, footsteps in the attic, and even the annoying sounds of a spectral hound scratching on the other side of the basement door to be let in. A former resident also said that books would tumble unaided from their shelves. Scariest was the fact that the Grosses had found a huge ice pick fastened over the basement door, as if in readiness for whatever wicked thing might be coming their way through it.

Hamilton House

Weird Michigan Sees Basement Billy!

Weird Michigan was minding its own business, hunting down the haunted Ramsdell Theater in the quaint tourist town of Manistee, when an even more spectacularly haunted place fell into our metaphorical lap. Directed to the old brick Baur building at the head of the town's main street by the knowledgeable emperor of Manistee's downtown museum, we stepped into Port City Organics, a health food store that occupies half the building at 319/321 River Street. There we were introduced by the store's owners to landlords Don and Darlene Van de Weele.

Darlene and Don, who lived in the now vacant upstairs apartment for six years, have come to accept as coresidents the three entities who make themselves known from time to time. The three are thought to be the son and two daughters of early Manistee residents Joseph and Anna Baur. The Baurs constructed the building to be used as a saloon around 1890, and some of their children apparently have had difficulty with the concept of closing time.

The large Baur family lived in a stately Victorian home (now torn down) across the street, but two of the older sisters, Nona and Rose, were given the apartment above the bar. Word on the street is that Nona and Rose were entrepreneurs of the evening, taking advantage of the tavern clientele to offer their own very private services. They surveyed the crowd from a special platform built behind a giant painting of the coast of Norway that is recessed into the upper wall of what was once the

tavern's bar area. The painting's dominant feature is a large lighthouse with cutouts in the windows of the tower, and the sisters were able to peep through them to see the bar's customers.

Weird Michigan asked Darlene if it would be possible to turn a light on behind the windows, and she replied that it would, if someone were to go upstairs and flip the switch in the platform room, but somehow no one got around to doing it. And yet, in one of our photos of the painting, the windows were lit anyway! In a second photo taken only moments later, they were back to the unlit appearance. Were Nona and Rose listening and playing?

Both Don and Darlene have witnessed the filmy figure of Nona in a white, "wedding-type" dress floating in their

Baur building owner Darlene Van de Weele stands in the basement where Billy's ghost often appears

bedroom. They recognized her from an old photo from the local historical society. Nona died tragically in the apartment on March 30, 1902, from appendicitis. She was only twenty-three years old. Former residents of that apartment have also seen a ghost that they were able to identify as the other sister, Rose.

The most mischievous of the ghosts, however, is probably the one Darlene believes is brother Billy, born John Baur. Darlene thinks Billy has resided in the low-ceilinged, dirt-floor basement since his death in January 1895. He hides in the unlit corners that probably once stored casks of alcoholic beverages. *Weird Michigan* was able to explore the unremodeled basement, which is mostly empty now, except for a few storage boxes and an old iron fence gate.

According to one obituary, Billy died of typhoid fever at the age of twenty-one.

Darlene says she has at times "felt" him following her back up the basement stairs, and she pointed to a light fixture in the upstairs room adjoining the staircase. "Billy keeps unscrewing that light globe so it crashes to the floor and breaks; we've had to replace it about five times," she said.

While we were examining the dirt-floor basement, both Darlene and I suddenly began feeling chills and goose bumps, which ghost hunters claim are sure signs that a spirit is hovering nearby. Darlene was confident that Billy is harmless, so she turned off the few tiny ceiling lights, and we waited in pitch-blackness for a few minutes to see if he would show himself. It's rare to actually experience ghostly phenomena on this type of investigation, so I wasn't expecting much. But in only a few minutes, I could see a white, semi-triangular form hovering near the ceiling on the right side of the musty room, near a duct covered in brown insulation paper. It was slightly transparent, about the size of a basketball with wings, and emitting a soft glow in the darkness. I was shocked, and I looked quickly away and glanced back again to see if my eyes were playing tricks. The form was still there, even brighter. It persisted for a few more long seconds, then slowly faded.

Darlene had said nothing through all this, but when I quietly asked her if she saw anything, she said she had seen the form of Billy smiling at us! Upon turning the lights back on, we examined the place where the white form appeared and could find no light or power source or even a reflective surface to explain it. It seemed like a good time to run back up the stairs.

Strangely, one of the photos we took of Billy's "corner" featured several orbs, or circular light areas, and inside one of the orbs appears what looks like the smiling face of a young person. "We've given him and the ladies permission to stay or to leave us," said Darlene. "But we don't ever want them to leave us. We love you, Billy," she added softly in the general direction of Billy's corner before following *Weird Michigan* back up the narrow wooden steps.

Cemetery
Safari

The pizza commercial that asks, "What do you want on your Tombstone?" poses an interesting question. Tombstones—the kind made of granite rather than mozzarella—are pretty much a person's last chance for self-expression in this world. *Weird Michigan* trudged through many a cemetery in search of strangeness engraved in stone, and we found plenty of it, left by those who just had to have the final eccentric say on their lives.

Of course, along the way, we also encountered the tattered, blood-soaked legends and stories attached to so many old Michigan cemeteries. Ghost hunters often declare that cemeteries are the least likely place to encounter ghosts, because spirits like to hang around the living. Some of our correspondents beg to differ. At midnight, while we wander among crumbling grave markers from past centuries, the legends that walk hand-in-bony-hand with our imagination come to life all too easily.

Here we respectfully offer the choicest of Michigan's bizarre burials. And we do mean respectfully. We always keep in mind, and hope readers do too, that even the oddest of graves is a place held sacred by someone. The living must obey cemetery rules . . . it's only the spirits who have free rein among the tombs!

A Haunted House with Its Own Cemetery

South of Bond Street in Niles stands the Beeson Mansion, a beautiful Greek Revival construction said to be haunted by the ghost of a long-dead child. If so, the baby ghost doesn't have far to travel from its final resting place. It can simply waft its way from across the street where, enclosed by a low stone fence, the old family crypt of the Beeson-Brownfield clan still stands as a private cemetery.

Originally built by a whiskey distiller who deposited one of his company's bottles in the home's cornerstone, the house was later purchased by lawyer Strother Beeson. Beeson had a grandson, Job Withrow Beeson, who was born in 1869 and died a year later. The parents, William and Harriet Beeson, were overcome with grief, of course. But they didn't need to look for a place to bury their little boy. Strother Beeson had already erected a tomb across the street, where he had laid his

mother, Judith, to rest. His infant grandson was soon interred in the mausoleum as well. The ornate little crypt was lined with fine marble, and the surrounding area was groomed and planted like a park, with urns full of flowers.

But watchful neighbors concluded that Harriet Beeson never came to terms with her grief. They said that the child's mother visited the crypt every night, removed the infant from its casket, and fed, bathed, and even diapered the lifeless body. And since he was afraid of the dark, she began leaving a lit lantern inside the crypt so he wouldn't be scared when she finally had to leave him each night.

According to legend, the young mother kept up her ritual of feeding and rocking the baby until one horrifying night when the shriveled eyes fell out of the tiny corpse's head. The shock was supposedly so great that the mother never recovered and was eventually institutionalized.

Relatives of the family have disputed the legend that Harriet actually took the baby's body out to care for it and that she "lost her mind." Whatever the facts about her mourning, Harriet died young, at age twenty-eight, and rests in the tomb alongside her baby. The mansion is also supposed to be haunted by the sobbing ghost of a little girl, although there is no record of a young female dying there. The home and cemetery are private, no trespassing allowed, but can be seen easily from the road.

The Silverbrook Witch

Also in Niles is a cemetery with a beautiful old, wrought-iron arched gateway, called Silverbrook. A witch is said to be buried there, although the location of her grave is unknown. If you happen to be there at the right hour of the night, the story goes, her screams reverberate through the chapel at the center of the cemetery.

Stairway to Hell

The Stairway to Hell is in Lake Forest Cemetery in Grand Haven, near the Civil War burial section. The legend goes that when a person is buried in that cemetery (and there are over 22,000 graves currently), the soul of that person goes to the bottom of the stairway. The "person" then walks up the stairway. As they approach the top, if they are meant to go to heaven, a beautiful white light will appear: the "doorway" to heaven. If the soul gets to the top and a white light never appears, they are doomed to turn around and walk back down, knowing that hell is waiting for them at the bottom. The stairway itself is paranormally active. Unexplained geomagnetic disturbances and temperature drops have been recorded on it.–*Nicole Bray*

Phantom Car Spooks Visitors

My partner and I drove through Coldwater Cemetery just before dark. There is only one road in, but behind the cemetery is a hotel and a path that leads to the back of it. Someone in a red truck was doing their last call, making sure everyone was out of there by 10. So we parked in the lot for the hotel, and walked in the back way of the cemetery. That way we could see if anyone was coming since there was only one way in (by car). I set up my camcorder and turned on my tape recorder and we walked the whole length of the cemetery. No one came in, and we didn't see a car or anyone walking.

Now we're up front and we see the one road where you can come in by car. We start to take pics around the gazebo towards the road, and we were heading towards the back again. All of a sudden we turned around to take more pics, and a car with parking lights was in the very back of the cemetery—no way could it have been there, as we would have seen it. They only had parking lights on, but then I looked at the car and in slow motion, I got extremely scared, sick to my stomach and was in a panic. Now there was no reason for it. The car wasn't a cop car, it looked like something from the '70s to me. And most of the time when you get caught in a cemetery they just tell you to leave.

Then I got what seemed like a vision—it said to get out of there, 'cause if I went up to this car or opened the door no one would be driving. For the first time in my life, I ran. I was in total fear and I ran. And the weird thing is that they didn't come after us. Still, let me tell you, I never ran so fast in my life. I fell and did something bad to my knee. But even that didn't stop me, because I was so scared that whoever was in the car was not what I call human—it was a spirit of sorts.

We walked back to the parking lot of the hotel, wondering how a car came in there. There's only the one

road and we didn't see a car come in. Keep in mind my camcorder was on the road. Well, my partner wasn't satisfied and wanted to go back in to see the car and who it may have been. So I told him, go ahead, I can't walk anymore. Well, off he goes and no one was there, no car, nobody walking around, nothing.

Well, that was enough for me! I knew right then that that car was not what we call "real." We watched the camcorder and no one came in—no cars, no nothing. So to eliminate every other possibility of what it could have been, I called the caretaker and asked if he has anyone patrol the cemetery at night, and he doesn't. I called the police and asked if they patrol at night at anytime. They thought I was nuts, because they laughed and said, "There's no way we're taking a car off the streets to patrol a cemetery!" I know what my vision was and I know I was more scared than I've ever been before.—*Julianna Williams Pluff*

The Green Lady, Comstock Park

Our organization (Grand Rapids Area Paranormal Enthusiasts) has received many emails telling us about an apparition of a woman in a green Victorian-style dress, observed kneeling and weeping at the grave of a child, in the Mill Creek Cemetery (a.k.a. Lamoreaux Cemetery). She is lovingly named the Green Lady. I have looked everywhere and I am not able to come up with anything on her or this cemetery.

I must add that this cemetery is a unique one. It's hidden from view, and there is no road in to it, only old stone stairs up a hill. It is very overgrown. Once inside the cemetery, there are graves in the side of the hill, scattered way into the woods, in some very odd places. It is not a large cemetery. I was told that it was abandoned, but the grass has been mowed at the top of the hill, and a couple of gravesites have been kept up, but everything else is very much overgrown. We did locate a grave of a child all by itself. I wonder if that is the one she is supposedly seen kneeling by? The cemetery itself is not marked at all, no signs or anything.–*Dave, Grand Rapids Area Paranormal Enthusiasts (G.R.A.P.E.)*

A Young Man Vanishes

In August of 2004, I was driving home from a paranormal investigation in Grand Rapids on M-104, just outside Nunica Cemetery. I was driving up to the cemetery when I spotted a young man walking up the side of the road, near the entrance. Just before I got to the cemetery, the man turned to the left and started to cross the highway. I was sure I was going to hit him, but when he got into the middle of my lane, he vanished. Seeing as how I am a ghost hunter and used to these types of experiences, it didn't freak me out. I just figured that it was either a resident of Nunica Cemetery or a victim of the many traffic deaths that have happened near there through the years.–*Nicole Bray*

Little Mary McNaughton

According to old records, in the spring of 1892 three of Mary McNaughton's sisters were stricken with diphtheria in Jackson but recovered. During that summer, the McNaughton family went to nearby Brighton to escape the typhoid and diphtheria in their own town. It was during that carefree family vacation that Mary died of peritonitis. The date was July 18, 1892, and little Mary was only seven years old.

She was brought home to Jackson and buried in the family cemetery, now Hillcrest Memorial Cemetery. The story goes that Mary's mother awoke screaming from a nightmare soon after her burial. Sweet little Mary was alive, she was sure!

To calm the distraught mother, Mary's grave was opened. Sadly, the small coffin was found to contain Mary's dead body and scratches on the inside of the lid. Had Mary been buried alive?

Some say she walks the cemetery and adjacent woods searching for someone to play with. During our own search for Mary's grave as dusk fast approached (and feeling rather foolish) we asked Mary to show herself. Speaking her name aloud in the cemetery made us instantly uneasy and we snapped several pictures of our surroundings and left. Imagine our surprise when we uploaded our pictures and found what appears to be a ghostly little girl coming towards us!–*Kelly*

Still Clawing Her Way from the Tomb

My first memory of hearing of Little Mary McNaughton was when I was around 6. My mother and grandmother were talking about it, and if I remember correctly, my grandmother had written to the *Jackson Citizen Patriot* regarding Little Mary. The story goes:

There was a little girl/young woman named Mary who was buried alive, sometime in the 1950s. She awoke after several days and scratched her way out of her grave, but really did die before anyone could discover her. She was reburied, same plot, a few days later, but every night can be heard trying to claw her way back out of her grave in Hillcrest Cemetery on Elm Street.

This of course became THE place to take a girl to scare her, or to show-off how brave you were. A lot of people took to vandalizing her headstone and the cemetery in general. Supposedly, Little Mary was moved to another location in an unmarked grave. My grandmother was pretty upset by the whole ordeal and had offered to help pay for the expenses.

I have never myself encountered the scratching of Little Mary there, but I have been chased out . . . er, scared out, of there by barking that got closer and closer yet never manifested as a dog in any form.–*Carrie in Jackson*

Eunice White's Journey

Every year the ghost of Eunice White is said to float down Reynolds Street in Jackson on its way to the cemetery, and the grave she seeks is that of her murdered father, Jacob Crouch. The crime dates back to 1883, when a massacre occurred in the Crouch farmhouse during a thundering electrical storm. When the storm had passed, the Crouch family was discovered shot in their beds by an unknown killer. The dead included seventy-four-year-old Jacob, the pregnant nineteen-year-old Eunice, her husband Henry, and a twenty-four-year-old guest named Moses Polley. Someone evidently had a vendetta against the Crouch family, because within months, Susan Halcomb, Crouch's surviving daughter, was also killed by forced ingestion of poison, and soon after, her husband and even the hired man, James Fay, were murdered. No one was ever convicted for any of the deaths. No motive was ever uncovered. It seemed a senseless tragedy.

The family did not all wind up in the same cemetery, however, and that is why each year on the eve of the mass murder, Eunice rises from her grave in St. John's Cemetery and travels to the cemetery at the corner of Reynolds and Horton about five miles away. The phenomenon was first noticed in 1884, and some residents of Jackson claim it continues to this day.

Reynolds Cemetery Glowing Mist

We've been to Reynolds Cemetery several times and it is a bit eerie. On the eve of November 21 it is said that the ghosts of a murdered father and daughter reunite in the very small, secluded cemetery. Also, in 1989 two ghost researchers insisted they saw an ectoplasmic cloud appear in the cemetery on Nov. 21–22. The glowing mist floated through the cemetery until it reached Jacob's Grave, where it suddenly vanished. Now, many people gather and keep watch. The last few years we went there on Nov. 21, there were probably a dozen people at any given time.—*Kelly and Shawna Loe*

Werewolf of Elmwood Cemetery

Put together a century and a half of burials, over 54,000 graves, and headstones etched with the names of Detroit luminaries such as whiskey distiller Hiram Walker and seven Michigan governors, and you have the perfect recipe for a legends cocktail. Adding to the dark mystery of Elmwood Cemetery is the Gothic chapel at its entrance.

The centerpiece of the cemetery's parklike design is the winding Parent Creek, also called Bloody Run for a gruesome battle that took place here between the Pontiac Indians and the British in 1763. As a result, the ghosts of slain Native Americans and Redcoats alike are said to roam the old creek bed to this day.

The cemetery's most publicized spookiness, however, probably came in 1939, when the mournful howling sounds of the *loup-garou,* or werewolf, were heard by neighbors of both Elmwood and the adjacent Mt. Elliot cemeteries. No one had actually seen the creature, but the fact that there was howling late at night in a graveyard . . . what else could it be but the fearsome shape-shifter that haunted Detroit in its earliest, French–Canadian–influenced days?

Well, try an escaped police dog. To the relief of area residents but the chagrin of die-hard *loup-garou* fans, the noises were found to be the wailing of a mutt that had ditched its job at the local precinct and fled to the relative wilds of the two cemeteries. Although it hid for some time in a tunnel it had clawed into the earth between the cemeteries, the beleaguered beast was eventually captured and died soon after. Whether it then returned to the cemeteries as an actual haunt-hound remains unknown.

Harrison Cemetery's Glowing Tombstone

Granted, it was hazy daylight when *Weird Michigan* went looking for a glow-in-the-dark tombstone at Harrison Cemetery in Schoolcraft, but the place still exuded a creepy aura. Those who have been there at night say that one of the tombstones has a glow that can be seen from a distance, but fades as soon as anyone comes within five hundred yards of the cemetery. Once inside, it is said to be impossible to tell which headstone had been illuminated.

Roselawn Thumper

Back in the summer of 1980, I was 16 years old and had recently received my driver's license. Naturally, this was a pinnacle step in the evolution of a Saginaw, Michigan, boy, soon to be a man. On this particularly nice late summer day in 1980, a friend and I had driven into a local cemetery named Roselawn Cemetery, located on M-46 directly across from the subdivision in which we both lived. We had discovered quite quickly that by frequenting the cemetery as opposed to the other local hangouts, we could relax, drink beer, party (quietly, of course), as well as entertain girls without ever being harassed by the local police.

On this particular day, my friend and I had gone into the cemetery to partake of some party essentials. After we had consumed the essentials in question, we proceeded to leave via one of the two roads that lead out of the cemetery. This area of the cemetery is very open, allowing for easy viewing of anything that is around the area. As we were about two-thirds of the way down this road, we heard a tremendous "thump" on top of my car. My friend and I were no strangers to a good confrontation so I slammed on the brakes and we both jumped out of the car.

I had assumed that whatever had hit the roof of my car was some sort of object that had been thrown by someone. Upon exiting the vehicle, I first examined the car for damage; there was no damage. Then I began looking around for the object thrown. To my amazement, there was no object and even more importantly, the distance required to throw an object and hit my car without being seen was at least 200 feet.

My friend and I were talking to each other over the top of the car, discussing the kind of arm required to make such a throw, when an even louder, more violent thump hit the roof. This thump hit with enough force to cause the roof of the car to depress (it popped back up), and was very loud. Since we were both staring at each other and the roof, we could obviously see that nothing had hit the roof. This was very strange, and it did not take long for us to get the hell out of Dodge.

I think about this episode once in awhile and I cannot come up with any explanation for what occurred, other than an explanation involving the paranormal. I am not one to fantasize and jump to conclusions. I always try to explain things scientifically using logic and reason; this incident defies both. It was this experience that opened the door to the unexplained mysteries in this world for me, and I have never looked back. For me, there is absolutely no question whatsoever that disembodied spirits do occupy our space and time, and can make themselves known not only ethereally but physically. –*Joseph Drago*

Dodge Brothers' Egyptian Mausoleum

Although they weren't Egyptian, Horace Elgin Dodge and John Francis Dodge got a sphinx apiece on their flamboyant, temple-inspired mausoleum in Woodland Cemetery in Detroit. Outsiders to the more established muckety-mucks of Detroit society, the Dodge brothers were nonetheless able to use their wealth to ensure a mausoleum reminiscent of the final resting places of Egyptian pharaohs. The brothers, although born four years apart, both died in 1920, and their widows became two of the richest women in America after they sold off their deceased husbands' successful auto manufacturing company.

Weeping Statue of Battle Creek

Every Sunday night around midnight (plus on full moons and Halloween) a statue of the Virgin Mary in Battle Creek's Oak Hill Cemetery is said to weep actual tears. The statue does appear to have traces or stains where something liquid has dripped, but some allege the marks have been painted there for effect. According to cemetery officials, there is no plumbing attached to the statue from below.

The statue stands at the family grave grouping for one Johannes Decker, who died in 1910. Many legends and rumors surround the woman buried there, ranging from stories that she committed suicide to more extreme tales claiming she killed her children and so must weep eternally through the eyes of the statue. (Some Internet stories have switched Johannes to Joanna.)

According to a 2004 story from the *Battle Creek Enquirer*, the tales have been in circulation since the 1940s. One cemetery worker told a reporter he believes the tearstains are from rain flowing down the sculptural depressions in the statue's face. Moreover, says the article, the statue is not the Virgin Mary but a Greek goddess!

The Witch's Chair and a Family Mystery

Historic Brookside Cemetery in Tecumseh dates back to 1853, and the parklike graveyard is filled with headstones from settler days. Toward the back of the large cemetery stands a peculiar monument carved from granite in the shape of a comfortable easy chair, known locally as the Witch's Chair. Engraved on the chair's back is the name of a prominent early family, Stacy. Local Tecumseh residents told *Weird Michigan* a woman in the family was rumored to be a witch, "or strange, or something like that." The one fact we did establish is that the old Stacy Mansion, which sits with many other beautiful Victorian-era homes on the town's main thoroughfare, has a very colorful background. A local history book says it was "inspired by an English castle, designed by a Scottish architect, and built on the site of an ancient Indian campground."

The house was commissioned by Tecumseh lawyer Consider Alphonso Stacy and his wife, Mary, in the 1850s. Known around town as the Judge, Stacy was a powerful businessman, ran for Congress unsuccessfully, and was local postmaster. He and Mary belonged to the Universalist church, a denomination considered suspect by more mainstream sects, and raised five children, including one girl, Loanna, who never married but worked in the post office with the Judge.

Perhaps it was Loanna's spinsterhood and the family's affiliation with the Universalists that got tongues wagging with the W word. Many an outbreak of whooping cough or cases of ailing farm animals were attributed to the supposed powers of the postmaster's daughter. At any rate, she outlived both parents and her brothers and lived alone in the giant home for years. And of course when *Weird Michigan* asked at the Tecumseh library if there were any haunted houses in town, the Stacy Mansion was the first one mentioned. Loanna, it seems, still lingers in the family home, roaming the halls at night.

Also located in Brookside is the ornate headstone belonging to the Silvers family, who became notorious in death as one of the town's most tragic and puzzling murder cases. Frank Silvers was involved in the town's budding horse racing business, and as far as anyone could tell, was a successful breeder and trainer. But for some unknown reason, on the morning of February 16, 1889, Silvers bought a new .32-caliber revolver and wrote out directions for his burial, asking for a family monument of black granite.

That night, in his tidy home on the southwest corner of Evans and Cummins streets, he shot his wife, Josephine, and his daughters Edith, eleven, and Ada, nine. Then he turned the gun on himself. Silvers was just forty when he died.

Neighbors found the bodies the next day. Josephine had been shot sitting in her willow rocking chair, and the two little girls were found together "white and cold as marble statues" in one upstairs bed with their father's unconscious body stretched across the end of it. He died that same day. The girls' dolls and school slates and even a letter Edith had recently written to a former classmate named Bertha were described in the local newspaper in touching detail. No furniture was disturbed, said the paper, and sheet music for "The Silver Bell Waltz" was laid out on the piano.

In a letter to two friends, Silvers had written, "Myself and family are going to take a trip, and we wish your assistance in disposing of our earthly possessions." The family had lived modestly and was quite solvent. He ended the letter with the cryptic statement, "You know us as well as anyone, and the whole thing is a mystery. That solves the problem for us all." But as far as the townsfolk could see, nothing had been solved, and it never was. Their black tombstone near the cemetery entrance remains a gruesome reminder of the awful day.

Brake for the Beauty in Westland

Possibly one of the most written-about cemeteries in the state, Butler, or William Ganong, Cemetery is renowned for its hauntings. The main legend is of a literally traffic-stopping blonde beauty in white who appears in the road in front of travelers, causing cars to swerve to avoid hitting her. Some drivers don't make the deadly curve. Tucked next to a schoolyard on Henry Ruff Road in Westland near Detroit, the isolated old graveyard was catapulted into the spotlight in 1980 when a well-known area psychic, the late Marion Kuclo, paid the place a visit.

Kuclo, also known by her Wicca name of Gundella, claimed to be descended from the Green Witches of Scotland. She wrote in her book, *Michigan Haunts and Hauntings*, that as she strolled through the vine-entangled gravestones one day, she thought that she spied a blonde wig lying on the ground. Walking nearer, she was horrified to discover that it was a human scalp, complete with strawberry-blonde tresses. She could also see a human bone sticking up through the earth and, nearby, pieces of an old coffin neatly stacked in a pile. Bits of what may have been either a white satin dress or a coffin lining lay about. There was a crumbled headstone on which the only name legible was Alice.

The police declared it a case of animals digging up a grave, but Gundella didn't believe that, having seen the neatly stacked boards. Other accounts claimed that rain had washed the coffin out of its burial place. Whatever the reason for the disturbance of Alice's remains, it seemed to set off a series of sightings of a beautiful blonde lady in white. Not long after Gundella's grisly discovery, a driver was killed when he veered off the road just outside the cemetery, on what is now called the Bad Curve, pouring more fuel on the rumors.

And the strangeness continues. Investigators still report hearing unearthly screams in the cemetery at night, with a high incidence of phenomena showing up on audio and video recordings. Is Alice unhappy? The best advice is to take your time when passing William Ganong at night on the Bad Curve and be ready to brake for transparent blondes.

Magician's Cemetery, Colon

Swirling capes, black silk hats, puffs of smoke, and ladies in skimpy costumes banished to dimensions unknown—the images of the stage magician are designed to captivate and confound. As supreme manipulators of assorted props, magicians may appear to cheat death, but even they need someplace to go at the end of the road show.

Such a place is the world capital of magical illusion, a tiny town in St. Joseph County with the unlikely name of Colon. For years, Colon has gained fame as a gathering place for magicians, all drawn there after the legendary Harry Blackstone made it his summer home. Others expanded the local tradition with a well-known magic store and annual festival.

But not only does Colon still attract live magicians, it lays claim to a permanent festival of dead ones too. Twenty-some deceased masters of prestidigitation are assembled for all eternity in the town's Lakeside Cemetery.

Their tombstones reflect their playful attitudes, each former entertainer enclosed within the one box from which no daring escape can be made. Harry Blackstone and his son, Harry Junior, are memorialized with a family stone in the shape of an eternal flame. Harry Senior, who was born in nearby Three Rivers, became famous for tricks such as the woman sawed in half by a buzz saw, the dancing handkerchief, and the floating lightbulb. He was greatly honored by his peers and wrote three books on magic, including the classic *There's One Born Every Minute*. His son followed in his dad's footsteps, continuing the act after Harry Senior passed away in 1965. Harry Junior died May 14, 1997. The pair were considered classical magicians, purists who scorned both Siegfried & Roy–type glitz and showy pop star trappings.

But other talented adepts lie here too. A headstone featuring an engraving of a hand with four billiard balls stuck between the fingers belongs to Bill "The Magnificent Fraud" Baird, who became known for his ability to pop objects in and out of view of the audience. The annual Abbott's Magic Convention gives an award in his name every year to the magician who shows the most skill at this type of trick.

Then there is the memorial block of juggler Fred Merrill, enlivened with a depiction of the batons he once whirled to the amazement of crowds across the country. Nearby is the headstone of comedian Ricki Dunn, "America's Greatest Pickpocket." The epitaph under his engraved caricature reads RICKI DUNN WAS A THIEF. Dunn was noted for an act in which he would neatly rob unsuspecting audience members of various possessions while they remained clueless.

Karrell Fox , co-founder of the Abbott's Magic Get Together, chose the words IT WAS FUN for his headstone. Faux conjuror John "Little Johnny" Jones's memorial reads NOW I HAVE TO GO AND FOOL ST. PETER. Lee Michael "Blackbird" Elliott's black granite stone says, eloquently, THE SONG IS ENDED, THE MELODY LINGERS ON, with a treble clef and musical notes to get the point across.

Are the magicians still pulling tricks out in Lakeside Cemetery when the moon is full and shadows enhance every illusion? Not one Colonite admits to having been spooked by any of the cemetery's inhabitants. It's fun to think that somewhere, however, the flamboyant entertainers are all still together, sawing ladies in half and then laughing uproariously because ghost ladies no longer care about keeping their halves connected. And once the memories of the real people buried here have faded from the townspeople's minds, rumors will doubtless begin to circulate about ghostly goings-on at the graves of the magicians in Colon. The place is a legend in the making.

Prison Wall and Binder Twine Plant,
Michigan State Prison,
Jackson, Mich.

Abandoned in Michigan

There's something eerie about an abandoned building. It's like a corpse left to decay by the roadside, bereft of either a proper burial or words of grace to mark its demise. And yet, the places we build to live, work, or worship in—and then suddenly desert—exert a strange attraction for most of us. It's hard not to stare past the CONDEMNED signage and wonder if mysterious clues to the former occupants remain behind the plywood barriers. Or, on the scarier side, whether residual energies from bygone residents may lurk under falling tiles and splintered timbers. "Haunted" and "abandoned" are almost synonymous in ghost lore worldwide.

Unfortunately, as interesting as these places are, their existence can be fragile. Some are crumbling into oblivion. Some may be in danger of undergoing sudden demolition, falling to developers' wreckers. And that's one big reason for this chapter. Somebody has to record these places and the legends that go with them before they vanish entirely. So think of this as your "Abandoned in Michigan" scrapbook. A pastiche of yellowing photos and cryptic notes mined from archives around the state, minus only the spidery handwriting of some long-dead collector of vintage architectural documents. We may abandon all hope, abandon our senses, but God forbid that we should ever abandon our memories of the Michigan that used to be.

Michigan Ghost Towns

Lumber camps and mining towns flourished around Michigan's northern parts in the nineteenth and early twentieth centuries, and their legacy is the large number of ghost towns that now dot the state wherever these two industries once boomed. Some estimates say there are as many as three thousand defunct settlements in Michigan, remembered for names like Killmaster, Podunk, Nonesuch, and Whore's Corner (reportedly a favorite of area lumberjacks). The little town of Seewhy in Chippewa County was named after its pun-loving founder, C. Y. Bennett. And tiny Gay on the Keweenaw Peninsula is famous for its only remaining business, the Gay Bar.

Not every ghost town has ghosts, of course. Fayette in the UP is now a preserved, official historic site in Fayette State Park. Others are little more than overgrown stubs of foundations in places so remote even the withered spirits have flown. Sometimes there is simply nothing left for a ghost to inhabit. Occasionally, the ghosts lurk right under our noses, as in Depot Town, on the campus of Eastern Michigan University in Ypsilanti. People walking through this area often report seeing spirit figures in period dress, presumably the wraiths of those who once lived in the little place named for its railroad depot. The old towns of Mandan and Sheldrake are also widely reputed to be haunted. *Weird Michigan* found them both, tiptoed through their weedy, ramshackle old streets, and lived to tell our tales.

Ticket to Paradise

The old Upper Peninsula village of Sheldrake (or Shelldrake), named after the playful ducks that dominated its shoreline, never was the kind of place to draw attention to itself. Whispered to be haunted for most of a century, it now is not only hard to find but also forbidden to explore, since it sits on private property a few miles north of the village of Paradise. Like many towns in the area, Sheldrake boasts a lake view. Unfortunately, it lacks viewers. Live viewers, that is.

Through sheer coincidence, we ran into one of the heirs to the village, who not only gave us permission to walk around and shoot photos; he also shared the haunted side of its history. Mike Biehl, whose family owns the Sheldrake building known as Hopkins House and most of the other buildings in town, lives in a nearby woodsy subdivision. Hopkins House has been rented out over the years, said Biehl, and many tenants have had "experiences" there.

"One couple staying there had a carousel music box that was not wound up, but it suddenly started going around by itself," he told us. "Another lady woke up in the middle of the night, and there was an Indian standing in the bedroom. He walked in by coming through one wall and walked out another."

The Hopkins House is just one of a row of weather-beaten, simple frame houses that stand facing Lake Michigan along an old gravel drive. The structures are all that remain of a community that once numbered between five hundred and one thousand people. In one house, which belonged to a schoolteacher named Mrs. Strobel, an old doormat with STROBEL'S neatly lettered on it still lies on eroded, gray-patterned linoleum inside the rickety porch. Tattered curtains hang on some of the windows, and although it was obvious the place was empty, we had the feeling unseen eyes were peering at us through the dirty glass. Our instincts were on target. Biehl told us that every afternoon at four p.m., someone knocks on the front door, but no one is ever there. Hmmm . . . four p.m. would be about the time a schoolteacher would return home.

During the 1890s, Sheldrake had several mills that served the many lumber camps busily denuding northern Michigan's forests.

"Another lady woke up in the middle of the night, and there was an Indian standing in the bedroom. He walked in by coming through one wall and walked out another."

The town's future looked promising until the mills burned down about 1916, and then things began to slow considerably. Another big fire in 1925 was the final blow. The remaining residents went to Paradise . . . the village, that is, and the forests reclaimed most of the land the town had once commanded. But perhaps not all the residents have departed. Several locals in the Paradise area have claimed to see unexplained, fast-moving, orange- and yellow-colored lights just over the shoreline on many clear nights.

Two Men Enter; One Man Leaves

Michigan's numerous copper mines left a trove of abandoned tunnels, structures, and equipment behind, and while most of the rotting hulks possess a haunting quality, many are downright legendary. My favorite is the Quincy Dredge #2, located about four tenths of a mile north of Mason on M-26 in Keweenaw Peninsula. It is nearly impossible to miss, sitting almost up on the beach across from the old Quincy stamping mill. The dredge itself is a silent and pretty creepy reminder of the copper mining boom days of the early twentieth century.

This suction dredge, and its predecessor, Quincy Dredge #1, were used to mine copper deposits off the bottom of Torch Lake. During the winter months, the dredges were anchored out in the lake until mining operations continued in the spring. Dredge #1, built in 1913, sank there during the winter of 1956 when its bilge pumps quit working. The slowly leaking hull was overcome by water and settled to the bottom. At the time, copper prices were low, so it was not raised or salvaged, and remains there today. When the water level is down far enough, you can see the roof protruding above the surface far out in the lake.

Dredge #2 was built to replace the sunken Dredge #1, and was used for about ten years before suffering nearly the same fate. Dredge #2 was anchored closer to the shore however, so when it sank during the winter of 1968, about three quarters of it was left standing above water, and still does to this day.

This dredge was also not salvaged, and until recently could be viewed up close. The last time I was there (summer 2004) the property was in the process of being fenced off, more than likely to fend off thrill seekers bent on climbing the thing. It's a massive and intimidating structure, about the size of a three-story house. Over the years, vandals have covered the interior and exterior with graffiti, but other than that, it is completely intact, although NOT structurally sound!

My dad and I used to visit the dredge every year on our annual trips to the Upper Peninsula and take pictures of it. One year, while we were walking around it on the beach, two adventuresome young men got out of their car, began climbing on the dredge, and entered it through one of the upper doorways. Minutes later only one came out, climbed back down, and left! Dad and I always wondered what happened to the second guy!–*Marc Sebright*

Exiled Nobleman's Secret

A few miles west of Kalamazoo lies a small lake named Bonnycastle, although some modern maps misspell it as Bonnie Castle. While it never did have a true castle on its shores, it was once the site of a sumptuous mansion built by a Scottish or English nobleman named Charles Bonnycastle. Obviously a very wealthy man, Bonnycastle arrived suddenly in 1837 and paid a shilling an acre for two hundred and forty acres surrounding the lake, which he then named after himself. Kalamazoo was not much more than a wilderness outpost at the time, and it appeared plain to everyone that the mysterious gentleman from abroad was looking for seclusion.

Huge amounts of goods and provisions were imported, and construction began on an immense house facing the lake. But while Bonnycastle's neighbors were all busy felling trees and creating plowed fields on their land, he merely fenced in his acreage and left the forest pristine. His chief occupation appeared to be hunting and fishing on his American "estate."

Of course, the rumor mill in Kalamazoo worked overtime trying to figure out the secretive man's true situation. He was rich and eligible, yet didn't appear interested in courting any of the local women for companionship in his luxurious home. He would not talk about his family or any part of his history. People concluded that perhaps he had to leave England quickly because he'd been caught in a heated love affair. Others believed he had beaten a hasty retreat after committing some crime.

Before anyone could find out for sure, Bonnycastle disappeared just as suddenly as he had come. A nephew, John H. Bonnycastle, arrived shortly afterward and sold the property. The mansion subsequently burned to the ground. In 1926, an eighty-three-year-old lifelong resident of the lake area told the *Kalamazoo Gazette* that he believed the strange nobleman had squandered his fortune and left because his funds were depleted, but that was never proved.

The newspaper article concluded, "Now nature, ever anxious to reclaim her lost possessions, has covered the shores with a dense wood and time has erased the charred remains of the palatial dwellings—erased the manifestations of a man's sorrow." Leaving Kalamazoo still to puzzle over the origins and exit of Charles Bonnycastle.

Midway Packing

Too bad Midway Packing is long since closed. That was Wayland's old slaughterhouse. It was REALLY creepy! I'm not sure how long it had been in operation, but it had gone out of business by the mid-to late 1980s or so. Supposedly it was forced out of business by the EPA. From what I've been told, the facility used to illegally dump blood and entrails in a cesspool out behind the building. When this became publicly known, it went out of business and sat abandoned for about fifteen years before it was knocked down. A friend of mine in high school and I used to explore that one on a regular basis. You could still get into the stables where the "condemned" animals were kept and everything! Since there was no lighting to speak of, it was pitch-black dark inside even in the middle of the day. A true "gotta check over my shoulder even though I know there's nothing there" kind of place!
—*Marc Sebright*

Jackson Prison: The Long Stone Wall

The rambling State Prison of Southern Michigan in Jackson was once the largest walled institution in the world, its stone ramparts enclosing six acres filled with a variety of buildings. The prison's inmates now "enjoy" a newer structure, on the outskirts of town, but much of the old wall still remains as a landmark in Jackson. Punctuated by a few lone guard towers, these days the wall surrounds only empty yards and city equipment fields. The original prison building has been converted to a National Guard armory, and those who enter the area once used as Death Row report feeling unseen eyes bore into them and hearing muffled, unidentifiable noises in the old hall.

West Wing of Cell Block, Michigan State Prison, Jackson, Mich.

Jackson's role as a prison town originated in 1838 when a wooden enclosure was erected for that purpose on a swamp, which couldn't have been great for the inmates' health. The first permanent prison, with its massive stone wall and cell house, was built in 1842. Its eighty-six prisoners wore classic black-and-white-striped suits and hats. They were chained by their ankles, forbidden to talk to one another, and soon began serving as a very cheap and convenient labor force for local industries. Prisoners weren't the only ones who disliked the massive

Bird's-Eye View, Michigan State Prison, Jackson, Mich.

place. A Jackson citizen wrote this unflattering poem about the prison and its effects on the nearby river in 1904:

> *And where the prison adds its prismy ooze*
> *Which to the fish and frog proves "knock-out booze,"*
> *Full gorged no wonder there the current mopes*
> *Like some poor fool the bland dive-keeper dopes;*
> *While up and down on weeds fermenting lie*
> *The "sewer creams" whose smells refuse to die.*
> (DeLand 1904: 437) from the Ella Sharp History Museum

Overcrowding caused a harrowing riot in 1926, and a new prison enclosing fifty-six acres was built in 1935.

The new building's huge cafeteria, the scene of frequent mayhem, became known as the Bigtop. The prison suffered another huge, four-day riot in 1952 over the prisoners' objections to the penal block known as the Hole.

It's little wonder that escapes were continually attempted. Some who tried to leave by diving onto the trains that passed near the wall fell to their deaths and reportedly still kept on trying in the afterlife.

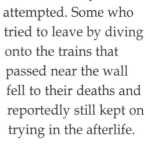

Abandoned Asylums

Every society in human history has shared a common concern—how to regard and treat those among us who are not quite in possession of their mental faculties. Some primitive societies thought of the mentally ill as holy, but for the most part, they have been misunderstood and often subjected to frightful abuses.

In the last quarter century of the 1800s, before we had psychoanalysis and modern drugs, compassionate physicians developed a new way to treat the mentally ill. They were inspired by the vision of Thomas Story Kirkbride, a founder of the American Psychiatric Association. Kirkbride believed that a beautifully landscaped natural setting and buildings full of light and flowers could actually heal these patients by giving them a peaceful place to mend their "disordered" minds. The word "asylum" was chosen for these places because it meant sanctuary, or refuge.

The hospitals that sprang up around the country to implement the new plan spared no expense. Huge acreages were planted and groomed for the most idyllic effects, while living quarters and other structures were built with lavish use of fine wood, artistic metal work, carpets woven in patterns that mimicked nature, and high windows to let in the natural light. Wards were decorated with hanging plants, paintings, and other soothing touches.

This was a big improvement over former options for the mentally ill, but the hospitals had their drawbacks. For one thing, many of the patients were there because of underlying physical causes such as syphilis or cancer. No amount of lovely scenery was going to cure them. Others resented being confined in any way and continually tried to escape. Some were just too far gone to be pleasant companions to anyone and had to be kept in isolation rooms for safety's sake. Naturally, many

unavoidable unpleasant events occurred, and patients died in the asylums from various causes.

With the advance of modern medicine and other living arrangements like group homes, the need for these huge places waned and they began to close one by one. The old brick buildings, tunnels, and other structures were not well suited to other enterprises, and the asylums became the white elephants of the very communities that had once clamored to host them. Trashed by vandals, haunted by every type of desperate spirit, the few remaining hulks have inspired their own peculiar genre of lore and legend. We stopped to pay our regards to a few of the ruins, and to the memories of those who lived and worked in them.

Not All Crazy in Kalamazoo

It's politically incorrect these days, and rightly so, to refer to the residents of psychiatric hospitals as crazies. But the 175-foot-high brick water tower of the old Kalamazoo State Hospital has stood on its hill overlooking the hospital campus since 1895, well before the national sea change in attitudes toward the mentally ill. The hospital, which opened in 1859, was once known popularly as the Insane Asylum (as in the poetry below); hardly surprising, since Oakland Drive, which fronts the huge campus for almost a mile, was then named Asylum Avenue and the institution's original title was the Michigan Asylum for the Insane.

According to one local historian, this hospital was a great improvement for southern Michigan's insane, who previously were locked in jail, hidden in attics, or even banished to hog pens. But the hospital had its dark moments. In 1904, a resident stabbed a doctor to death. In 1954, another resident, eighteen-year-old Louis Smith, killed a young nursing student, Marilyn Kraii. Some patients also died violently. And of course, these incidents always fueled the legend machine. People expect ghosts to result from that kind of troubled scenario.

The old hospital's crenellated, castlelike tower is still a city landmark, although its tanks are no longer in use. It is the only remaining structure of the original buildings, and it and a few of the older buildings are reputed to house hosts of ghosts. Visitors and workers over the years have witnessed mysterious lights, watched writing appear on a wall from an unseen hand, heard strange noises, and observed numerous misty forms waft through the old halls. Some say that as long as the tower stands, the ghosts will keep their connection to the place and continue to appear. And landmark that it is, the grand old tower is not going anyplace soon.

> The Michigan Insane Asylum
> Is up on the top of the hill,
> And some irresponsible crazies
> Meander around there at will,
> And they frequently talk to a stranger,
> And they sometimes escape, it is true,
> But the folks are not all of them crazy
> Who hail from Kalamazoo.
> —J. B. Smiley, 1886 or 1888

The Asylum Named for a Postman's Daughter

For over one hundred and fifty years, the Wayne County Infirmary, Psychiatric, and General Hospital Complex, known collectively as Eloise, served thousands of metropolitan Detroit's needy, diseased, and mentally ill. Throughout that time, the facility grew to seventy-five buildings and then was reduced to four. The mystery surrounding the grounds has intrigued many.

Eloise came to be the infamous name of the institution in the 1890s after a post office branch was established on the grounds. The name Eloise was submitted as a last resort after the postmaster general in Washington had rejected all others. She was the four-year-old daughter of Freeman B. Dickerson, the postmaster of Detroit and the president of the governing board. The name was finally chosen, and a U.S. post office was established on the grounds under the name Eloise. You can still see Eloise, frozen in time as a young child with her St. Bernard, hanging in the front lobby of the old D building, now known as the Kay Beard.

Many a lost soul is said to haunt the grounds surrounding the four remaining buildings. A cemetery sits virtually unnoticed across Michigan Avenue. Here many of the poor and those without family to claim them have been buried, without a name, just a numbered plot marker. Medical and death records have been lost over time, and because the buildings were demolished, the names of the cemetery's occupants will most likely never be revealed.

Most of Eloise was abandoned in the late 1970s. That left it as prime ground for area teens looking for a thrill. The Eloise tunnel system, where staff members transported patients from building to building, has been rumored to house medical waste and other strange items from a bygone era in medical science. A golf course exists today above where these tunnels once ran.

Explorers were rumored to have discovered jars of human body parts, documents outlining strange medical procedures, and creepy snapshots of patients in the abandoned buildings that were torn down in the 1980s. More recently, a spectral woman wearing white has been rumored to be seen in the upper floors and on the roof of the old D building, which now houses government offices—though all but the first floor is off-limits to the public. Some have reported hearing strange moans, screams, and roars on the old grounds.

My husband and I were exploring the ruins of two buildings that were part of the women's insane hospital in a small wooded area by the Rouge River when we encountered a strange black form. We had just discovered another large sewer grate that had the words ELOISE HOSPITAL boldly stamped into the metal, when my husband noticed a figure behind the shopping complex on the other side of a large trench that was enclosed by a chain-link fence. We both ducked down, as we were out in the open at this point, thinking it was an employee taking a smoking break. We quickly learned otherwise. Its movements were so fluid that it obviously was not running. This figure seemed to float above the ground, moving quickly and quietly in the darkness before disappearing down the side of a small hill. It made the hair on the backs of our necks stand up.

Perhaps the most intriguing thing about Eloise is what we do not know and what we may never know. What was done to the people who were sent there for care and kindness will most likely never be known, and we can only begin to imagine some of the horrors they faced.

There is definitely an impression on the grounds that stems from so many memories of suffering and death. If you listen hard enough, you can hear the stories and feel the emotions that took place so long ago. They want to be heard and felt.—*Erin Derry*

Exploring an Asylum Called Eloise

I live in the downriver area of Michigan, but the asylum in which the story takes place is in Westland. The place was called Eloise, named after the founding physician's daughter. The whole area of Westland had once been a city that housed not only the insane but also the poor who had terminal conditions and couldn't afford to seek the more expensive care they needed. It is said that back in the early 20th century diseases such as TB were highly unresearched and caused the affected people to behave in such a way they were thought to be insane.

By the time I was in my teenage "I want to be scared" stage, there were only three dilapidated buildings left standing on the hospital side of Michigan Ave. The piggery, cannery and train depot were left on the farm side of the avenue.

My friends and I were very taken with the buildings and had toured them many a late night. We always contained a sense of well being upon entering and though we had seen many cops patrolling the area, they had never seen us and we were never caught.

Upon entering the first of the many steel doors in the back area of the Old Hospital building itself you could either go directly downstairs or directly up. We chose to go down first. In the ruined basement our flashlights played upon five-foot tall metal crib-like enclosures and a metal straight-backed chair with leather straps on the armrests and legs. Turning an immediate right you faced the morgue, complete with pull out drawers and metal table with leather padding.

One other room in the basement we found disturbing; we were never sure what it would have been called. The room was about 8 by 6 and along the left side there was a cell with a swinging door leaving just enough room to walk. Contained in the cell was a metal cot bolted to the wall and a place where the toilet had once been. When the cell door suddenly slammed behind me as I searched I quickly ran out.

My friends and I also searched the farm side of the area and entered first the piggery, complete with ton scale, meat hooks, and 10 x 10 coolers. The cannery had lost all resonance of its former use and looked as if it had most recently been a file storage area.

Though now all but two of the buildings are gone forever the place still gives off an eerie feeling as you drive past the lone sentry, the smoke stack, on which is still clearly printed ELOISE.—*Nite Wolfe*

Northern Michigan Asylum

If walls could talk, building 50 at Traverse City's Northern Michigan Asylum (later called the Traverse City State Hospital) would be a veritable Tower of Babel. The old building is a thousand feet long, after all. And what its walls would have to say would probably be difficult for most people to hear.

It's a tribute to the citizens of Traverse City that this four-hundred-thousand-square-foot, 1885 brick edifice still exists. Only a grassroots effort kept it from being pulled down after it closed in 1989, although some parts of it were later demolished due to fire hazard. Still, the arched windows and soaring cupolas of what remain make this place more closely resemble a palace in some European capital than a home for the mentally ill. If ever a building were worth preserving, this would be it.

Now called Grand Traverse Commons and in various stages of redevelopment, the complex once encompassed some five hundred acres, three hundred of which are designated park land. On those acres were gardens, greenhouses, and a dairy farm where patients could labor as part of their therapy. The farm produced a world champion milk cow, Traverse Colantha Walker, whose stone grave marker still stands near the few preserved barns. And although various enterprises are now under way to adapt the buildings to modern use, rumors still swirl about what happened there during nearly a century of the asylum's life.

Some fifty thousand patients entered its doors during that time, and locals still whisper about the electroshock therapies, lobotomies, and other, experimental forms of treatments visited upon some of the patients. Heidi

Johnson, author of a beautiful book of essays and photography called *Angels in the Architecture*, noted that more than thirty thousand electroshock treatments had been given to patients at the state hospital by 1947.

Johnson's book captures many strange and personal stories of the asylum. One story from a former attendant told of a nurse who was driving home for the weekend when she suddenly saw a favorite patient lying in the road in front of her in a long red dress. Of course she swerved and stopped, only to find no one there. However, if she hadn't stopped, she would have gone over a cliff! When the nurse returned to the asylum, she was told that her favorite patient had been acting strangely and at one point threw herself onto the floor. It turned out that the patient's actions occurred at the same time the nurse saw her on the road and that the patient happened to be wearing a long red dress she had just found in a closet.

The asylum buildings were connected by a large system of steam tunnels, used by the staff to move around the campus, especially in winter. The tunnels still exist and are the subject of much Internet speculation and debate. Some "urban exploration" sites claim the hospital tunnels are connected to other tunnels under Traverse City, but those familiar with them say they only lead around the old hospital grounds. But the dark underground corridors gave many staff members the heebie-jeebies from the beginning. Over the years, they've become a

favorite hangout for various groups of intruders, and we don't like to speculate about what's gone on down there.

Urban legends concerning the Northern Michigan Asylum abound. Many people who have walked the grounds express a feeling of being watched everywhere they go. Some have felt impressed by strong emotions such as anger or sadness in certain spots on the campus, as if old patients were projecting their feelings onto the living. The strangest legend is that of the Hippie Tree, located somewhere in the vicinity of building 50. The story goes that if someone walks around the Hippie Tree, at one certain spot a vortex may be entered that carries the circler straight to hell. The main problem with the story is that the exact tree is never identified, making it difficult to either find or avoid!

By the time all the subdividing, developing, remodeling, and reconstruction is finished, it's anyone's guess how much of the old state hospital will remain. Luckily, there are several books and photographic collections documenting this wondrous and emotional place. Also, both building 50 and the famous cow grave have been designated official historic sites, so that the Northern Michigan Asylum will be better remembered than most of the two hundred or so similar hospitals built around the country in the second half of the nineteenth century. And well it should be. They literally don't build 'em like this anymore.

Detroit, Demolition, and Disney

Nobody can argue with the fact that Detroit has more than a few too many abandoned buildings. What does cause dissension is the problem of what to do with them all. Rehab or wrecking ball? One small, anonymous group of fine artists has decided that no matter the final fate of these dilapidated homes and former factories, it's time that people stop looking past them and begin looking straight at them. To ensure that this happens, the group has started a guerilla art operation. In July 2005 they began taking paintbrushes in hand and splashing the fronts of abandoned buildings with orange so bright it's only a few tones removed from Day-Glo. The shade is called Tiggeriffic, to be exact, a Disney Collection color found at Home Depot.

"Every board, every door, every window is caked in Tiggeriffic Orange," said a press release the group sent to various city publications. "We paint the façades of abandoned houses whose most striking feature is their derelict appearance."

Weird Michigan spoke with one of the artists, who preferred to be identified by only his first name, Jacque. (His three cohorts are Greg, Mike, and Christian.) "At first, people see these houses as a social travesty," said Jacque. "But by painting them orange, we say look, they are here."

As the group's press release urges, "If you stumble upon one of these houses colored with Tiggeriffic Orange, stop and really look. In addition to being highlights within a context of depression, every detail is accentuated through the unification of color. Broken windows become jagged lines. Peeling paint becomes texture. These are artworks in themselves."

And yet, strangely, many of the buildings seem to be demolished by city workers soon after receiving their extreme art makeovers. Jacque said he didn't know

whether that meant his group had the psychic ability to choose only doomed structures or that the city was trying to remove the brilliant reminders of neglect and decay as soon as each became highlighted. "On one hand, we were sort of upset that they're gone," said Jacque, "but by knocking them down, the city is at least acknowledging what's happening."

Jacque and his friends do have day jobs besides their building-painting careers. Jacque describes himself as an installation artist. But using the derelict places of Detroit as their prime exhibition space has become the group's passion. And while they don't advocate any specific outcome—preservation or demolition—they hope that their work will have some positive impact on their hometown. As they conclude in their release:

"The dialogue is going. Our goal is to make everyone look at not only these houses, but all the buildings rooted in decay and corrosion. If we can get people to look for our orange while driving through the city, then they will at the same time be looking at the decaying buildings they come across. This brings awareness. And as we have already seen, awareness brings action. Yours truly, the DDD Project."

INDEX

Page numbers in bold refer to photos and illustrations.

WEiRD MiChiGAN

By

LINDA S. GODFREY

Executive Editors
Mark Sceurman and Mark Moran

ACKNOWLEDGMENTS

Weird Michigan was a total team effort, starting with my weirdly excellent editor, Mark Moran, who entrusted me with the Wolverine weirdness. I also owe major thanks to some special people who took turns riding shotgun on my road trips—my husband, Steven, who racked up brownie points I'll be paying back forever, and Weird Road Warrior Princesses Janet Marcuccio, Sally Gavic, and Mary Pagliaroni, whose collective prowess with notebooks and maps cannot be overestimated.

To name every last person who helped would take the rest of this book, but for starters it would include all the gas station clerks who gave us directions, every historical society member who hunted up old maps and prints for us, every public and college librarian who directed us to the vertical files of old newspaper clippings or faxed me needed articles and documents, the brave souls who e-mailed their personal adventures, and all the interesting people and owners or originators of roadside oddities who generously shared their stories.

In particular, Bruce Johanson and William Kingsley contributed reams of background research far beyond their print credits. My old friend Steve Cook deserves continued thanks for his generosity in granting print permission for the lyrics to his song "The Legend" and for giving us the legacy of the Michigan Dogman. Other persons special to this project include Julie and Lynn of the Media Mavens Breakfast Association and Terri the Bookworm for moral support;

Richard
Hendricks for
throwing Michigan
news culled from his
anomalist.com files my way;
Todd Lemire, Jeff Wilson, and
Bill Konkolesky for their crop circle,
UFO, and other related research; and
Kim Del Rio and Patricia Hodgell just for
being there.

Finally, I have to mention the Paulding Light, the Fairy
Infestation of Ann Arbor, Bigfoot, Dogman, five decades
of alien intruders, the Detroit airport kangaroo, and ghosts
too numerous to mention for being the stuff legends . . .
and books like this . . . are made of.

Publisher:	Barbara J. Morgan
Managing Editor:	Emily Seese
Editor:	Marjorie Palmer
Copyeditor:	Alexandra Koppen
Production:	Della R. Mancuso
	Mancuso Associates, Inc.
	North Salem, NY

CONTRIBUTORS

NICOLE BRAY, based in the Grand Haven area, is a paranormal researcher and founder and president of the West Michigan Ghost Hunter Society. She is also cohost of WPARAnormal.com Paranormal Radio talk show.

ERIN DERRY is originally from the Detroit area but now lives in the Florida Panhandle with her husband, who is in the United States Air Force. She runs a Web site dedicated to Eloise Asylum, http://www.talesofeloise.com.

MICHAEL A. DOTSON is a researcher in the weird and paranormal of Upper Michigan.

RICHARD D. HENDRICKS is a Guinness-swigging researcher and writer partial to Poe and Baudelaire and based in Madison, Wisconsin. He is the co-author of *Weird Wisconsin, Your Travel Guide to Wisconsin's Local Legends and Best Kept Secrets,* news editor of The Anomalist Web site, and maintains his own site on strange and paranormal topics titled "Weird Wisconsin" at www.weird-wi.com.

BRUCE H. JOHANSON is the president of the Ontonagon County Historical Society, a staff writer for the *Ontonagon Herald,* and a retired teacher from the Ontonagon Area Schools where he taught instrumental music and later Michigan and American history.

WILLIAM KINGSLEY is a writer and collector of voluminous research based in Mt. Pleasant. He has contributed many articles on strange phenomena to various magazines and publications.

DAVID A. KULCZYK was born in Bay City and raised in nearby Linwood. He is the winner of the 1996 Heintzelman Trophy for best fiction and has had four other short stories published. He has written for numerous print publications and is currently an associate editor for *Maximum Ink Music Magazine*. Kulczyk currently lives in Sacramento, California.

DOUG MASSELINK lives in Jenison. Through procedures based on GPS techniques, he has done extensive research in the alignment characteristics of ancient sites in Michigan, Ohio, and throughout the Mississippi Valley. His e-mail address is djmasselink@comcast.net.

JOHN P. RIBNER is a writer and martial artist who lives and works in Flint, a town known as much for its high standard of living as it is for its ability to show kindness to strangers.

MARC A. SEBRIGHT is a graduate of Kendall College of Art and Design in Grand Rapids. He spent many summer vacations exploring the sights and history of the "Copper Country" in Michigan's Upper Peninsula. He lives in Grand Rapids with his fiancée, Stephanie Cox, and his hobbies include photography and restoring vintage snowmobiles.

MELISSA TROASI is a friendly person with a lot of great stories who lives in Grand Rapids.

BILL WANGEMANN is the city historian of Sheboygan, and a weekly columnist for *The Sheboygan Press*. He is the author of *Meet Me Down by Prange's*.

DR. HARRY WILLNUS, a Michigan educator, has been involved with the UFO phenomenon for nearly fifty years. He has been an investigator for the Center for UFO Studies (CUFOS) and the Mutual UFO Network (MUFON).

DANIEL J. WOOD is a writer and researcher based in Three Rivers. He is a frequent contributor to *FATE* magazine and other publications.

PICTURE CREDITS

All photos and illustrations by the author except those noted below.

SHOW US YOUR WEIRD!

Do you know of a weird site found somewhere in the United States, or can you tell us about a strange experience you've had? If so, we'd like to hear about it! We believe that every town has at least one great tale to tell, and we're listening. It could be a cursed road, haunted abandoned site, odd local character, or bizarre historic event. In most cases these tales are told only in the towns in which they originated. But why keep them to yourself when you could share them with all of America? So come on and fill us in on all the weirdness that's lurking in your backyard!

You can e-mail us at: Editor@WeirdUS.com,
or write to us at:
Weird U.S., P.O. Box 1346, Bloomfield, NJ 07003.

www.weirdus.com